# DEMOCRACY IN A REVOLUTIONARY ERA

# DEMOCRACY IN A REVOLUTIONARY ERA

## THE POLITICAL ORDER TODAY

*by Harvey Wheeler*

★★★★ PUBLISHED BY
THE CENTER FOR THE STUDY OF DEMOCRATIC INSTITUTIONS
SANTA BARBARA, CALIFORNIA

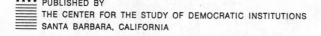

*For Mimi*

# CONTENTS

Preface
  Harry S. Ashmore  *vii*

CHAPTER

1  Introduction  *3*
2  An Authoritarian Era  *23*
3  Democracy and the Politics of Cultural Development  *41*
4  The Rise of Bureaucratic Cultures  *79*
5  The Scientific Revolution  *102*
6  Ideology  *138*
7  Balance-of-Power Politics, Old and New  *161*
8  World Order  *193*

# Preface

"World order is not inevitable. It is only necessary."

This has been a central thesis of the considerable body of work turned out by Harvey Wheeler, one of the most innovative and provocative of contemporary political scientists, in the ten years since he joined the Center for the Study of Democratic Institutions as one of its original Senior Fellows.

Wheeler argues that mankind has reached a point where radical restructuring of our political institutions is required by a technological imperative that does not necessarily coincide with traditional revolutionary ideology. Asserting the Aristotelian claim that politics is, and must be, the archetectonic science, he dismisses the compromises and confusions of contemporary pluralism as inadequate to meet the threats and opportunities of the nuclear age:

> Gone is the possibility of viewing the vicissitudes of waxing and waning cultural orders with detached Toynbeean philosophic serenity. The task of human self-preservation has now become a problem whose dimensions are as large as humanity itself. One of history's clearest lessons is that problems cannot be solved on a scale smaller than that on which they arise. This was the lesson the nation-state taught to the medieval baronies it superseded. It is the lesson the nation-state must learn from world order.

At the Center, Wheeler has directed a variety of studies testing his view of the world he sees coming into being. He caught sight of the political implications of systems theory when most of his colleagues still consigned it to the scientific laboratories. Years before ecology gained recognition in headline parlance he made the term common currency in the Center dialogue. With his colleague, the mathematician and philosopher, John Wilkinson, he is currently addressing himself to the explosive issues raised by what he defines as a clear need to constitutionalize science.

In 1968 Wheeler summarized his concepts in a major work commissioned by *Encyclopaedia Britannica*. This was one of a series of thirteen related essays ultimately published in a special volume of *Perspectives* commemorating the Encyclopaedia's two hundredth anniversary. Some of these also were published as separate volumes by Frederick A. Praeger.

The Center actively collaborated in the planning of the *Perspectives* articles, and I served as editor of the series. The prospectus from which the authors worked thus described the undertaking:

> Fundamental to the notion of the *Perspectives* article is the understanding that the world always has been characterized by dominant issues — great unresolved conflicts that are related to, but go far beyond, the level of academic dispute, professional quarrel, political argument, or international violence. Such issues ignore academic departmentalization, cross religious, economic and political demarcations, and jump over national boundaries.

This also could serve as a description of the notion that underlies the Center dialogue in which Wheeler's concept of democracy and revolution has been forged. In the *Perspectives* series, as at the Center, his sweeping vision of world order flowing from a technological imperative has not gone unchallenged. The French sociologist, Raymond Aron, who treated the social order in tandem with Wheeler's discourse on politics, wrote:

> The transition from *many* sovereignties to *one* sovereignty is neither logically nor materially impossible, but it would be *essentially* different from the transition from city-state to empire. Empires eliminated or integrated sovereign states; they did not eliminate all external sovereignty. United under one sovereignty, mankind would no longer have any enemy — unless it be on another planet. This would be a mutation *of* history itself, and not a mutation *within* history.

Since these polar ideas are central to the Center's concern with the basic issues, Wheeler's treatment of *The Political Order Today* should be of special interest to those who sample the dialogue through the Center's membership publications. This edition has been specially prepared for distribution as an *Occasional Paper*.

HARRY S. ASHMORE

*Santa Barbara*
*April, 1970*

viii

# DEMOCRACY IN A REVOLUTIONARY ERA

# *Chapter* 1 Introduction

THE POLITICAL ORDER! A resounding phrase. And as quickly as it is uttered an argument is begun. The political order seems to take for its province the world and all that's in it. So it does. And so would this essay if I could make it do so. For the underlying assumption of this essay is that politics is the architectonic science. First off, then, an issue as old as political speculation itself is joined. For the first query that comes to mind is whether or not this is too idealistic and too utopian. Are not the day-to-day events of politics actually determined more according to the dictates of power?

The first reply is to agree, in part. Much that actually takes place in politics does appear to derive from little more than the power struggle of contending political forces. But power is no better understood than is justice, or the architectonic idea expressed above. Usually what power really means is organization. But if this is the case the dispute disappears. For organization is closely associated with what political philosophers have always meant by the architectonic art.

In the second place, the power argument seems to identify itself with what "wins." And if by definition you put yourself on the side of what wins, how can you lose? But this again is misleading. Do we mean what *appears* to have won at any given moment? The Nazis appeared to have won in German politics. Stalinism appeared to have won in Soviet politics. For a while McCarthyism appeared to have won in American politics. There was a time when Nkrumah-ism appeared to have won in Ghanaian politics. If politics is to be identified with what "wins," the notion of winning must be broad enough to avoid entrapment in the perishable victories of passing phases. Otherwise we are left with a composite of capricious, transient, or whimsical events making up our notion of politics.

To help clarify the point let us take two examples of politics as the architectonic art. One would be the entire process by which the American Constitution was (1) brought into being, (2) subjected to intense public deliberation, (3) adopted, and then (4) embarked on the process of application, clarification, and development that has gone on continuously ever since. A second example would be the entire process of (1) preparing, (2) deliberating, (3) inaugurat-

3

ing, and then (4) applying, clarifying, and developing the vast social and cultural plan that was announced in 1961 at the 22nd Party Congress in the U.S.S.R. Some of the people in each of these two countries may look unfavourably upon the way politics is conducted in the other. But taking politics as it is engaged in and evaluated by the people involved, these are two familiar examples of one of the highest meanings of politics as the architectonic art.

Ancient Greeks were the first to speak of politics as the architectonic science. But of course they did not interpret "science" so narrowly as is often done now. Science meant all rational knowledge and wisdom. To men like Plato and Aristotle it seemed obvious that science ought to be devoted to the common good. Science left to itself, so they believed, would only produce chaos. To prevent this and to harness the sciences to the common good was believed to be the special province of politics.

Such a view implies that politics is architectonic in two ways. First, its facilitating tools are the separate arts, sciences, and technologies; so it uses them in building a state the way architecture uses the separate crafts to make a building. Second, the proper object of politics is the common good, the architectonic good, so to speak.

Here the pragmatic man of affairs again registers a protest. Does politics mean the description of *things as they are* or the *principles* of politics that men of wisdom have devised? Wisdom, lamentably, is not the way of the world and politics cannot be cavalierly defined as if it were. No argument. Philosophers, whose profession is the pursuit of wisdom, know better than most how true this is; and how false it is as well. But here we reach a very profound problem. For it is also true that no architect, laying out his designs on paper, has ever drawn a perfectly accurate line. Does it follow that architecture must be defined as the science of inaccurate designs? Furthermore, the architects who win contracts are sometimes less skilled than those who lose. Do we define architecture, then, solely on the basis of that which wins? The science of whatever is actually built, no matter how ugly and faulty its design may be? So far we have mentioned only deficiencies of design, assuming their perfect execution. But execution of plans is never faultless, and this moves the discussion of the problem to a new level. Take the simplest plan imaginable and turn it over to the most perfectly skilled craftsmen. Even under these ideal conditions the ultimate building inevitably will contain numerous imperfections. Does this mean the plan itself was wrong? Is the validity of a plan determined by how well men carry it out?

Suppose it is not a simple plan. Suppose it is the most sublime conception of which the genius of man is capable, a plan, let us say, for the Taj Mahal. And suppose this plan is turned over to carpenters who only know how to build crude cottages. Must we judge the practicability of architecture by the ability of the cottage carpenter? Possibly we must. For it seems reasonable to say that

4

in a nation of jackleg carpenters architecture must be defined as the art of the crude cottage. Is this what is meant by those who claim that politics must be descriptive rather than architectonic? We may say this, knowing that there is a level of meaning on which it is true, but a level also on which it is false. Not only false, it is ignoble. No one who has ever lived has been content with such a purely descriptive view of man's capability in any field, especially in politics.

But does any of this have a plain meaning for everyday politics? Consider a law—a statute. Laws are to politics as blueprints are to architecture. That is why those who view politics as the architectonic science also view law, though sometimes the term constitutionalism is preferred, as the central concern of politics. Laws may contain imperfections, but each law always aims at some ideal. It prescribes how men ought to behave. Any dispute here? But if politics —the rough-and-tumble, everyday, practical world of politics—issues in laws prescribing how men ought to behave, how can we describe politics fairly if this element is left out? Compare men attempting to follow their laws with carpenters following orders on a job. From the moment workers accept employment they must do such and such according to the work plans, or they may lose their jobs. Citizens are in a similar position. From the moment they adopt a law they must follow it or they risk punishment. There is never perfect compliance in either case. Citizens, like carpenters, are never perfect at carrying out their duties, but this alone is not sufficient reason for scrapping their plans and laws.

No fundamental law or charter of human rights has ever been perfectly observed and none will ever be. But this merely proves to all how sorely such laws are needed rather than that they must be repealed and the effort to follow them abandoned. What is true of man's noblest charters is also true of his everyday laws and ordinances. Some are the result of quite low and corrupt forms of the architectonic art, just as there are corrupt designers who will connive at the creation of faulty buildings. But it is not by their corruptions that we define the professions of man. Neither is it merely the descriptive or the actual that defines politics.

In all of the professions—lawyer, doctor, minister, teacher, citizen—we have in mind a standard of excellence that forms an essential part of our definition of them. These definitions remain true even in times when professional skills have suffered decline and their practitioners have succumbed to corruption. The assumption of this essay is that politics is a kind of profession, a profession engaged in by citizens. Citizens are practicing members of the political order. Like some carpenters, they may be poorly prepared, jackleg citizens. In that case their politics must be of a very low order. But, as with the architecture of the jackleg carpenter, this doesn't mean that nothing higher is practicable. The sciences and the professions experience their vicissitudes, as do all human institutions. Politics is no exception. Where the physician is judged by his wealth

5

surely it is not surprising for the citizen or the politician to be judged by his power. Power is real and necessary; no one ever advocated powerless politics. But neither is power the whole truth. Even in times of widespread corruption it is inaccurate to identify the professions, medicine, for example, solely with profits or politics solely with power.

The delights of wealth and power have never been absent from the interests of men. However, some societies have emphasized them more than others. In many societies wealth has been held in common. In some it has even been the object of contempt. In Western feudalism the profession of arms held first place, and manorial estates were evaluated, sought, and managed in the light of that profession. The Chinese of the Mandarin epoch reserved their highest esteem for the profession of letters. For several centuries, on the other hand, Western man has esteemed the individual creation and possession of wealth and power. But as the 20th century nears its close this seems to be changing. Men want a good life—a life that is always improving—but in the most advanced industrial nations there is an increasing demand for cultural development. Not only men's values but also their professions are undergoing change. So is their politics. It is becoming more architectonic.

The architectonic view of politics forces us to the most general levels of speculation about the common good. Two overriding issues emerge immediately: the scope of politics and the practice of politics. The first is the question of the arena within which politics occurs, the second is the question of the quality of political relationships between people. Each problem arises in our day with a new force. The first is the problem of world order, the second is the problem of democracy.

The challenge of world order is an old one, so old it may seem to be the same problem today that it has always been. But today's world is different. The world conquerors and the philosophers of world order of the past were freer than are we. For them world order was a glorious possibility; for us it is a grim necessity. World order is the precondition for the survival of the species.

That democracy is desirable requires no argument. It is extolled with near unanimity throughout the world. So much is this the case that we often despair of finding a common meaning for this common ideal. The older nations of the West speak of liberal democracy. The newer nations speak of collectivist democracy. Those countries just emerging from the burdens of Western imperialism speak of nationalist democracy. Moreover, we know that Greek democracy was different from these three modern forms, and Roman republicanism differed from them all.

Democracy has always drawn its meaning from the specific type of despotism it was designed to counteract. The common fact is that democratic forces are regularly called forth in opposition to despotism. The substantive ingredients of democracy change, and must change, from place to place. But equally true is the fact that democracy's inner logic remains always the same.

## The Unique Condition

Biologists who ponder the story of the evolution of life from simple cells to complex plants and animals often present us with a stark fact of fate: life on this planet seems to be a one-shot affair. Of course scientists, like everybody else, differ among themselves violently when they trace problems to their most fundamental levels. Yet they seem generally agreed that if a thermonuclear holocaust were to exterminate all living matter it would end life on earth forever. Nowhere on earth today are living cells being generated naturally out of lifeless protein molecules.

Eons after its fiery formation, as the earth slowly cooled off, water began to form on the earth's surface and an atmosphere began to appear above it. Much later, it is suggested, a time arrived when conditions throughout the earth were just right for the widespread generation of life forms. The hot, soupy plasma which seems to have covered the earth's surface became like a vast laboratory test tube for transforming lifeless molecules into living cells. But once that evolutionary point was past, the earth ceased to function as a life-making laboratory. Had life not evolved then, or had it accidentally disappeared at any time later, its chance would have been lost forever. Life in the large is like the life of each individual. It is mortal. Once gone it is beyond recall.

What is true concerning biological life seems to apply also to human society, though here we are on more speculative ground. Perhaps man, the creature biologists define as this planet's *Homo sapiens,* has always and everywhere been exactly the same. But as the article in this series on HUMAN NATURE shows, this has not been true of mankind. Mankind has experienced several different conditions. One of these occurred when herding creatures invented rudimentary social institutions, another came with the appearance of literate civilizations. Each new developmental stage seems to have arisen naturally, as did life itself.

Before the first appearance of social institutions like the family and the tribe the condition of mankind can be compared to that of the complex proteins just prior to their evolution into living cells. Social organization developed fortuitously in several places on earth under similar conditions. Mild, constant weather, plentiful water, rich natural fertility, and abundant year-round food and game occurred in much the same way in several of the world's rich plains and great river valleys: the Yellow, the Tigris-Euphrates, the Nile, and the Ganges. In each of these places similar forms of social organization sprang up. Even after they had developed agriculture and urban centres, their people always preserved in their myths the memory of a remote primordial time before society had existed. They told of a Garden of Eden, a Paradise, or a Golden Age in the past when life was simple and natural.

A climate that is constant and mild means that people can exist on minimum amounts of food, shelter, and clothing. Life is cheap, cheap to produce and cheap to maintain. Combine with this the natural productivity of grain and you have a real revolution. Seeds carefully invested in the fertile earth of spring will yield autumn profits of over 100 to 1. Nature was man's first factory and her natural profitability persuaded him to master simple principles of sowing, irrigating, and harvesting crops. Then it was merely necessary to invent organization—despotism it is often called—and apply it to the ingredients lying naturally at hand. Civilization appeared. Capital formation, militarism, caste systems, urbanization, bureaucratization, symbols for communicating and calculating, religion, and law all sprang forth naturally and developed along broadly similar lines everywhere. The result was almost as different from what had gone before as had been the earlier difference between man and animal. A higher form of life, man as a social animal, had been produced. Once again the laboratory conditions had been just right.

One searches the earth in vain to find those same environmental conditions today. Climate seems to have changed. The once fertile river valleys long since seem to have become leached out and exhausted. Their fertility is again being recaptured, but only through intensive fertilizing and elaborate irrigation schemes requiring highly artificial dams and power plants. If some future catastrophe were to wipe out the memories of men, taking from them all knowledge of their social and cultural institutions but preserving them exactly the same otherwise, it is doubtful if the resulting cavemen could ever do the same thing all over again. Social life seems to have been like other forms of life. The conditions that made its birth possible may have occurred at only one remote moment in the earth's development. Moreover, what is true of the origin of the multiform civilizations of ancient man seems to be more applicable to the preservation of the higher, more intensively organized, convergent civilizations of industrial man.

For countless thousands of years human societies persisted, listless and indolent in one place, surging and irrepressible in another, sometimes each by turns. Yet the basic components of society were remarkably similar everywhere. The cultural systems of East and West were isolated from each other but they were as different members of one great family. Local differences and specializations did not obliterate family resemblances. The story of the higher civilizations can be pictured on the model of a vast evolutionary oak tree, similar to those biologists use to portray the evolving species of the animal kingdom. From the central trunk spring huge branches that are labeled Mesopotamia, China, India, Egypt. They differ from each other in the special institutions they seize upon for em-

8

phasis and for development: religion, warfare, law, technology, commerce, and so on.

The ancient Egyptians tried to elevate the upper levels of their civilization into the heavens, making their pharaohs into immortal gods.

The Greeks, working like Olympian jewelers, designed a different civic gem for each Hellenic valley and cove. With infinite lapidary patience and care they polished and refined the separate cultures, bringing out in each one its unique qualities.

The Romans concentrated on perfecting the quality of their imperial cities' sinews and connective tissues: law and citizenship. They then proceeded to load these with opulence and stretch them abroad to contain all the foreign peoples that could be reached, like a child intently blowing up a balloon.

The Chinese seized upon the efficacy of ritual and extended to all of life and to all human relationships the principles which lay behind primitive fertility rites. For some reason, perhaps owing to the very success of their stylized customs, they never quite hit upon a system of gods like those of the others.

In different times and different places, various other features of social organization were selected for overspecialization in much the way the animal kingdom evolved its different overspecialized species. The overspecialization never stopped, not even with modern man. During the past three centuries Western man has been discovering what happens to human culture when man selects industrialization for his dominant concern. As the 20th century draws to a close, man seems determined to choose science for his next experiment in overspecialization.

During all this time, no matter what happened to its individual branches, the basic tree of human culture was never threatened with complete extinction. When any one branch had reached out to its limit and fallen victim of its own overextension, there were always others in reserve ready to move into the breach. The tree of civilization was never dependent upon the vitality of any one of its branches. A cosmic observer looking down upon the human struggle could contemplate the decline of Mesopotamia and Egypt with serene detachment. For close by were hardy survivors in Phoenicia and Crete, able to furnish channels of cultural transmission out of which the brilliant efflorescence of Greece and Rome could spring.

So long as a plurality of autonomous cultural systems existed, unconcern about the fate of human society as a whole was justified. This remained true until the close of the 19th century. Then, speeded by a series of world wars and revolutions, there began a massive process of worldwide cultural homogenization. Human society gradually ceased to show many different faces and came instead to exhibit everywhere the same dominant pattern. Cultural differences persisted, but they were attributed to vestigial remains of the old or to different

9

stages of development toward the new. The differences between human societies began to be more the differences of degree than those of kind. A permanent irreversible change was introduced into the condition of mankind. Men came to belong everywhere to the same cultural species. A new stage of human development had been reached. Twentieth-century man is faced with the political consequences of this fact.

No doubt there will always be large differences between places like Nigeria, Mexico, Indonesia, China, the Soviet Union, and the United States. Probably this will remain so even after the old cultures have disappeared from the memories and habits of the elderly, the lower classes, the former elites, and the remote communities. There will remain widely different styles of life, folkways, arts, and ceremonies. But these continuing differences promise to be like those which distinguished the Corinthians, the Spartans, the Athenians, and the Thebans of ancient Greece: minor variations among members of the same cultural family.

In the world's capital cities, in its industrial centres and universities, and among its new ruling classes, the old order has been uprooted. The results have been roughly the same everywhere. As the mind's vision follows the path of the great airliners, anticipations of the strange and the exotic are evoked by the thought of seeing Tokyo, Peking, Bangkok, Rangoon, New Delhi, Tel Aviv, Athens, Cairo, Accra. The names alone are enough to stir the imagination with romantic pictures of the world's many different cultures. But the actual experience grievously disappoints the expectations.

The airlines themselves illustrate the point. They bear excitingly different names: El Al, Cathay, Varig, Sabena, Panagra, Lufthansa, Alitalia, Aeroflot, Aer Lingus. But this is almost their only mark of distinction. They all come from a few of the world's great manufacturing centres. The scurrying businessmen, diplomats, and sightseers who inhabit them seldom leave the culture of the West, no matter where they travel. The world's capital cities have come to look as if they were all constructed by the same builder. There are the same international languages and the same cosmopolitan shops. The restaurants, hotels, and taxicabs are filled with the same people who dream the same dreams and struggle against the same frustrations. Modernization is under way everywhere. Modern man is the only kind of man that is being produced. For the first time since the beginning of human society the history of mankind has converged into a single story. A most awesome consequence follows from this fact.

As we look back over the civilizations of the past we see that cultural obliteration was a common occurrence. Arnold Toynbee founded his story of the sweep of human history on this fact. And when one culture died the story merely shifted to another. But what if some dread natural or man-made catastrophe were to strike at the roots of modern industrial society? Suppose something

10

were to prevent our utilization of the major sources of energy? What if somehow a bombardment of nuclear particles from outer space made electronic communication impossible? The only civilization man has would be destroyed.

The tree of human culture has changed. It must be pictured differently. Gone are the separate cultural systems which served in the past as alternate offshoots from which high cultures could evolve in historical succession. If industrial man should falter in his headlong dash through cultural time, there is no different cultural system standing by ready to grasp the baton of civilization and carry on the human race. The tree of civilization has changed from a sprawling oak into a great single-trunked sequoia. Anything fatal to its solitary stalk would mean the end to everything. Gone is the possibility of viewing the vicissitudes of waxing and waning cultural orders with detached Toynbeean philosophic serenity. The task of human self-preservation has now become a problem whose dimensions are as large as humanity itself. One of history's clearest lessons is that problems cannot be solved on a scale smaller than that on which they arise. This was the lesson the nation-state taught to the medieval baronies it superseded. It is the lesson the nation-state now must learn from world order.

Human society has come to the political point of no return. In unconsciously creating a unitary industrial society throughout the world, man has made his survival depend upon his ability to follow it with a consciously created world political order. From now on, and for as long as man may exist, one item of business will dominate the agenda with which he begins each day. It is a problem man has never before had to face: safeguarding the survival of human culture itself.

Nothing in the nature of things insures that regardless of what man does civilization will always survive. The successive eons of the past are the historical graveyards of biological and cultural species that turned out to be incapable of coping with the catastrophes that confronted them. World order is not inevitable. It is only necessary.

## The Problem of Democracy

The problem of world order is directly related to the second issue, that of democracy. We are accustomed to thinking of democracy as a problem that applies only to individual persons and only to the internal conditions of a nation. But nations are also persons. They are corporate, artificial, man-made persons, to be sure, but they are persons, nonetheless. This is what is meant by national sovereignty. When its defenders insist upon the inviolability and the inalienability of the sovereignty of their nation they attribute to nations the characteristics of a person. The hardest problem besetting world order is to determine how all the corporate persons of the world should be brought together and what their relationships to each other will be.

11

In one sense the problem of world order is that of revolution rather than inauguration. For the last 300 years the world has been an oligarchy: a government of the many by the few. Asia and Africa were dominated by the Western powers the way feudal barons dominated their serfs. And if someone should object to this and claim that the world was not a true political order and that the idea of an oligarchy cannot be applied to it, well then, the reply is quickly made: For the last 300 years the world as a whole has exhibited almost exactly the same degree of political order as did France and England in the early days of European feudalism. The world had just about as much of a political order as did Italy and Germany and the nations east of the Danube until far into modern times.

Today the history of the dissolution of feudalism inside the early-modern nations of the West is being repeated inside the contemporary world seen as a whole. What happened earlier to the estates of the realm is happening now to the nations of the world. Imperialism is dying. The former colonies and dependencies of the Western nations are assuming first-class citizenship in the world community. In fact, to say that a world order is only now emerging for the first time in history is just as wrong, but also just as right, as it is to say that England did not emerge as a nation until after the Wars of the Roses in the mid-15th century. The world is shedding its former marks of despotism and acquiring revolutionary new traits of democracy based upon the individual integrity of each of its corporate components, no matter how rich or poor, or how advanced or retarded, they may be. But world order is striving for birth with much greater urgency than did its national predecessors. And well it might. It has a more insistent goal. In addition to the implacable revolutionary pressures from below, and in addition to the thermonuclear apocalypse which threatens to burst from the skies, there is a less obvious but even more insistent necessity. For as we have seen, mankind has now wagered all his stake on one civilization, one gamble for survival. Like it or not, this puts the whole world together in the same game of politics. It had better be an architectonic one.

Just as the overthrow of Europe's feudal despots required a revolution, so does the overthrow of world imperialism. Revolution entails violence. Always. The violence need not be physical. It is not bloodshed that is necessary. What is necessary is the deeper violence involved in wrenching and transforming men's habits and ways of thinking into entirely new patterns. This is what happened when feudalism was overthrown inside nations. It will also happen when imperialism is finally overthrown in the world as a whole.

The overall shape of a community affects the relationships that can take place within it. To be a serf in a feudal regime was a quite different thing from being a farmer in an industrial order. The office of citizen is quite different in collectivist democracies from what it is in the liberal democracies. These are violent differences. Something comparably violent is in store for the world as the imperialist oligarchy of the past is supplanted by the novel principles of a democratic world order. There is no way of knowing in advance exactly how nations, organizations, professions, and individuals will be affected by the advent of world order. The story of European feudalism is instructive. But perhaps an even more ancient example, that of Athens, will fit the modern situation better.

Athens was a democracy for many decades but it was always a strange example of democracy. It would be almost like calling prisons democracies if all managerial tasks were distributed among the guards by lot. Athenian democracy applied only to those who had inherited full citizenship. This was about one-tenth of the whole population of the city. Not only slaves but also resident aliens were specifically excluded from Athenian citizenship. Some modern critics of Athens have argued that a minority ruling class that rests on a base composed of slaves and second-class citizens can hardly be called a democracy. This is much the same argument Western critics apply against the collectivist democracies and the developing countries. Socialist critics of American democracy make the same point about the inferior status of Negroes. And yet, in all these cases, democracy was real within the restricted realm of its operation. Of course, for those outside the ruling classes and parties the democracy they lived under was also a form of imperialism and dictatorial exploitation that worked the same way when it was turned against outsiders as it did inside the country.

This was seen clearly in ancient Athens. The government confronted the majority of the population the way modern imperialist powers confronted their colonial possessions. And when Athens behaved this way at home, how could she behave differently toward the other Greek city-states? In fact she did not. In her various attempts to form international leagues and confederations Athens never really thought of the other city-states as her equals. They were like the noncitizen residents of Athens and were treated in the same despotic fashion. Accordingly, Athens was never able to organize a genuine federal union of Greek city-states which might have insured her own survival.

Until quite recently the nations of the West treated the rest of the world the way Athenians treated their noncitizen population. Internally most of them were democracies. But it has never been clear to what extent their internal democratic institutions were made possible by the imperialist servitude forced upon the rest of the world. Many economists argue that after the 19th century imperialism ceased to be profitable—just as they argue that slave labor is uneconomic except for crude earth-moving and extractive operations. But this is not the point. What is at issue is the injustice of a despotic world order and the evils its maintenance caused inside the ruling nations of the West. For in the end we must apply to them the same criticism that is applied to Athenian democracy. Both were despotic, and because they were they were not complete democracies. Neither learned the full lessons of self-government. Both were like wealthy families accustomed to depending upon staffs of servants. What will happen when the Western family of nations is thrown on its own? Their democracy will then be put to the test. Will it mature, or will it suffer the fate of Athenian democracy? For today, just as in those days, democracy and imperialism are closely related to each other.

In ancient Greece, imperialism gave way to outright empire. The Hellenic city-state system was superseded by Alexander's world empire. Alexander the Great may have been a personal despot but his empire was put together on a nondespotic principle. It was a postimperialist union in which peoples and nations surrendered their previous autonomy to become members of a sovereign imperial state. This new basis for citizenship required a new and more universal conception of mankind. And while the Alexandrian system lasted only a short time, its principle of universal citizenship was soon reborn in imperial Rome. The ultimate problem of democracy—the complete elimination of despotism—was not solved by Rome. On the contrary, economic exploitation was carried to a high point of refinement. But one of democracy's impulses, the just application of law to all equally, was almost completely realized in Rome.

## The Universal Revolution

Will today's world have something similar in store for it as it struggles to eliminate despotism from the relationships between peoples and nations collectively and also between individuals? If so, the disappearance of modern imperialism will be followed by the advent of new forms of democracy. These promise to bring a world revolution as profound as that represented in the shift from autonomous Greek city-states to universal Roman law. We cannot say exactly what these new forms of democracy will be, but we certainly must make an effort to clarify the salient issues that seem to be emerging in this universal revolution against despotism.

The problem of supplanting a world feudal regime with a more democratic world order led us into the problem of democracy. It turned out that imperialism in the large was related to imperialism in the small. Seen in this light the conclusion follows that despotism, in one form or another, has been present in every political order that has ever existed. But what is despotism, and how has it been combated?

The beginnings of political relationships are shrouded in mystery. Anthropologists tell us that politics may have begun in many ways. A large family unit, or tribe, may have captured or acquired slaves to perform menial tasks. A band of invincible marauders may have captured a thriving community intact and planted itself at its head as an aristocratic caste. A group of migrants may

14

have settled in a new territory and forced the native population into subservient roles. Most of today's nations have experienced this latter condition in some form.

Archaeological records indicate that the aristocratic ruling class of ancient Greece may have been descended from prehistoric northern invaders. England experienced many waves of invasion, the most recent being the Norman knights who accompanied William the Conqueror and adapted English feudalism to their needs as a ruling class. The ancient records of India, China, and Japan yield a similar reading. In Eurasia the White Russians were counterparts of England's Norman conquerors. Africa, colonial Asia, Latin America, and the United States south of the Mason-Dixon line, all developed similar forms of despotism. The rulers and the ruled were sharply distinguished from each other. They obeyed separate codes of morals and of law. Leadership and control were the exclusive monopoly of one, inferiority and servitude the preordained lot of the other. All property, with but insignificant exceptions, was owned by the ruling class.

Despotism is a form of imperialism with the forces of exploitation turned inward against a subject population. The masses are kept in a permanent state of underdevelopment. They are, in their own country, like the natives of an exploited colony. The profession of arms is among the highest callings of a despotic ruling class. This is not only because it permits the monopoly of power and is accordingly a ruling function; equally important is the need to guard against a rebellion by the subject population.

The maintenance of solidarity against the lower orders is the overriding obligation of all members of the ruling class. Deeds which they would regard as reprehensible and intolerable among themselves, such as rape, personal indignities, cheating, and murder, are perpetrated against the lower orders and remorselessly condoned in the interest of class solidarity. This is a despotism without a homeland. It recognizes neither ethnic boundaries nor barriers of time. It is one of man's primordial forms of government but also one of his most perishable.

Despotism has always fallen victim to its own success. This occurs because it is an economic as well as a political system. It is an imperialist (*imperium* is the Latin for authority and power) device enabling the ruling classes to enforce the division of labour and specialization of function and monopolize its benefits. The result is the accumulation of wealth. The community expands. It becomes more complex and acquires impressive buildings. But the wealthier it becomes, the more valuable the producing classes also become. An instrument that can produce many highly prized items is more valuable than one able to produce only a few primitive ones. In a dynamic society even slaves must be induced to acquire special, new skills and to apply them efficiently and industriously. The value of each person increases with the increasing splendour of the society. As the value of people increases so does concern for their living conditions. At the very least they must be treated as exceptionally valuable domestic animals.

But in the end, in wealthy and complex societies, slave systems must succumb to the facts of genetics. *Homo sapiens* is everywhere essentially the same. There are no "natural" slaves. And even where humanitarianism ignores this fact, economics puts it to work. Time and affluence are the natural enemies of despotism. At one extreme, revolts of the oppressed stimulate democratic reforms; at the other extreme is some form of *Caesarism*. Usually both have worked hand in glove.

Caesarism is the classic maneuver employed by the disaffected or thwarted members of a ruling class. Their response to being thwarted is to capitalize on the grievances of the subject population. The people are promised reforms in return for their aid in overthrowing the elite. The Gracchi initiated this maneuver in ancient Rome, but Julius Caesar made it successful. The means were military.

The American Revolution was a form of Caesarism. With the slogan "no taxation without representation," leading members of the colonies made clear to the political elite in England their wish to be included in English governing institutions. When this was denied they resorted to the classic Caesarist device. They championed the grievances of the lower orders—organized them into a successful revolutionary force. A few decades later Jefferson applied an electoral version of the same maneuver. He organized the people into voting, rather than fighting, legions. When this electoral version of acquiring power became reinforced and institutionalized a little later by Andrew Jackson, the American party system was born.

Much earlier England's King Henry VII had relied upon the support of the yeomanry in consolidating his own regime. From this, ultimately, there grew the opposition of the Roundheads and the Cavaliers, the civil wars, and finally England's party system. France went through similar experiences prior to the birth of her political parties. Indeed, Western political parties were everywhere the vestigial remains of earlier despotisms. They retained throughout their lifetimes characteristics derived from the special types of despotism out of which they grew. Elitist parties longed nostalgically for the return of an aristocratic state. The popular parties never lost the myth that gave them birth: riches and rights had been unjustly withheld from them by despotic classes.

Societies can only persist because of their ability to preserve habitual patterns of action from generation to generation. By the same token, however, institutions whose origins trace far back into the reaches of time continue for centuries to influence the way things are done. Western political parties are instances of this. Although many forces conspired to produce them, the fundamental fact to be borne in mind is that they were the residues of prior forms of despotism. This is not a disparagement of Western party systems. That would be like criticizing the automobile for having been developed from the horse-drawn carriage. However, it does help provide a larger perspective for evaluating both Western and non-Western political systems.

## The Nature of Despotism

Still, we have not disposed of the essential nature of despotism. Is it a matter of form or of substance? Suppose a dictatorship or an aristocracy were to exhibit a sublime degree of wisdom and fairness. Would this absolve it from being called despotic? Or would the mere fact that some people were held permanently inferior to others be an ineradicable mark of despotism regardless of all the other virtues of the regime?

Put it another way. Suppose an exceedingly enlightened and virtuous imperial power governed the natives of its colonies with unexceptionable justice. Would this absolve it from being called despotic? Or does imperial subjection alone—the mere form of imperialism—constitute despotism? The historic impulse of democracy has always been to answer this question with an unqualified yes. So said both the lower orders of ancient Rome and the middle classes of 17th-century Europe. So say the colonial peoples of the 20th century. This brings the problem of world order into the same framework as the problem of democracy. The overthrow of despotism has always required some form of revolution, violent or not. The converse has also held true. Wherever democracy has been introduced it has had a revolutionary impact. The reason for this derives from the form of despotism.

The most extreme instance of despotism is slavery: the outright subjection of servants to masters, enforceable at law. Imperialism represents a master-slave relationship between a nation and its colonies. Caste systems, such as those traditional to India and those found in the many forms of feudalism that have appeared throughout history, are the same and they usually contain many grades of legally enforced subordination.

In one respect they are like the hierarchy of ranks found in an army. In an army there is the one major division between the officer class as a whole and all the lower ranks. Then, inside both classes there is a separate hierarchy. Despotic orders are usually the same. The many hierarchically arranged castes and classes yield to one overall division: that between the governing class—the nobility, the descendants of the gods—and all below them. Ancient philosophers classified such governments as aristocracies, and many of the wisest men of history have reserved their highest praises for the aristocratic form of government (or rather for their own description of how an ideal aristocracy of the wise and just might function). But the fact remains that an aristocracy, no matter how just and enlightened it may be, is still a form of despotism. It rests upon a sharp, legally enforced distinction between the rulers and the ruled.

The Western middle-class revolutions, which began in the 17th century, aimed at destroying once and for all the legal foundations of despotism within their own natural borders. This was unquestionably one of the most glorious efforts in all human history. For although anthropologists believe they have some evidence of nondespotic regimes in various primitive settings, complex societies had never before completely eliminated the legal basis for despotism.

The great visionaries of the middle-class revolutions, Rousseau and Locke, believed that once legal barriers were eliminated all men would be able to aspire to any level of wealth or status and to any political office, no matter how depressed their original station or how elevated the office sought. "The career open to talents," rather than inherited status, became a motto of the French Revolution. Constitutionalism is the term usually employed to express these ideals. However, in the course of the 19th century, constitutionalism was criticized by those who detected that legal reform was not enough to eliminate the fact of despotism. The law was blind not only to persons but also to the operation of certain economic and social forces.

Aristotle had pointed out long ago that all societies are divided into the haves and the have-nots. Karl Marx agreed, adding that this fact contained the hidden explanation of the way every society actually functioned. He claimed that law was ineffective against economic power, especially the new kind of power represented by capital. Marx gave painstaking sociological description to the deeper despotism that was embedded in the exploitation of labourer by capitalist. The old despotism had been political. The political revolutions of the 18th century had eliminated the legal basis of the older despotism. The remaining task was to carry out an economic revolution to eliminate the despotism based upon capital.

The Marxist argument made much more sense in Europe than it did in the United States, though in theory it should have been the other way around. In America, where capitalism's victory was complete, class warfare failed to appear. In Europe, where feudalism was never quite vanquished, class warfare never ended. The 18th century political revolution did not ring truly around the world. Its echoes faded sharply the farther one traveled from the point of revolutionary detonation in the North Sea countries.

Marxism thrived only where the bourgeois revolution it disparaged remained unconsummated. In such countries the new economic relations accompanying industrialization engrafted themselves onto the old social demarcations of feudalism. Marx's diagnosis turned out to require adjustment. Economic power certainly reinforced any underlying sources of despotism it encountered. But in America, where there were no feudal vestiges to overcome, one could see that the source of injustice was based upon forces even more irrational than was economics. The cause lay deeper in the cultural system. The poor tended to develop their own locked-in subculture. This culture of poverty, like the patrimony of a French peasant proprietor, was preserved intact and passed on from generation to generation. The members of this subculture were prevented from participating fully in the opportunities open to others. This was the lesson contained in the American Negro Revolution. It was a revolution that harked back to the themes of 18th-century constitutionalism but then hurried on to carry the fight against despotism to new and deeper levels. Those who were products of the culture of poverty found it necessary to wage a perpetual struggle to see that the underprivileged were provided with compensatory cultural enrichment from early childhood throughout their entire lives. This was the inner meaning of the Negro Revolution. And this was what linked it directly to the ongoing struggle against despotism that has occupied the political efforts of civilized men since their first appearance on earth. This essay is an attempt to describe the many facets of that struggle.

Despotism, whether it is legal, economic, or cultural, is a form of subordination and discrimination. It drives a line through society, separating the unfortunate from the fortunate without regard to intrinsic individual merit or potential capacity. Admittedly, it is impossible for all individuals to be absolutely equal in every way. No one would want that to happen anyway. But it *is* possible to continue the struggle against artificial and accidental barriers to individual development and cultural enrichment. It is such barriers that constitute despotism. The gravest problem about such barriers is that like all other social forces they become self-perpetuating. The entire social system adjusts itself to them and thereby works to preserve them. So it is that nothing short of revolution suffices to eliminate them. This is why an essay on the political order must, in this day, also be an essay on revolution.

Revolution does not necessarily mean violence in the streets—though that has often been its accompaniment. It means the alteration of the social system as a whole in a fundamental way. It is applicable when the causes of ills are so deeply embedded in the structure of society that reform and evolutionary change will not suffice. This requires the highest application of the art of politics, politics at the architectonic level, directed to the problem of the overall system of relationships among men. This political meaning of revolution is far from implying violence. Rather, it suggests the antidote to violence.

Revolution is not only controversial as a tactic—as a means of political action—it is also controversial as a matter of historical fact. Scholars conduct elaborate debates about whether or not there is in fact any such thing as a revolution. For whenever we look intently at any so-called revolution of the past it

19

is always possible to uncover foundations that had been at work years and even decades before the outbreak of what later was called the revolution.

The American Revolution is a perfect example. The individual colonies had been developing local self-governing institutions for a hundred years before their disputes with England came to a head. Few of the colonial leaders initially wanted or proposed a revolution. They felt excluded, ignored, and discriminated against, but they refused to believe their grievances could not be corrected without a structural change in the imperial system managed from Britain. Their reaction was to devise a number of carefully worked out schemes for reforming British politics and the empire. They hoped that through these reforms the British would accommodate themselves and resolve the complaints of the people. Had that been possible, colonial allegiance to the British crown would not have been endangered. Until the very last moment the colonists thought in evolutionary rather than revolutionary terms.

Even after the War of Independence had been won the confederacy that was instituted provided for only a minimum degree of union among the colonies. National liberation had been achieved, but the separate colonial governments were maintained just as they had been before the revolution. The only change was to substitute a feeble confederate assembly for the imperial crown that had been thrown away. Even the new federal Constitution, when it was instituted a few years later, was little more than an improved surrogate for the missing crown. The new federal government was a studiously transplanted and republicanized crown; a little, self-governing and self-contained empire of New World colonies, adding to the old functions only those they had long felt it was appropriate for the crown to exercise. The separate colonies jealously retained for themselves the autonomy they had originally sought from England by petition and diplomacy.

Viewed in this light, the revolutionary aspects of the American Revolution seem to fade into the background, and its evolutionary aspects—its direct and intimate ties with the traditions and governing experiences of the past—assume dominant significance. This, in effect, was the judgment of Charles H. McIlwain, the great authority on the British constitutional tradition. He claimed there was nothing revolutionary in the American position. Of course, the moment McIlwain's ideas were announced they became the subject of a vigorous academic debate. But that is just the point. Those who know the most about the revolutions of the past are the ones who are the most doubtful about whether or not they ever really occurred.

The French Revolution has long been the subject of a similar controversy. A few years ago this debate was revived and brought abreast of recent scholarship by the English historian Alfred Cobban. Even Russia's October Revolution has suffered this fate. The debate was brought to a head by the massive volumes of

E. H. Carr, the historian of the Bolshevik Revolution. Contemporary sinologists are similarly divided about the Chinese Revolution. World War II had not been long in the past before the same issue arose among historians of German Nazism and biographers of Hitler.

The problem carries right into the present. Experts who work in and advise the world's foreign ministries are divided among themselves by precisely the same issue. What is the true nature of the new nationalism arising in the developing nations as they throw off their colonial bonds and assume the status of free and independent nations? Can the developing nations realize their aims only by revolution, or is it possible for them to introduce a series of gradual reforms and thereby achieve their ends through evolutionary means?

Perhaps Edmund Burke was right. His voice comes to us out of the heart of the revolutionary turmoil of the 18th century. In his day revolution meant republicanism: the overthrow of kings and aristocratic elites. Thomas Paine was stirring Europe with the revolutionary republican creed. Burke answered Paine's *Age of Reason* with a plea for prudence. He argued that revolution is just too expensive. You never get your money's worth. It is a get-rich-quick scheme that leaves you poorer in the end. The surer way is that of reform. Established institutions are repositories of a cultural prudence that is wiser than human reason. It is a hard lesson to teach, especially in an age of turmoil. But, said Burke, one distinguishes the statesman from the demagogue by his unflagging efforts to teach the people this hard truth.

But how does all this sound when one is listening to it from below? Is demagogue merely the Establishment's word for spokesman for the oppressed? Does not Burke's view imply that structural evils *never* occur in any social system? But once one sees that an evil is the result of a defect in the social structure does not one then become a revolutionary, violent or not? This was the light that finally dawned upon the American revolutionaries. It is merely that they proceeded in two stages. External despotism was first overthrown by Washington's guerrilla operations. Next, internal despotism was brought under siege by Jefferson's electoral partisans.

The late 20th century is experiencing turmoils and upheavals like those of the late 18th. Its statesmen and politicians daily ponder up-to-date versions of the debate between Burke and Paine. The dominant issue dividing them is surprisingly like that of the 18th century. The Western nations have taken the place of kings and nobles. Imperialism stands above the non-Western nations as European monarchs stood above their subjects. The United States implores the non-Western world with the themes of Edmund Burke. The collectivist democracies counter with the ringing challenges of Paine and Jefferson. Of course, the actual names the East and West hurl back and forth to each other are often Adam Smith and Karl Marx, but the issue is really the older one—whether the elimination of despotism requires a fundamental change in the political order: whether revolution or reform is the better solution to despotism.

World order, despotism, democracy, revolution, constitutionalism: these are the themes that permeate the issues of our times. We shall follow their impact by turning first to the political changes occurring in the most advanced nations of the West. Next we will turn to the developing nations. Third will come a discussion of life in bureaucratic cultures. Then will follow discussions of ideology, of the scientific revolution, and of the problems of diplomacy and war. Finally we will turn tentatively toward the future and consider the political implications of world order.

# *Chapter 2* An Authoritarian Era

THERE IS A LOGIC embedded in events that often evades that which plays before the mind. England's 17th-century King James I was a competent philosopher and theologian, but he could not decipher the meaning of the philosophical, religious, political, and economic revolution that was breaking out all around him. The ancient Romans achieved their best military results in the East, but they failed to understand the connection between these and the northern rebellions that overwhelmed them. For when they mounted a massive attack on the East they disrupted the intricate web of political interrelationships that reached from Persia up to the Black Sea area. From there secondary reflexive disturbances sped across the North and soon the northern nations were in arms, pounding on Rome's back door in belated response to her own sorties out the front. As we search throughout the late 20th-century world we are struck by a similar discord between the logic of political events and that of political discourse. Democracy furnishes the rhetoric of politics, authoritarianism its content. This is true in the West no less than the East, in the Northern no less than the Southern Hemisphere. Nor is contemporary authoritarianism any more respectful of tradition than it is of rhetoric. The forces of science, technology, urbanization, industrial development, the mass media, and world integration all work against the proletarian dictatorships from one direction, but they also work against the constitutional democracies from another. This is seen from a consideration of recent political changes within four of the most industrially advanced nations, the United States, Britain, France, and the Soviet Union.

In the late 1920s the West was still innocently bent on profits and naïvely trusting in peace. The world revealed a quite different political face from the one it now displays. The Soviet portent was blithely ignored. Only a few voices warned of harder times and graver wars to come. The future of democracy, as it was then defined, seemed very bright. Where it was not already flourishing, it was momentarily expected. Only the impolite called attention to the pervasive world hegemony of the West. Indeed, the average Westerner could not even perceive that the world was in fact a feudal order administered from an oligarchic headquarters in the Atlantic community. The fact that the world was divided into haves and have-nots seemed natural, certainly not something caused by the West. In this larger arena of the world democracy held no sway at all. Who, in 1920, would have dreamed that a scant quarter century later the great powers of the West would be vying anxiously and unfavourably with Communists for the friendship of African tribal chiefs and Asian guerrilla leaders? Who could have then foreseen the advent of the relations among nations? Who could have predicted that the internal political systems of the world would take on a new authoritarian structure, one that seemed to recognize neither political boundaries nor differences of technological advance?

There are great differences in the authoritarianisms of the East and the West, but they are not so great as is usually assumed and by no means so sharp as is proclaimed by the opposing ideologues on each side of the Cold War. Both style themselves democracies. But while the problems of democracy may pervade the language—especially the polemics—of politics, it is authoritarianism that furnishes its content. This is a statement that will attract little agreement. The collectivist democracies discount the failings of the present in the light of their dream of a better world in the future. The liberal democracies explain away their growing restrictions in the light of the freedoms of their past.

Any category that finds a kinship between East and West is certain to be a disturbing and a controversial one. When it goes further and incorporates the underdeveloped world as well, it may, without losing its controversial nature, run the additional risk of seeming useless. Yet this is the second aspect of the rise of contemporary authoritarianism. The underlying structure of politics in Africa from Tanzania to Angola, in Latin America from Cuba to Brazil, in the developing nations from Egypt to China, and in the West from America to Russia springs from similar roots and issues in institutions whose familial similarities belie their highly publicized differences.

The forces of science, technology, urbanization, industrial development, the mass media, a generation of Cold War, and world integration carry the same imperatives with them wherever they reach. There is an "Establishment" of military, industrial, and party chiefs. Government is by a professionalized corps of experts. Access to the mass media is monopolized by the Establishment to mobilize consent and control behaviour. These ingredients of authoritarianism are much the same throughout the world. In one place the military may seem dominant, in another the party apparatus, and in yet a third, the technical-industrial chiefs. Contemporary authoritarian societies are like vast paternalistic bureaucracies. Individuals are surrounded by rules and orders over which they have little direct influence. The possibilities of remonstrating with or talking back to the authorities are meagre and sporadic. It is not so much that democracy has been killed—in world politics, as we have indicated previously, it is just being born. It is rather that 19th-century forms of democracy are no longer adequate to cope with the complexity of governmental issues and the massive power available through modern governmental institutions. The likelihood is that contemporary authoritarianism is a transitional stage—as was the authoritarianism of the absolute monarchs of Europe just prior to the middle-class revolutions. One of our purposes in studying contemporary authoritarianism is to uncover the conditions for the resurgence of democracy.

## The Executive Role

Authoritarianism in the West is revealed most clearly by considering the changing role of the executive. This is perhaps most dramatic in America, where the fear of executive authority has been traditionally most strong. The American idea of the executive grew in symmetry with early ideas of democracy and constitutionalism. The original Constitution confronted the president with a series of potentially antagonistic powers: the states and the other two federal branches. The president's authority was checked and counterbalanced at every turn. In order to be effective he was forced to be forever mollifying his governmental opponents and rallying his supporters. In the American democratic ideal, government was to be held as close as possible to the interests and desires of the common man. It was deemed appropriate for popular forces, immediately and also through intermediate pressure groups, to focus attention directly upon the president and attempt to influence each of his acts. Ideally, the American president was to function as a neutral broker of political power. He was supposed to accommodate a multitude of autonomous governmental and political forces and employ his brokerage talents to transform them into official policies. War and crisis frequently frustrated realization of the ideal, but America's greatest presidents have been those who were most adept at the orchestration of univocal authority out of the vigorous play of numerous independent forces. It could almost be said that the American political tradition provided no place for positive leadership. The very idea seemed undemocratic. But at the same time Americans met each great crisis with a cry for strong presidential leadership. And they have awarded the mantle of historical greatness only to those presidents who have been strong and forceful. This has been the paradox of executive authority in America.

Abraham Lincoln was certainly one of America's greatest presidents. He was also an embodiment of the special form of democratic leadership typical of American politics. Lincoln is always classed among the "strong" presidents. He is among those few who stepped boldly outside established constitutional boundaries. By his own presidential fiat he freed slaves and suspended civil rights. But one thing Lincoln never did was to ignore the ground rules of the American political game. Those rules required that a president appear to be reactive

25

rather than dominant. It was not prohibited that an American president have ideas or programs of his own. But it was prohibited that he assume the role of a personal saviour. The ideal president was one able to voice the demands and needs already present in the people, even though previously their presence may not have been fully recognized. Then it was quite proper for a president to arrange and manipulate indigenous political forces so that his policies would be, and also would appear to be, forced upon him by a broadly based popular demand. The American president was in one way the political counterpart of the business entrepreneur. He had to produce a better mousetrap, but in the final analysis the only judgment that mattered was that of the mass political market.

Lincoln's achievement would have been a masterstroke in any country at any time in history. He presided over a bitter civil war, and yet emerged as the nation's symbol of unity. His judgments were sure. His methods were as American as his wit. With one hand he arranged for intemperate proslavery editorials to be printed in Midwestern journals, thereby isolating his opposition on the right. With the other he privately advised Eastern abolitionist leaders that "we shall need all the antislavery feeling in the country and more; you can go home and try to bring the people your views; and you may say anything you like about me, if that will help. Don't spare me!"

The formula for presidential success that emerged from American politics was applicable only for Lincolnian types. A man like Wilson might fall victim where a Franklin Roosevelt would rise in victory. Americans could claim to have produced a genuinely democratic form of leadership, so democratic as to be almost invisible in the hands of its greatest adepts. But it was limited by the conditions of its exercise. It looked to the grass roots of politics rather than to its heights. It was reactive more than it was directive. This was the American style of politics in all areas. Legislation was to grow out of indigenous forces. The economy was not to be directed, but to be cultivated and regulated. Foreign policy was also to be reactive rather than directive.

In order to work, the American political system required a rich land whose people were of generally equal status and power, a people who could provide most of their needs by their own individual efforts. It required a country so isolated from the rest of the world that the resolutions which emerged from its internal processes could not be frustrated by forces from abroad. Otherwise, a deeper and more profoundly architectonic form of political leadership would have been required from the start. Had America been part of Europe the Wilsonian rather than the Lincolnian tradition might have become dominant. Reactive isolationism is the only face such a politics could present to the outside world and still remain true to itself. Anything more positive ran counter to the pluralistic social and economic forces upon which the political system rested. So long as community problems—schools, roads, health, welfare, and the like—could be solved satisfactorily on the local level and so long as laissez-faire conditions obtained throughout American industry, America's pluralistic, inward-looking form of grass-roots democratic leadership remained adequate. But as the 20th century matured none of these conditions any longer held true. Problems of the world impinged directly on every domestic issue.

The internal structure of American society had changed more rapidly than political awareness. There were no longer any purely local issues. The federal government became involved in every serious local problem from water to education. The nation's economy became a vast constellation of world-bestriding corporations and intertwined forces, which could yield only to centralized control and direction. The people themselves had changed. They were no longer self-sufficient. They were no longer rooted in local communities. They communicated their common problems to each other indirectly through the mass media rather than in personal intercourse. Political problems became too complex for the understanding of the common mind. A great corps of professional experts and engineers arose in response to the technical complexity that invaded the city as well as the states and the nation. Traffic control was no different from atomic energy; both were presided over by experts no one else could understand. All of this meant that the traditional form of American democratic leadership had become outmoded. Popular decision-making was impossible, yet popular consent was indispensable. Complexity expelled democracy from the concrete issues of politics and from the people. The only place it still held sway was in the relationship of the people to their highest elected officials. The people and their leaders strove for new ways to reach each other. Out of their joint struggle came a new form of plebiscitary presidential leadership. It matured during a long, tense generation of war and cold war. Its historical models seemed to draw from the Rome of Augustus and the France of Napoleon as much as from the American past. And yet the old pluralistic political machinery survived alongside the new politics of mass consensus. The America of the Kennedy brothers and of Lyndon Johnson seemed to be living simultaneously in two different political systems, the parochial intransigence of the old set stubbornly against the transcending impulse of the new.

The covert logic of crisis silently invaded the overt processes of American politics. Born of the discord between the vested institutions of local consent and the novel, centralizing imperatives of mass consensus, a constitutional impasse developed that could find fitful resolution only at the apex of power. Distant though the people were from the sinews of national power they had come to feel closer to the President than they did to any precinct politician or local leader. They saw, read, and heard more of him than they did of any but their closest friends and relatives. For his own part, the President nervously courted the people like an anxious suitor of a much-besieged beauty. Needing constant proof of their unflagging affection, he sought reassurance everywhere, studying polls and opinion indices the way an overextended market investor studies the latest stock quotations. President and people were bound together in a public drama of mutual fascination. And, as in a drama, the relationship was intense, but it was also unreal. The people seldom got behind the President's carefully contrived public image, and the President knew not the people themselves but the public opinion profiles of them constructed by his pollsters. This was the new face of bureaucratized democracy: a mass media image presiding over a statistical profile. The result was an aggrandizement of the presidency, a development which by historical standards was virtually un-American. The traditional forms of grass-roots democracy were inapplicable to the national and world problems constantly besetting the nation. Above all else, America prided itself before the world for its tradition of participational democracy, yet it was here more than anywhere else that revitalization was most imperative.

## The British Model

If the American president traditionally percolated to power from the bottomlands of politics, the British prime minister descended to the people only after he had won party leadership over his political peers at the heights of parliamentary power. Even then, when the prime minister appeared before the people, it was not in his own name but in the name of his party. The electoral program for which he stood was not his personal creation. Its broad outlines had emerged gradually from the party conventions. Specific issues arose from the dialectic clash of opposing parliamentary parties. The Crown was politically mindless and, in theory, merely stamped its seal automatically on whatever the majority party wanted. A conflict that could not be resolved in Parliament would be referred to the people in a general election. The people were supposed to be presented with a choice between programs rather than persons. The program which won became the substance of its party's popular mandate. British democratic leadership took place on a programmatic rather than a personal plane. In fact, according to the theory of the constitution, party leaders hardly existed at all. It would have made little difference if paid performers had been hired to give their election speeches. This was the working theory of the classical British constitution.

So long as the system worked, and it seemed to work well until after World War I, British democracy was the marvel of modern politics. Students of its intricate machinery were accustomed to stating that the British prime minister was the most powerful political leader in the world—all ministerial and legislative authority was concentrated in his office—but no one was alarmed by the fact. The British, alone in all the world and indeed in all history, seemed to have solved the riddle of contriving to make authority always adequate but never arbitrary. Somehow the British seemed to have acquired a marvelous set of constitutional instincts not found in any other people. However, their basic political style was aristocratic rather than democratic. This was always revealed in times of crisis and change. British democracy, like the game of cricket whose imagery it often applied, was an orderly spectator sport, not a rough-and-tumble free-for-all. While its processes were adaptable to the growing complexity of government they did not fit well with the new politics of mass media and mass movements. These tended to subvert the tradition of parliamentary sovereignty by depositing political power in the hands of those who were most effective in making personal appeals to the masses.

World War I was the turning point. In Lloyd George Britain produced a leader whose strength was as firmly based in the people as it was in Parliament. The portent could be attributed to the war emergency and ignored. Then came the Great Depression and the cabinet crisis of 1931. It was a far smaller crisis than that of the war but it had similar political effects. Ramsay MacDonald had little trouble in using the mass media to play both Crown and people against the deadlocked factions in the Parliamentary parties. What emerged was a new form of personal political power.

The British financial crisis of 1931 was a prescient one for another reason. Because it sprang in part from sources outside Britain it could not be resolved by internal political forces alone. Its solution required lengthy international negotiation. This was alien to the conventions of the constitution whose principles required that the conflicts Parliament could not solve be referred to the people for resolution. There was no point in calling a general election if there was no program to take to the people. A program could not be devised without the aid of foreign financial powers. This presented a genuine constitutional crisis, for the centres of international finance could not negotiate a stable financial settlement unless there was in Britain a stable government. This was the new logic of politics and it stood in direct conflict with the old. It was typical of the domestic crises which were to occupy the political landscape of the 20th century. The affairs of the world had become so intertwined that the stability of each nation could be preserved only by insuring the stability of the web of interrelationships that enveloped them all. This demanded a new world constitutionalism with processes commensurate to the scale on which political problems arose. Otherwise it would be like the residents of Soho trying to eliminate only that portion of the London smog that hangs over their own precincts.

In 1931 the local conventions of the British constitution were vetoed by the larger forces of world politics. When Ramsay MacDonald ignored the party system to form a coalition cabinet and ask the people for the blanket authority of a "doctor's mandate" he was unwittingly acknowledging the end of the traditional form of British democratic leadership. The party system, which could not have recovered in any case, was given no chance to do so. The rapidly on-rushing war saw to that. And during the war the chance innovations of the crisis found their most adept utilization in the hands of Winston Churchill. Vowing in ringing phrases to preserve the empire, he was instead forced to pre-side at the wartime liquidation of Commonwealth, constitution, and empire. But Churchill was more accomplice than author. The war, and the Cold War that prolonged it, magnified the forces that were removing decision-making from the people, and escalating local issues to the most elevated councils of world politics.

So long as nations held on to their customary forms of politics, World War II could not really be brought to a close. It had opened the domestic forums of the West and the politburo of Eurasia to the play of strong new international politi-cal forces. The Atlantic community and the Eastern land mass paired off to threaten and to ward off each other. In doing so they began slowly to break out of the confines of the nation-state.

The United Nations was disappointing as an arbiter among the great pow-ers, but as an incubator of new nations it was prolific beyond all expectations. It began in 1945 with 46 founding members. In 20 years its membership had considerably more than doubled. Previously the acquisition of nationhood was a mysterious process tightly controlled by the great oligarchic powers of the West. Now it involved little more than registration with the General Assembly. Formerly nationhood required an elaborate and expensive outlay for embassies and staff. Now small countries like Niger and Chad can command the world's attention in a way that previously was reserved only to the great Western pow-ers. All this occurred without any direct modification of the state, either in Britain or elsewhere in the West. Not only the United Nations but also a host of new organs of European and international cooperation grew up alongside the state. Britain's political problems increasingly arose from and required resolu-tion in these new arenas, but her constitution remained the same as when Britain could assume that the forces of diplomacy were generated at home for application abroad.

As the winds of world power buffeted British domestic politics from the four corners of the earth, her statesmen rose and fell on foreign issues beyond their control. Purely domestic issues had almost ceased to exist. The natural result was the multiplication of crisis. Every issue that arrived at the borders of Brit-ish politics from abroad was processed through inward-looking political cus-toms, now better able to frustrate than to resolve. The consequence was an augmentation of executive power with which neither the parliamentary opposi-tion, the party system, nor the electorate was able to cope. The British people watched from afar as their Prime Minister turned into a replica of the Amer-ican plebiscitary president. Britain's tie with America led to an endemic dollar crisis. America's thermonuclear supremacy colonized the Foreign Office and the defense establishment in the same way that her economic power had the Exchequer. But traditional institutions, though they could not cope with the expanding universe of politics, were still too hardy to give up. The British were the victims of their own constitutional virtues. Had British institutions been less excellent they might have been less resistant to reform.

## Crisis and Stalemate

Similar forces impinged upon France, making their way more easily because of her weaker constitution and her more powerful government bureaucracy. In France, the revolutionary forces of world power, which ignored national boundaries, mass politics, and party baronies, made much faster headway than in the United States or Britain. For one thing, the French had never produced adequate parliamentary institutions. Indeed, the 20th century was in general somewhat unsuited to the French taste. She began it under the shadow of German military and industrial might. The strength of her glorious cultural heritage kept the industrial revolution always somewhat at arm's length. Atelier craftsmen in France had differed from their English counterparts. They were either unwilling or unable to climb the corporate ladder of capitalism. Her peasant proprietors long refused to convert their lands into American farm factories. Her tradesmen persisted as urban peasants, frugally cultivating the same commercial allotment year on end. Landed proprietors and industrial moguls maintained their preserves in relative serenity. French labour, perhaps the only true proletariat in the world, worked and plotted in the molds their Communard forebears had established in the 1840s. It was as if France could never quite let go of the 19th century. Its hold upon her body politic exerted itself most strongly through the party system. The cultural forces, the social classes, and the ideologies of the past congealed into a panoply of small political parties more dedicated to the settling of old scores than new problems. The result was the politics of crisis and stalemate. Seldom could one party get enough votes to carry out a consistent parliamentary program. Only by forming a coalition of parties could a parliamentary majority be achieved. But all such coalitions were inherently unstable. As a result, a parliamentary veto was easier to organize than was a governing majority. The French parliament became an engine of opposition rather than achievement. A programmatic vacuum developed and lasted with only occasional interruption for over half a century.

Behind the facade of parliamentary frustration a more hopeful, if less spectacular, tradition was in the making. The French civil service became a marvel of administrative expertise and integrity. Here too, the traditions of the past were at work, patiently and effectively constructing a professional governing cadre. France had never really broken with the glorious administrative tradi-

31

tion begun under the mercantilist kings of the *ancien régime*. This virtual priesthood of the bureaucracy stood her in good stead throughout the period of entrepreneurial capitalism and parliamentary deadlock. The combination of a parliament that could not govern and a bureaucracy that could prepared the way for De Gaulle's remarkable acquisition of unchallengeable authority in 1958. De Gaulle found he could turn the mass media against the traditional political system and free his hands of both constitutional restraints and governing details to follow the ambit of world power along its international circuit.

The new Fifth Republic appeared to represent a sharp break with 150 years of French democracy. De Gaulle, more apparently than the British prime minister or the American president, was a plebiscitary president. With consummate skill he managed the mass media, especially television, so as to envelop his person, his authority, and his policies with an almost irrational charismatic mystique, seemingly alien to the Cartesian rationalism so long identified with French politics. The French succumbed to a cult of personality superficially reminiscent of Hitler's Germany and Stalin's Russia. But the differences were as important as the similarities. Traditional personal freedoms were only slightly abrogated. And though the means De Gaulle employed appealed to the irrational in man, the ends of their exercise were remarkably rational. France exchanged rational parliamentary processes, which in fact had produced little but irrational policies, for the opposite.

De Gaulle's models, consciously or not, came from Plato's *Republic* and Bacon's *New Atlantis* more than from Fascism or Stalinism. In drawing about himself prominent French intellectuals from all parties—they thought of themselves as latter-day Mandarins—he installed in positions of authority a kind of collegiate, or oligarchic, philosopher king. His elaborately contrived appeals to the French masses were reminiscent of what Plato had described as the "noble lie": the tricks a wise leader plays on his people in persuading them to follow the arcane dictates of the common good.

One might have thought that the intellectuals of France, always noted for their fierce individualism, would have been De Gaulle's most adamant opponents. Why were they not? In the long run the answer to this question may be the most important thing to be learned from the phenomenon of Charles de Gaulle. Throughout the world the intellectual and the scientist are growing in social and political significance. What we cannot as yet foresee is whether they will ever become a ruling class, like the capitalists and Cavaliers before them. Would Gaullist France set a pattern for the future?

It is hard to see how Europe, especially France, can look kindly toward the 20th century. It brought unceasing waves of warfare, economic devastation, and totalitarian holocausts that swept through nation after nation, ravishing societies with man-made diseases of the body politic, as medieval plagues had once ravished the physical body. Before the century was half ended the imperial and cultural dominance Europe once exercised over the world had been dissolved. Peoples who were once her pupils and servants rudely shoved Europe aside. As the plagues of old subsided they left upheaval and revolution in their wake. So did the social pestilences of the 20th century.

French intellectuals felt the effects of this turmoil more intensely than all others. As the 20th century approached, France had been the unquestioned cultural leader of mankind. The creative work of her leading painters and writers influenced the styles and patterns of speculation of the entire world. A chance Parisian salon discussion might reverberate for years throughout the discourses of Europe's intelligentsia. Two wars later, physically debilitated by the first and morally emasculated by the second, France was dishonoured and ignored. Many Frenchmen sought and found moral rebirth and invigoration in the anti-Nazi underground. The effect on France's intellectuals was especially profound. Through it they seemed to acquire an intuitive understanding of the conditions of freedom under mass, bureaucratic conditions.

Franz Kafka's strange books, *The Castle* and *The Trial,* had early depicted the amorphous, low-grade terror that permeates even the most gentle and benevolent of bureaucracies. His was an extreme portrait, a caricature, but like all good caricaturists Kafka painted truer than the truth itself. He spoke directly to bureaucratic man's sense of estrangement. He wrote of the baffling new ways of life which can only be compared to an underground existence. The underground struggle waged by Frenchmen against the Nazis was comparably true to life. It was not what contemporary conditions are really like, but what they often feel like. The problems and crises that arose among the Maquis were not the direct counterparts of the problems of liberty and survival in bureaucratic cultures but rather their most extreme and revealing analogues. The French became pioneer settlers forced to master the conditions of survival at the frontiers of bureaucratic culture. Their lives were given new meaning. Their endeavours and examples were once again shown as beacons for the world. They were like the 19th-century Americans who had settled the frontiers of the industrial revolution. And like those pragmatic predecessors, they too produced a new philosophy—a new ethic—suited to the conditions they met. The existentialist ethic was not born in France—neither was the Protestant ethic born in America—but it was first applied and dramatized there. And it was from the writings of French intellectuals, Camus and Sartre most prominently, that it pierced to the troubled spirit of bureaucratic man everywhere.

With the end of World War II came the end of the exhilaration and significance that had characterized life during the occupation. Normality returned, and that was the whole trouble. France subsided back into insignificance as a nation. Indochina, East Africa, and even North Africa demanded independence, and Frenchmen were torn between injured pride at the prospect of losing their empire and shame over the excesses required to retain it. She submitted with mingled gratitude and resentment to U.S. economic and military colonization. Her intellectuals refused to return meekly to the trivial charades of the Third Republic and remembered with nostalgia the heady days of the underground.

De Gaulle, who had kept French prestige alive during the war, now promised to do so again. On returning to power in 1958 he asked for, and was given, a new hand-tailored constitution modeled after the contours of his political personality as carefully as his elegant uniforms were fitted to those of his imposing stature. The new regime was a mutation in French politics, but it was no accident. It seemed to be a denial of the French democratic tradition, and it was, taken literally. However, in a deeper sense, it represented a profound consensus. Quickly it substituted an aura of rejuvenation for that of disease. The economy, already the beneficiary of extensive U.S. aid, was now inspired to new heights of performance. Foreign policy was at one stroke freed of the irrational impediments of both the Cold War and 19th-century imperialism. Leading social strata, including both intellectuals and industrialists, felt meaning had returned to their lives and glory to their nation. Nagging problems of distribution and agriculture persisted but compared to the past the French economy was a model of orderliness. And if this nation, which above all others had learned how to resist Nazi totalitarianism, accepted with equanimity the authoritarianism of the man who had symbolized the resistance, her self-confidence was not without some foundation.

Gaullist France had turned her back on the pluralistic, multiparty parliamentary democracy of the past. That she had also turned her back irrevocably on democracy was far from apparent. For a moment, during the opening years of the Fifth Republic, what struck the eye was the dazzling authoritarian spectacle of the imperious General. In many ways it appeared to be pastry-shell politics, splendid to look at but too fragile to stand for long. But behind the contrived mass-media charades with which *De Gaullism* was embroidered there developed the solid *Gaullist* governing institutions and traditions.

The traditional democracy of France was gone, but, as we have seen, so were the traditional democratic practices of England and America. The times were making two new demands on democracy. One issued from the arena of world politics, the other from scientific and technological forces. These latter led to a new kind of professionalized government. Many French political philosophers argued that liberty would find protection from the newer professional and scientific classes rather than from traditional democratic institutions. A world democracy of peoples meant that the desires of the world would have to take precedence over the desires of individual nations, no matter how democratically those internal desires were expressed. It is not a new problem. The American federal union foundered, and fought a bitter civil war over this same problem. Now that the same problem had appeared in the world arena, nations were being forced to learn what Lincoln had taught the American states. The France of De Gaulle might stand as a lesson to the West. Henceforth national interests could be accomplished only in conjunction with the common interests of the international community. The other demand came to democracy from internal professional and technological forces. In France, as in the other nations of the West, science and technology seemed bent upon undermining the older institutions and practices of democracy.

## The New Mercantilism

In the newer nations, however, especially in Russia, the impact of science and technology had the effect of preparing for the emergence of democracy. In Russia the initial Bolsheviks had been as political magi heralding an ideological star that refused to rise. They anxiously searched the western heavens beyond their borders, trying to anticipate the political imperatives of the expected new, world, socialist authority. But even had their international vision materialized, the internal problems of Russia would not have changed. Most perplexing was the problem of devising a political system for converting quickly unskilled labour into industrial capital. It was the problem of subordinating economics to politics in a most un-Marxist fashion. But crisis often deals harshly with dogmatism, and the nations who later won independence were to run head on into the same problem that led to Stalinism in Russia: rapid industrialization of a pre-industrial economy.

The wealth that Stalinism forcefully extruded from the Russian people could not be squandered on romantic foreign revolutionaries. The doctrine of world revolution in primitive Marxism also had to go. Russian industrialization was not for others to partake of, only to emulate. But what sometimes escaped Western notice was that the Russian model for rapid industrialization was a modern and more terroristic version of a hallowed device. Wherever it has succeeded, industrialization has been prepared for through central economic organization and development programs. History knows them by the name *mercantilism.*

Mercantilism appeared in the West as early as the 16th century and was not supplanted by capitalism until the 18th and 19th centuries. Mercantilist planning migrated to America under the auspices of Alexander Hamilton. Its principles were adjusted to 19th-century conditions, first in Germany and then in Japan. It finally assumed 20th-century form in Soviet Russia under the slogan "socialism in one country." From there, with local variations, it spread rapidly to China and the other new nations.

35

The general prerequisites of industrialization are everywhere the same. The capital foundation must be laid down before industrial growth can take place. Public utilities must precede. The problem is to provide for power, transportation, exchange, communications, technologies, and skills, and to do so primarily out of indigenous human and physical resources. In England and France this process took 200 years. The new nations of today are more impatient. They want their basic capital equipment installed in a hurry and are prepared to pay the political price of impatience: dictatorship. Adam Smith pointed out that the accumulation of private capital often can be stimulated through policies that make high profits possible. But even then the mercantilist stage must have already occurred. The only way to get the basic public foundations and utilities into being is through collective programs for converting labour into the needed capital foundation. Labour must be organized, trained, and motivated in accordance with a long-range capital formation plan. It is no small undertaking. Peasant and tribal institutions must be dismantled and urban institutions substituted in their place. An integrated legal order must be substituted in place of discordant provincial customs and codes. Consumption must be held to a minimum to maximize the share of production available for capital formation. Under whatever auspices this process has been accomplished—from the New England Puritanism of the 17th century to the Fidelismo of the 20th—it has required dictatorial organization. The more primitive the initial state of human and physical resources, the more impatient the people, and the more advanced the stage of technology, the more totalitarian must be the scope of the dictatorship.

It bears repeating that many Englishmen and Frenchmen who lived under mercantilist kings thought their regimes were unconscionably dictatorial, so much so that ultimately they rose in revolt. In retrospect, the absolute monarchies of the mercantilist kings of Europe seem to have been quite humane. They were certainly leisurely. Gothic England stumbled into industrialization, taking 150 years to make the necessary transformations of her late feudal economy and family systems. Twentieth-century underdeveloped countries must resort to stringent totalitarianism in order to do the same thing on purpose and in a hurry. Moreover, one can only industrialize at the technological level of one's own times. England and France industrialized when nearly all products were still handcrafted. Nineteenth-century Germany, however, did not go back in history to start out from 17th-century levels of handicraft technology. From the beginning she needed the railroads and ironworks which England had taken a hundred years to produce. Only the government, or enterprises which are huge from the start, could command the resources necessary for undertakings at such a level. Accordingly, the small entrepreneurs who provided the base for English and French industrialization had to be skipped over in Germany in favour of government-sponsored cartels. Japan's industrialization started from an even higher stage of cartelization. Possibly Russia could have followed the Japanese model, but when one wants everything in a hurry—General Motors, I. G. Farben, and Mitsubishi virtually overnight—state trusts and collectives may be the only answer. Today, even the United States has reached this point. Private industry can no longer finance her most serious new capital needs. To desalinate water, to provide atomic energy, to pioneer new air transport planes, and to explore outer space are all beyond the capabilities of private financial resources.

Westerners, Americans most of all, know what it is to be in a hurry. They may also recall the terroristic slave compounds, the authoritarian construction camps, and the cruel industrial slums which sprang up in response to their own insatiable industrial appetites. Production for markets rather than subsistence requires the forced relocation of peoples, whether it is the Irish peasants of the 1820s or the Russian peasants of the 1920s. Industrialization has always been ugly and inhuman and it has always employed authoritarian methods. The earlier forms were simpler, they proceeded at a more leisurely pace, and their authoritarian devices appeared to be more private and more the consequence of circumstances for which no one was politically responsible. In 19th-century Europe sometimes it seemed as if private authoritarianism was produced by the same unseen force that was supposed to regulate the marketplace; it was nearly as invisible as the acclaimed invisible hand. But it was different in the 20th century. Industrial violence could not be kept invisible where the state took the economy into its own hands.

First in Stalinist Russia and then in the developing countries that followed her lead, the 20th century witnessed the appearance of a new mercantilist totalitarianism. On top of the historically familiar authoritarianism required to impose modern industry on primitive cultures were revealed the special forms of authority and mass manipulation required to officially mobilize labour and relocate populations.

There were a few specially favoured exceptions, most notably Puerto Rico, Yugoslavia, Israel, and Egypt. But these were quite special cases. Capital that can be squeezed out of diplomacy need not be squeezed from land and labour. Even here, however, the need for authoritarianism was given an additional spur. Only strong governments—those with forceful and ruthless executives—could apply extortionist pressures against the capital-supplying centres of East and West.

Authoritarianism has always accompanied the initial stages of industrialization. The more advanced the technological level, the larger must be the organizational units of industrialization and the greater must be the degree of authoritarianism. As the impulse to modernize and industrialize spread to the

37

new nations of the 20th century, it carried dictatorship with it wherever it went. The late 20th century was converted into a volatile collection of dictatorships beset by the internal discords that always accompany rapid transition.

## Interlocking Patterns

World interrelationships were so closely interwoven that instabilities in one place were transmitted everywhere instantaneously. In the 1920s a coup d'etat in Latin America seemed almost like a musical comedy diversion. By the 1950s it was quite the opposite. Every world power had an immediate stake in everything that happened everywhere. Indeed, governmental changes were no longer left to chance by the great powers. They struggled against each other clandestinely throughout the domestic political systems of the world. This accelerated the trend toward authoritarianism in two ways. Democracy could find no friend among the great contending powers. Both sides feared it might prove unreliable. Secondly, as the great powers invaded the domestic politics of other nations they tended to convert all domestic issues everywhere into international issues. Just as in Gaullist France and Cold War America, so also in Cuba and Korea the internationalization of domestic politics added to the forces tending to undercut the prospects of democracy and to magnify the role of the executive. At the same time, however, this revealed to the world the extent of its interconnectedness.

Arenas of politics are followed ultimately by institutions of government. As world politics matures and stabilizes its forms of action, it is destined to constitutionalize the dictatorial authority of national leaders in the same way that parliamentary politics ultimately constitutionalized the despotic authority of despotic feudal barons. We may also expect this tendency to be reinforced from within the world's new nations as their goals of modernization approach realization. This was the lesson of the end of Stalinism in Russia. If violent developmental programs really succeed they must die of their own fruits.

Terror was employed in Stalinist Russia to solve the problem of motivating peasant-based masses to increase their productivity without increasing their levels of consumption. When standard-of-living increases were awarded, they came as a result of a central political estimate that they would bring more than proportionate increases in productivity. Later on, however, industrialization in Russia generated on a nationwide scale the same moderating forces that the mature industrial enterprises of the West had already experienced. This is the nature of an industrial civilization; the carrot soon becomes more effective than the stick. Slave labour is notoriously uneconomic except for the most primitive purposes. The introduction of expensive capital equipment may reduce the value of the craftsman but it increases enormously the value of the common labourer. Marx had foreseen the former but not the latter. The whole purpose of politically induced industrialization is to increase the economic value of people. This is the meaning of increased productivity.

As an industrialization program succeeds, its initial modes of crude coercion are moderated, first by the imperatives of economics and then by those of politics. Compare the common people of a preindustrial society with those of a vigorously expanding industrial society. The people who are brought forth as a result of industrialization are highly educated, technically advanced, economically mobile, and intricately organized, especially when compared with what they were before. They require a special environment to elicit their optimum utilization. Terrorist control systems may have worked with their predecessors, but with industrial development terror becomes unwieldy, overly expensive, ineffective, and politically dangerous. The requirement of economic efficiency carries its own rationale with it wherever it reaches. These imperatives, which must be forced upon a lethargic and tradition-bound people at the start, soon become broadly comprehensible to the new intelligent, skilful, and highly motivated people who are naturally produced by an industrial order. Such people can be managed more efficiently through some form of democratic consent than through terroristic imposition. Managers and leaders, though their personal preferences may be authoritarian, soon find professional success depends upon their ability to stimulate the voluntary cooperation of their subordinates. Parallel to this is a process in the political order that tends to bring forth rule-of-law principles. Maintaining a terrorist police system becomes more threatening to the top officials than to ordinary citizens. The elite soon finds that the price of insuring its own security is to extend political security to all. This is the inexorable, universal logic of liberalism. It has found many different institutional forms of expression. In the West it first resulted in a demand for laissez-faire. Later came rule-of-law reforms, then trade unions, cooperatives, and welfare programs. Similar forces, or their counterparts, underlay the dismantling of Stalinist terror in the U.S.S.R.

The reforms that were initiated under Khrushchev and carried forward under Kosygin and Brezhnev were at once the signal of industrial achievement and the precondition to its further consolidation. There would never appear in Russia a mirror image of the liberalism that flourished during the 19th century in the West. Indeed, the West's own liberalism never took precisely the same form in any two countries. Sometimes it even took radically different forms within the same country. This can be seen by recalling the 19th-century contrast in America between the agrarian South and the industrial North. But whatever the form, and regardless of the name, something like liberalism appears wherever people become extremely valuable.

The fact that 20th-century Russia experienced some of the same general developmental forces as did 19th-century Europe and America, produced a curious result. As the 20th century drew to a close, the only place in the world experiencing a trend away from authoritarianism was in the older of the People's Democracies. Americans who diverted their attention from the oppression of the Negro, the Germans and Italians who dismissed Fascism as a momentary lapse, and Britains to whom imperialism recalled Kipling rather than Warren Hastings, might complain of how much reform was still needed in Russia rather than applaud what was accomplished. The fact of Russian liberalization was nonetheless real. It rested upon the same general forces that had brought Western liberalization everywhere.

The Stalin era had seen several distinct bastions of power rise alongside the Party: the armed forces, the security forces, the industrial complex, and the administrative bureaucracy. In addition, increasingly insistent forces began to appear from agriculture, from urban centres, and from the talent trades—performers, writers, teachers, students, athletes, and above all, scientists.

Intruding from without Russia came other novel forces. The Communist regimes of Eastern Europe were progressing from subservience to semiautonomous dominion status, occasionally even outright defiance. Yugoslavia's break with the Communist commonwealth had upon it something of the same effect that America's breakaway in 1776 had upon the British commonwealth. Next, China became a national threat to Russia as well as a rival force in world affairs and within foreign Communist parties. Finally, there were the more general international forces which impinged upon Russia, just as upon America, from every corner of the earth. Scholars who ponder this catalog of the forces that influence Soviet politics often remark on its similarity to those at work in America. But the same forces are at work in all Western nations. We shall even discover them affecting the institutions of the developing nations.

It does not follow automatically that the nations of the future will be impelled to develop along similar lines. At least this has never happened in the past. There were marked differences between the types of feudalism produced in Europe, Islam, China, and Japan. Within medieval feudalism itself there was great diversity. Ancient city-states were all quite similar, and yet between Rome and Carthage as well as between the individual city-states of ancient Greece there were many significant differences. Cultural systems have never been produced in mirror-image likenesses of each other. However, the contemporary forces of homogenization ignore border guards and secret police. They travel on passports of necessity, out of the East as well as into it. World interrelationships and interdependencies were never in the past so intense as they became as the last quarter of the 20th century approached. While a complete convergence and accommodation of the world's cultures cannot be expected, we should not be surprised if the future brings an international homogenization more thorough than ever before in history.

# *Chapter* 3   Democracy and the Politics of Cultural Development

LIKE ALICE TRYING to enter a strange new territory in Wonderland, we feel the need of a special talisman or a secret formula as we seek to understand today's new nations. They are singled out as the developing nations. Their problems have a familiar sound. Today's new nations are nationalistic. Their unity is being forged by militaristic regimes reminiscent of the unifying role played by the national army when the European nations were born. They are bent on industrialization. They proclaim their ultimate devotion to democracy. This combination of nationalism, military unification, industrialization, and democracy had been the special historic creation of the West. These elements can hardly be imagined separately, much less in combination, without holding before the mind the recent historical experiences of England, France, the United States, and the U.S.S.R. The impulse is sound, up to a point. First we will consider the differences between the new and the old nationalisms. Later we will seek to uncover some of the common political problems shared by all of the developing nations known to history.

The institutional patterns of the West are not really applicable to the politics of development in the New Nations. Indeed, the politics of development has appeared throughout the past and it promises to dominate man's concerns for as far as we can see into the future. If we wish to understand the politics of development in today's new nations we cannot refuse to give attention to the more general and historical settings within which men have faced the problems of development. Conversely, a consideration of the politics of development in today's new nations will enhance our understanding of the political implications of man's ongoing developmental problems. The new nations are intensely nationalistic but theirs is not the nationalism familiar from recent Western history. Ho Chi Minh, Nasser, and Nkrumah did not play the roles of Talleyrand, Metternich, and Disraeli. The Organization for African Unity that met in Addis Ababa in 1963 was not the counterpart of the Congress of Vienna that met in 1815. Today's new nations should be the world's most adamant defenders of sovereignty—and they are. But they are also the world's strongest supporters of the United Nations. Beyond that, they are the world's strongest advocates of world order.

41

One of the most striking characteristics of the developing world is its militarism. Military dictatorships abound. The first impulse is to compare this to Western 19th-century militarism. But they are not really similar. Nineteenth-century militarism was a part of 19th-century nationalism. It was directed toward the increase of national power in competition with other nations. Europe was the marketplace of world power and all the nations of Europe were locked in a struggle to monopolize as much of the world as possible. This older form of European nationalism is rapidly changing its nature, as was seen in the previous chapter. Imperialism was the aim of 19th-century nationalism; it is the enemy of the new nationalism of the 20th century's developing countries. This is the first distinction between the old and the new nationalisms. It helps explain why the two nationalisms represent opposing drives.

If we seek back beyond the 19th century, however, Western history is more instructive. The nation-state was a product of the national army. Through the army, kings and dictators were able to disarm the private armies of local barons and build an integral national community. This has been the function of militarism in the developing nations. It is directed at the resolution of internal strife and at guaranteeing the security of national boundaries. Israel and Egypt are relatively far developed along these lines. The new nations of Africa, however, appear to be in for a long arduous period during which internal pacification and the rationalization of the irrational boundaries, left over from Western colonial divisions, takes place. This would appear to indicate that the new nationalism is, after all, much like the old. But while it is true that both represented community-building episodes, there the parallel ends.

The old nationalism of Europe looked inward for the creation of law and outward for the creation of power. The new nationalism of Asia and Africa is the opposite. The new nations could not have been born if it had not been for the external authority of the United Nations. They must look outward for the source of legality that gives them national sustenance and guarantees the integrity they need to develop their own institutions as they see fit. Moreover, they do not create power abroad, out of colonies, as did the buccaneering states of Europe. What power the new nations create must be built out of their own peoples and resources. When they look outward for treasure they apply methods that turn the old nationalism upside down. They must design their foreign policies so as to attract capital, not capture it. This gives the new nations a direct interest in the creation of an international rule of law, an intent that was absent from 19th-century nationalism. The new nations want to be sought after but not fought over.

The old nations regarded world law the way 19th-century entrepreneurs regarded state planning. They wanted a free market for competitive world exploitation. "Every nation for itself," cried England's Canning, adding that concern for the common good of the world was best left to God. If nations fell to quarreling among themselves war was their only arbiter. We have seen that while the new nations are militaristic they are not imperialist. Theirs is a militarism that is far older than nationalism. It is the immemorial militarism required to create an integrated community.

The militarism of the old nations looked outward. It was, as Clausewitz said, the extension of diplomacy. But diplomacy itself has changed. The old diplomacy implied the resolution of conflicts in war, world war if necessary. The new nationalism implies a new diplomacy that can find resolution only in a world political order.

The third great goal of the new nations is the rapid achievement of industrialization, cultural development, and modernization. Again, this is a goal that sounds familiar to the Western ear, and there is indeed a similarity between the two. But the difference is that Western industrialization had an especially harsh impact on precisely those which are now the new nations. The motif of Western industrialization was not so much development as it was exploitation. This was certainly the impact it had upon colonial areas. Exploitation and imperialism began in unison and always remained interrelated. They ushered in a classic form of despotism. Western nations ruled the world as feudal overlords. The relation between imperial power and colony was that between master and servant. Whole regions were administered as if they were concentration camps, designed for the maximum exploitation of raw human and physical resources.

Western industrialization made the state into a vast machine for processing and exchanging resources. In England this was the program of the Manchester liberals, in the United States it was the program of the so-called Radical Republicans, who monopolized power after the Civil War. Lenin started the Russian state on pretty much the same track. Socialism, he said, was electrification plus Soviet power.

But Russia marked a turning point. Industrialization and imperialism had been developed by the older Western nations into closely related forms of economic and political exploitation. By the time Russia's turn to industrialize came the world was all parceled out. Russia's form of exploitation also had its own closely related political and economic features. It also was a form of imperialism. But since it could not look outward for the exploitation of colonial subjects it was forced to turn inward on its own people, its many ethnic subcultures, and later its satellites. The exploitation of satellites was quite different from the exploitation of colonies, as we shall see later. All this added up to the economic meaning of what was called the dictatorship of the proletariat. It was a self-confessed form of despotism. Stalin employed the slogan, "socialism in one country," to explain it away. But if we bear in mind the industrial content

Lenin gave to Russian socialism, Stalinism can be understood as a new form of imperialism in one country.

## The Chinese Model

Compare Chinese and Russian industrialization with that of the West. Russia in 1920 was at a stage comparable to that of England in the mid-17th century. However, China in 1950 was more like mid-16th-century England, just after the feudal wars had subsided. Because China had to start from a much lower level of development she was forced to concentrate on agricultural production as much as, or more than, on industry and manufacturing. It was a sound impulse. It was the way the first Western nations had inaugurated their industrialization programs. China also made use of the basic organizational innovation of the Russians, imperialism turned inward. All of this made the Chinese model more attractive than the Russian model to the developing nations. When nations such as Ghana and Cuba won freedom China was still in her first stages of modernization. Russia, on the other hand, was comparatively well developed by 1960. She was even acquiring some of the traits of a have rather than a have-not nation.

The Chinese also had in their favour their pigmented skin. The cry of the independence movements in the new nations was to throw out the white imperialist oppressor. Having raised a successful revolution with this cry it was discordant for them to turn back to the white man for help and inspiration, even when he was a Russian Communist. The Chinese not only had the right colour but they also had struggled against Western imperialism, and they had done so recently.

Russia's quarrel with the West was as old as her revolution. The joint Allied invasion of Russia after World War I very nearly succeeded in bringing down the Bolsheviks. But Russia had never really been colonized by any but her own indigenous masters. Moreover, the Cold War was the contemporary form of Russia's struggle against the West. The developing nations often got caught in the middle, seemingly confronted merely with a choice between two competing forms of imperialism.

The colonies of the imperialist powers were not only suppressed cultures, their economies were dominated by the operation of a few extractive industries. The effect was to funnel colonial resources into the industrial centres of the West. Regions that had been developed to serve Western markets for jute or sugarcane or cocoa cannot one day cut those imperialist ties and the next day run a thriving, independent, and economically self-sufficient economy. For on top of everything else, the expelled Western power sometimes boycotted the products it had once absorbed. Unification of a group of former colonies was of little help. A collection of ex-colonies, no matter how cooperative they may

44

wish to be, cannot provide each other with markets to rival Bremen, Manchester, Marseilles, and New York.

The new nations faced a special set of difficult problems: distorted economies, surplus crude commodities, insufficient commercial and industrial facilities, untrained and inefficient labour and management, capital shortages, adverse trade balances. Topping it all were the uprooted native populations. Independence found them deprived of their traditional cultures and of the work that imperialism had substituted. In all but this last problem the situation facing Africans, Arabs, and Southeast Asians seemed quite similar to that confronting the Chinese Communists.

In addition to the large number of economic similarities between China and the developing nations there was an even more important political kinship. The Chinese had perfected the successful new technique of underground guerrilla opposition for overthrowing a Western-oriented and Western-supported puppet regime. The victory of Mao Tse-tung over Chiang Kai-shek spurred the hopes of native revolutionaries throughout the world. It was an eminently exportable revolutionary technique. Mao's doctrines found avid disciples among oppressed peoples everywhere. Che Guevara, an exceptionally adept pupil, even went on to improve on the doctrine of the master. Independence leaders everywhere who came to power through such means felt a strong ideological kinship with each other.

Nor was this surprising. The middle-class revolutionaries of the 18th century had also employed kindred methods and ideologies against 18th-century monarchs. The Monroe Doctrine of the United States was announced in her own self-defense—European monarchies then opposed the spread of republicanism the way 20th-century America opposed the spread of Communism. However, there was also a strong feeling of ideological kinship with the revolutionary struggle against monarchy everywhere. But the differences between the centuries told not only in their different enemies but also in the political aftermath of victorious revolution. Two factors, one political and the other economic, made it almost inevitable that the inaugural regimes of today's developing countries would be strongly authoritarian. First, they were forced to construct tightly-knit military organizations in order to achieve power. Second, once in power they found that authoritarian methods were necessary to create the special inward-looking imperialism necessary to cope with the stupendous problems of developing and organizing their peoples' human and physical resources.

Neither factor was actually as novel as it appeared to Western eyes. None of the Western nations had been democracies at the beginning of their own industrial efforts. We have already noted that the early monarchical despots of Europe had been able to build nation-states out of divisive feudal baronies only through the invention of the modern army. Once they had secured their power through military means they turned their attention to economic development. Chartered mercantilist enterprises were formed to increase the wealth of the crown. Outside their national borders the same motive dominated royal operations, and modern imperialism was born. Western imperialism operated in much the same fashion throughout the world, first in Latin America and North America, later in Asia and Africa.

Later, when the white settlers won their independence from Europe it often made little difference in the organization of colonial economies. In the United States, south of the Mason-Dixon line, the traditional colonial pattern was maintained until after the Civil War. In Latin America and Africa it remained in force a hundred years later. The Dutch Afrikaans program of apartheid in South Africa was especially noxious; the Portuguese of neighbouring Angola were only slightly more humanitarian. The fact remained, however, that everywhere and in all times the structure of developing nations has been remarkably similar. Ghana under Nkrumah may have seemed to look to the future, and Portuguese Angola to the past, but a visitor from a far planet, traveling through the developing countries of Africa, would have had a hard time telling the difference between the two. Their authoritarianism, their one-party systems, their jails full of political prisoners, their developmental programs, and the sharp differences of status between the administrative elites and the unskilled masses showed how the process of development always poses similar problems and elicits comparable solutions.

Every advanced civilization known to history has employed a similar form of despotism to achieve economic development. But contemporary development contains one great difference, and this difference may carry the seeds of a revolution new to mankind. The nations of the past have often avoided the full internal implications of development by turning despotism outward, that is, by imperialism. The exploitation and subjection of foreign peoples has permitted the imperialist power to institute internal reforms but still preserve intact its old elites.

The saying that England's empire was a vast outdoor public relief system for the aristocracy was more than a clever witticism. And while economists carry on learned debates about whether any nation's empire has been a source of profit, there is no disputing the fact that firms and individuals have reaped huge profits from imperialism. The West has yet to appreciate the full implications of the fact that it is no longer possible to do this. However, the future of democracy in the world may depend on the fact that the new nations are beginning their efforts at development under the new conditions which prevent imperialist exploitation. The logic of the world situation runs counter to imperialism. The ideologies of the new nations are anti-imperialist. This combination may force the new nations to learn a lesson that no civilization has ever learned before: how to institute the principles of democracy in the world community as well as domestically.

## The Democratic Goal

Democracy is the fourth of the motivating goals of the developing nations. And while the nature of democracy is perplexing in any setting, it is especially so in developing countries. Democracy has been one of the oldest quests of mankind, as old as the quest for immortality. Indeed, one of democracy's first forms was a demand by the lower orders of antiquity to enjoy the same kinship with the gods and the same prospect of immortality as was claimed by their priests and great chiefs.

So astute an analyst of democracy as Alexis de Tocqueville identified it with the desire for equality. But this is saying both too much and not enough. The early Americans that Tocqueville wrote about accepted many gross inequalities unquestioningly. Inequalities of wealth, of social position, of authority, of knowledge, and of talent were largely unquestioned. Indeed no society has ever tried, or has even desired, to make all its institutions egalitarian. But the differences between the various historical forms of democracy have depended in large part upon the particular functions and institutions that have come within the popular demand for equality.

In the West, for example, authoritarianism is broadly accepted in military organization, in the management of businesses, in schools, in science, in churches, and in team endeavours such as athletic contests and orchestras. On the other hand, the mature form of Western democracy was influenced strongly by the early self-governing churches, associations, and communities. Their present-day descendants retain vestiges of those early forms of democracy even though conditions are quite different. The industrial cartel of Germany, the English trust company, and the American corporation were once forces for democracy. So were the cities of London, New York, and Paris. They stubbornly retain archaic democratic forms which could be effective only in the small cities that instituted them.

Political theorists of all times have agreed that it is almost impossible to make democracy work in large, congested communities. We have discussed previously the way democracy is expelled from operations that are so complex as to require the talents of professional experts and scientists. A simple gravel road can be designed and even constructed democratically, but not a complex network of interurban expressways. As Plato pointed out, the passengers of a ship would perish if they insisted that problems of navigation be solved by majority vote.

The nations that undertook industrial development at the beginning of the modern period faced economic problems at the gravel road level of simplicity.

Those who began development in the mid-20th century did so at the interurban expressway level of complexity. And though the first nations to industrialize were actually authoritarian until long after the industrial revolution was well under way, it is conceivable that they might have been democratic from the start. At least, democracy was not excluded by the complexity of their tasks.

The opposite was true in the 20th century. Nations like Ghana, Egypt, and China needed the highest technical skills from the start. They had to begin at levels of complexity that the West had worked centuries to produce. One of the costs of technological advance is the restriction of the applicability of participational democracy. In the West democracy was expelled from any function taken over by the expert. What gradually became true of London was true from the start at Lagos. It was simply impossible to think of submitting the complex development programs of mid-20th-century Nigeria to the deliberations of a population that still retained many of the vestiges of tribalism. And yet Nigeria and all other developing nations required broadly based popular consent in order to pursue their developmental programs.

This was the dilemma facing all the would-be leaders of the developing nations. A constantly nourished and refreshed popular mandate was a necessary condition of getting anything done, but what was done had to be accomplished through experts and by authoritarian means. The traditional forms of Western democracy were obviously inapplicable. Moreover, any expectation that replicas of Western democracy might gradually appear in the developing nations was doomed to disappointment. They would never experience the simple organizational conditions that had fostered participational democracy in the West. Any effort to impose early Western democratic forms on the new nations is foolhardy or worse. In any case, the leading Western nations themselves have long since moved away from those forms of democracy they criticize the new nations for failing to adopt.

Twentieth-century Americans who seemed to expect Africa and Asia to institute promptly a two-party system filled their foreign listeners with bafflement. From the outside both of the American parties looked so much alike that foreign critics often regarded the country as a one-party state. On the other hand, to institute a true multiparty system in the new nations would amount to setting off a full-scale civil war.

It had been pretty much the same throughout all the countries in the Anglo-American political tradition. Radically different alternatives of either left or right were seldom presented to the voters. England's Lord Balfour had explained the reason long ago. He said that a system of competing parties presumed the people of a nation would have so profound an agreement on the fundamentals of their society that different political parties could alternate in and out of power without changing the country's basic social and political system.

The leaders of the new nations understand this perfectly. But widespread unity and agreement on fundamentals is exactly what they don't have and are trying to bring about in their own countries. Rampant factionalism, vestigial tribalism, and incipient civil war are what they must overcome if they are to achieve social and political order at all. This can be produced only through constant efforts to educate the masses and through deep-reaching programs of social unification. This effort is democratic, but it is the kind of democracy that occurs when states are being created. It is the form of democracy special to revolutionary regimes.

Revolutionary regimes cannot be judged or understood by the standards that are applicable to those that are securely established. In times of violent transition, such as are now occurring in the developing nations, it is each day an open question whether or not the revolution can be consolidated. There is always an *implicit* two-party system struggling for the allegiance of the people. The nation is torn between the defenders of the *ancien régime* and the would-be founders of the new revolutionary order. Quite frequently the Western nations have participated in this implicit two-party struggle as supporters of the *ancien régime,* with Russia or China supporting the revolution. For the West to do this and at the same time to criticize the revolutionary regime they oppose for not instituting party competition is a strange complaint. It would be like criticizing President Thomas Jefferson for not including proponents of reunion with Britain in his cabinet.

The developing nations of today are at the primordial community-building state of political development. Their problem is the problem of Moses and Solon and Lycurgus and Hammurabi, not the problem of Andrew Jackson and Edmund Burke and Léon Gambetta. None of history's new nations have started off with gentlemanly multiparty systems. The underdeveloped countries, especially those of Africa, must reach far back through the stages of political development to find appropriate models. They must look back beyond the stage when electoral machinery was formed, back beyond the stage of laying the foundations of industrial development, back even beyond the stage of mobilizing agricultural production to accumulate capital for industrial foundations. Their first problem is the primordial one of creating a unified political community. They must produce the "agreement on fundamentals" without which further political development is impossible.

This is the meaning of the "nationalism" and the militarism that are spreading through the underdeveloped world. And it is also the explanation of why they are not the nationalism and militarism of Bismarck and Disraeli. The developing world is following the lead of the great lawgivers of history. It is striving for the principles of civic order celebrated by the ancient Greeks in the Orestean trilogy when the rule of law, symbolized by Apollo, supplanted the retaliatory tribal law of an eye for an eye and a tooth for a tooth. We cannot look back at the likes of Solon and Moses and criticize them for having been authoritarian—for not having instituted a two-party system. And yet, Solon and Moses were profoundly popular leaders. They saw the need for putting down the divisive leaders of the traditional tribes and factions. In the light of what went before them their roles were democratic. The same is true of England's William the Conqueror. History books celebrate him as the fountainhead of the liberties that followed. Yet in his own time he was a military dictator ruthlessly crushing tribal centres of opposition. This is the first perspective in which the problem of democracy must be viewed in today's underdeveloped nations. But will anything like Western democracy ever appear in the non-Western world? It is a question that must be returned to later. For it may be that all nations together will have to develop a special, postindustrial form of democracy.

Just as it is impossible in the 20th century to begin industrial development at 17th-century levels so also is it impossible to begin political development at ancient levels. Leisurely historical processes must be focused into one frenzied forced march upon tomorrow. President Julius Nyerere of Tanzania had to try to be Solon, Pericles, William the Conqueror, Bacon, Washington, Bismarck, Gambetta, Lenin, and Mao Tse-tung, each modernized and brought up to date, and all of them rolled into one. Economic problems range from building jungle trails with road gangs to producing atomic energy with native scientists. People that have known neither the wheel nor the plow must undergo the agrarian, the urban, the industrial, and the scientific revolutions all at the same time. Peoples whose organizational achievements have rested upon tribalism and slavery must develop a community, a sovereign authority, a central police, rule of law adjudication, industrial corporations, legislation, a professional bureaucracy, and mass democracy all together. That is, all of a sudden they must produce an advanced civilization. This means producing an urban order, for the city has been man's instrument for developing the politics of modernization. The two great examples were the ancient city and the industrial city.

## Civic Order

The word civilization has the same root as the word *city*. Civilization was born in the city and ever since the link between the two has been an intimate one. But this is no sooner stated than we realize that something more than merely life in a congested urban setting is at issue. The Greeks and Romans were city dwellers, but so is bureaucratic man. The people of today's new nations either are or shortly will be urban dwellers. The civilization of the Orient is urban. Half of the world's ten largest cities are outside the circle of advanced industrial powers that reaches across the Northern Hemisphere from America to Russia: Tokyo, Shanghai, São Paulo, Cairo, and Peking. Rio de Janeiro, Seoul,

Buenos Aires, Mexico City, Tientsin, Jakarta, Bombay, Calcutta, Teheran, Nagoya, Karachi, and Madras are among the world's largest cities. All are larger than Detroit or Hamburg. Japan has as many cities of over a million as the United States does. In numbers alone China and India win hands down. They lead the world by a substantial margin in urban concentrations of over a million. In Africa, where there are about as many people as in North America, six cities have either arrived at or are pressing the one-million mark, and the urban population is increasing at an unprecedented rate.

Urban problems are by no means identical everywhere. Bangalore and Ibadan have the ancient rather than the modern problems of urban congestion. But everywhere the trend toward urbanization is accelerating. And in today's developing areas, just as earlier in Europe, the city is the entity in which modernization takes place. In this the city continues to play its immemorial role. All complex societies, among the social insects as well as among men, have been produced in cities. As with most other human institutions, the city has seldom been the result of rational design. With very few exceptions it has remained the creature of accident. Ancient cities, which in many cases were states, were also in some ways like modern factories. They provided a milieu in which captial could be accumulated. They permitted the demand for specialized functions to find expression. They facilitated the exchange of goods and services. These functions were seldom either the result or the continuing object of rational organization and design. Instead, the typical city of history was unaware that it possessed an underlying principle of organization. Cities usually provided for their religious, political, economic, military, educational, and reproductive needs through a hierarchical system of castes.

Looking back beyond these caste systems one can surmise how they may have developed, first out of tribal institutions and then through the introduction of slave systems and the imposition of supervisory military and priestly orders. This was roughly the way Plato accounted for the institutions of the ancient city-state. A smoothly functioning caste system eliminated the need for explicit social organization. Government could be held to a minimum so long as the traditional caste system was rigidly enforced.

Urban order, again like the regime of the modern factory, had two imperatives. One was individual and the other collective. The first necessity was for everyone to do his job properly and with good grace. This meant that each citizen should believe in the justice of his own lot and in that of all others. If this happened the entire system could maintain itself in harmony. The result would be the growth of a city which was more than a mere random collection of functions. It was more like a living organism. It had its own integrity and its own spirit or personality. It was the collective counterpart of a living person. When this occurred one could describe the second imperative of the city.

51

With an organic city, as with a man, one could speak of a just or proper function for the body politic taken as a whole. This could only be to achieve the good life. Achieving the good life of the city as a whole also required a way of insuring that each member performed his proper function. So, what was right, or just, from the standpoint of the body politic taken as a whole could not really be different from what was the just and proper functioning of each individual. Two orders of justice were involved but each had to be in harmony with the other. However, a serious problem arose because the identity between justice in the large and in the small might not be immediately apparent to the individual citizen. Each individual's self-interest leads him to disparage the humdrum circumstances of his own lot in comparison with that of those more fortunate. If the traditional bonds of the caste system weaken, the city experiences discord and crisis.

Plato pointed out that this reveals the deep logic of politics implicit in the city and in civilization: a logic of justice and of justification. The office of politics was to insure that the good of the whole corresponded with the good of its parts, and to reveal to all the truth of this correspondence. When the office of politics is unrealized or violated, civilization falters and the city fails. Accordingly, Plato conceived of the city essentially as a school. For the basic necessity was to make it possible for each citizen to engage in a lifelong education concerning the individual and collective requirements of the quest for the good life.

In this Plato, the Athenian, echoed the traditional claim of his *polis* that while other cities might be noted for special artistry in the making of things, the business of Athens was to make men. Indeed, it is hardly possible to imagine any other purpose for civilization in general or for the political community in particular. However, all attempts to induce in citizens a self-conscious appreciation of the principles of civic order ultimately have failed. Political communities have approximated the same end by developing special religions, systems of authority, and belief systems to reinforce the dictates of civic order.

## City versus Tribe

Throughout history, just as in today's new nations, civic order has stood in opposition to tribalism. It is true that a few relatively high Oriental cultures were little more than extensions of tribal foundations. Even so, they developed in conjunction with walled-in pockets of urbanization. For city and tribe possess two different types of justice and order.

To be outside the city was to be outside the reign of law. On the outside, human relationships were governed by the principles of self-enforcing retaliatory justice, an eye for an eye and a tooth for a tooth. But even the most primitive of human inventions are capable of elaborate sophistication, and this has been true also of retaliatory justice. It is possible to develop retaliatory justice into highly articulated codes of gentlemanly behaviour and on that basis produce a high culture. This was the way of ancient China. But no matter how sophisticated, such a way of life always stands in contradiction to the corporate organization principles upon which a complex civilization depends. It produces disruptive explosions and clan feuds rather than political order.

Urban civilizations have been marked by a suppression of feuds. The individual settlement of grievances is superseded through the offices of a great redeemer—a god of atonement, such as Apollo or Jesus, or a godly messenger such as Mohammed. The divinely sanctioned urban lawgiver is by no means merely a relic of musty myths. He appears over and over throughout history whenever men begin to create new civic communities in place of tribal institutions. The 20th century can witness in Africa modern versions of this. The new African nations are no different from those that emerged earlier in history. Before they could embark on the industrial revolution they had to undergo the urban revolution.

The divisive retaliatory justice associated with tribalism had to yield to a new urban legal order. This was the first task confronting the new African leaders, and many of them went about it aware that they were following in the steps of history's fabled lawgivers. Kwame Nkrumah in Ghana assumed the title *osagyefo*, the Redeemer. He waged a modern, often violent, version of the primordial struggle to supplant a tribal society with the principles of urban order.

This is one explanation of why the first-generation leaders of the developing nations sometimes preferred to follow the Chinese model of modernization instead of the Russian. For in China the prerequisite to industrialization was the dissolution of the traditional family system in favour of the principles of law and order that are brought to men through the urban revolution. Mao, Nyerere, Castro, and Nasser were in the first instance the urbanizers of their people. For it was civic order more than industrialization that they had been deprived of by Western imperialism.

## The Urban Theology

The new redeeming god of civic order is the god of each citizen. An injury to any citizen is more than a personal injury, it is a civic injury, an affront to that god and to justice itself. A man who does not keep the peace ruptures justice. The civic order he has broken can only be made whole again through atonement. Feud retaliations would only aggravate the rupture. This is the theology of the urban rule of law. This is what St. Paul may have meant in suggesting that the strength of sin is the law. That is, the strength of a people's determination to avoid sin is the measure of their devotion to the law. What urban man may not learn through reason he perceives through the strength of his faith.

Consequently, the cities of antiquity were designed as the abodes of the gods. The great residential palaces of the gods commanded the civic heights. Civic centres were composed of the temples of the deities who presided over the chief departments of nature and of human affairs. The typical ancient city, like the contemporary Vatican, was a "holy" city. The Roman Catholic Church retains to this day structures, modes of operation, and principles of citizenship remarkably similar to those of the ancient imperial holy city it supplanted.

Ancient cities, moreover, were theocracies—ruled by the gods through human vicars whose performance of liturgical functions was inseparable from the conduct of their civic offices. When the city convened itself to conduct its public affairs it did so as an ecclesia, a church of true believers. Warfare, even when monopolized by a special caste, was an engagement of the city as a whole. Gods were not only military consultants, they were active field participants. In laying siege to an enemy city, one made its temples the object of attack. Their fall, together with the outright capture of the gods, was the sign of victory.

A residence for gods and a factory for making men and ordering their functions—these were the ingredients of urban civilization when it first took shape. Each element reinforced the other, to yield a civilizing process. In retrospect we distribute praise or blame among ancient cities according to the level of civilization they were able to produce in their people. Athens, Rome, Peking, Alexandria, Kyoto, Constantinople, and Florence are among those with the highest historical marks by any standard.

The bond between civilization and the city remained vital long after the fall of Rome. During the early Middle Ages and for as long as the term Christendom had meaning there was a close connection between Christian civilization and its holy imperial city. Christendom was a self-styled city of God, grounded on spiritual rather than territorial ties. The political thrust of feudalism was to rupture the connection between civilization and the principles of civic order. As its dominant political principle, it substituted relationships to land for relationships to civic order.

Feudal forms of organization, law, justice, and politics were more reminiscent of the times of Homer than of the ancients who had experienced the urban revolution. Neither Western Europe nor its cultural progeny in the New World ever fully recovered from this rejection of urban civilization, whose counterrevolutionary ideology was first announced by St. Augustine in the 5th century A.D. Centuries later, when industrialism tried its hand at revolution, it turned against almost everything in feudalism but the property foundation on which feudal ties had rested. The great paradox of the industrial revolution was that it spawned cities—conurbations—without producing a truly urban civilization.

A true city, as Lewis Mumford has said, is different from all other institutions by virtue of its architectonic synthesis of diverse functions into a coherent organism. But just as an industrial revolution cannot be produced merely by placing an assortment of modern factories in a jungle, neither does it follow that an accidental collection of people and industries will automatically produce the synthesis of functions and the forms of justice required by an urban civilization. Western industrialization broke the restrictive bonds of feudalism, but then convinced itself that no different ones need be put in their place.

## The Feudal Heritage

Industrialism appeared to be essentially and completely an urban development. Indeed it was. But it was urbanization of a very special and a very partial kind. It was urbanization without the urban revolution. It was like the Golem, the legendary creature with the body of a man but lacking a soul. Western politics was witlessly doomed to build great urban communities like cities in all respects save the presence of the civilizing soul that is the essence of the city.

In the place of a civic order, industrialism preserved a number of feudal vestiges. It continued to found its politics on property rather than civic goals and human functions. Human functions were left to the determination of economics; territory became the basis of the state. Associations, interests, sects, and factions, which sound quite modern when we refer to pluralism and constitutional protections for freedom of association, were actually the surviving residues of late feudal society with their restrictive bonds broken and their autonomy guaranteed. Parliamentary democracy, in one light as modern as the automobile, was in another light as medieval as a jousting tourney.

The trouble was that the modern state had never really gotten knit together. Christendom had transposed the principle of social cohesion from the city of man to the city of God. The modern, secular, industrialized nation-state never really brought it back to earth. The ancient city-state had been an organic body; the industrial nation-state was a loosely connected assemblage of autonomous components.

Ancient philosophers pictured their statesmen as physicians applying the principles of political hygiene to the body politic. Their counterparts in the liberal democracies were seen as lawyers arranging contracts and settlements. They functioned as brokers negotiating deals. The ancients could not have played politics according to such rules even had they wanted to. Their political systems contained no internal, pluralistic centres of autonomy. Almost all the institutions and practices that modern Western man has identified with the essence of politics were unknown to the ancient world.

The urban civilizations of antiquity contained nothing comparable to the private associations that populate the Western world. The commercial and industrial corporation did not exist, neither did labour unions, nor professions in the modern sense. Ancient factions and cliques never functioned like the political parties of the industrial West. The large collection of practices and institutions which surround the nomination and election of governing officials and legislative representatives in the modern West had no counterpart in antiquity. Pressure groups, which always envelop and sometimes smother the Western legislative process, were nonexistent.

Classical political theory dealt with the nature of the overall political community. Modern Western political theory dealt with the freedoms and contractual interrelationships of the autonomous persons inhabiting a given geographic area. In the ancient world men thought of freedom as the opposite of slavery and barbarism. It meant the freedom to partake of the benefits of civilization. At its best it was something like the freedom that the members of a good college create for themselves. Western European freedom was individualistic. It was like that of traders in a marketplace or strangers assembled in a hypothetical state of nature.

The violence of the dialectical birth struggle that the modern world had to wage against medieval culture still obscures from its view the measure of its debt to feudalism. But as in all dialectical struggles, the victor was fated to bear the indelible marks of the foe that was overcome. The industrial contents of the modern state were revolutionary but the political container itself remained remarkably constant. The very pluralism which sets off modern from ancient politics has its origins in the Middle Ages.

The corporations, guilds, trade associations, fraternal orders, professions, social classes, markets, cities, nations, parliaments, and universities that characterize modern Western society and set it off from ancient culture are all of medieval origin. It was not their sudden novelty but their chartered autonomy that stamped modern Western politics with the features that distinguished it sharply from every other political system in human experience. The countervailing, retaliatory, balance-of-power struggles of autonomous interests, groups, agencies, and classes ultimately congealed into modern political institutions. But the result was only an apparent political community.

The political party was invented and for a time it seemed to weld everything together, but this too was more apparent than real. In actual fact, politics was held back while economics was given free reign. Like most other human institutions, Western political parties arose accidentally. They functioned in the absence of an integrated political order. For a brief moment during the struggle against feudalism it was even possible that they might not have arisen at all.

## The Incomplete City

Industrial civilization was grounded in the market city. It brought new gods and new tasks and transformed the nature of the city to suit them. Location, structure, population, and function followed the dictates of industrial production and distribution. A few great old cities such as Paris, London, Moscow, Berlin, and New York preserved some of the characteristics of their classical predecessors. But in addition there arose the more specialized cities with exclusively industrial characteristics: Manchester, Chicago, Hamburg, Detroit. In some physical respects the industrial city looked much like its predecessors. It occupied a definite territory and it had the special technical problems of city life: bringing in water and supplies, disposing of wastes, maintaining order, facilitating communication and transportation, keeping accounts, providing education, amusement, health, and so on.

In one important respect, however, the cities of the industrial order were not urban civilizations at all. None of the great industrial cities of modern times exhibited a coherent civic order. No one of them embodied a complete cultural system. Each was dependent upon a host of others like themselves. But the network of their interrelationships, the nation-state, never itself became a civic order.

The industrial nation-state never produced a true civilization. It never addressed itself self-consciously to the task of creating a high culture. Its overall principles of organization were based upon property relationships and principles of accumulating wealth. This is expressed in the differences between the political philosophies of Hobbes and Locke compared with those of Plato and Aristotle—philosophies that based law upon property rather than upon justice and civilization. Modern political science, like modern economics, mirrored the state on which it was based and excluded justice from its purview.

In this sense, the West has known civilization only through its contact with the ancients. It has lived in a long, 500-year period of renaissance, without ever having either reproduced a civic order on the classical model or invented a new model of its own. In Europe this dependency on the past has always been appreciated, if not honoured. In the United States, where the rejection of European standards became an early dogma, the greatest cultural leaders always recognized that what Arnold Toynbee has said of America was true: the United States was never able to bring into being the essential features of a civilization. In this, however, America merely revealed more starkly what Europe could hide from itself by an occasional reverent obeisance to the past.

The creation of a civilization, a true civic order within which contemporary man can express the collective and individual goals of the good life and set about their realization, stands as the great political challenge of the coming age. To conceive of such a civilization requires superseding the politically disintegrative principles of the industrial revolution with a new politics which builds upon human needs and functions rather than upon property relationships and industrial needs.

Until quite recent times the city as a physical entity was indispensable to the cultivation of the arts. Great research laboratories, libraries, universities, coliseums, museums, and theatres required great cities in order to exist and attract patronage. This has ceased to be true, and as a result, one of the last remaining defenses of the industrial city has been undermined. The growth of the print and electronic media of communications has severed the historically essential bond between the city and the talent trades.

We learn from the article in this series on THE FINE ARTS that what André Malraux called the museum without walls belongs to neither a city nor a nation, but to the mass media and to the world. Computer systems for the storage and recall of all human information release libraries from the confines of specific buildings, cities, or nations. The physical assembly of persons in conventions, convocations, audiences, and spectators no longer requires halls, arenas, and stadia, or even urban facilities to accommodate the attending throngs. Worldwide television audiences are becoming commonplace through the communications satellites. Microelectronic feedback devices make it possible for masses of dispersed individuals to participate directly in remote events. The entire world can soon meet together on computerized multichannel two-way television networks. Certain types of competitive events—athletics, political debates, and scientific discussions, for example—may take place with the contestants as widely dispersed throughout the world as are the spectators.

What is already possible in the talent trades may move quickly to industry. The idea of the museum without walls leads us to visualize the factory and the office without walls. Vast and complex automated production and clerical processes can be programmed, monitored, and controlled by dispersed employees through microelectronic equipment in their homes and autos. One visualizes society's connective tissue disappearing into the memory banks of a huge public computer system able to do for coordinational needs what telephone and highway do for communication and transportation needs.

What of the city—even the miserable industrial noncity of the present day—under such conditions? Earlier it was suggested that Christendom had translated the ancient city into the heavens—into the spiritual bonds and goals of Christianity. It is surely much less fanciful to conceive of a future translation of the city into cybernated systems of mass communication. *Translation?* No, this is not the right word, for a true city does not really exist to be translated into a new form. *Invention,* or *rediscovery,* are better words.

It may soon be possible to rediscover the city, and with it civilization, for the first time since the Ancients. Of course, the highest ideals of civilization will never become completely realizable, but to refresh our minds about their ancient principles helps us appreciate the magnificent challenges and prospects of the future city.

## The Search for Coherence

Ultimately we must think of the city as the smallest coherent unit of association in which it is possible for the human being to realize his maximum potentials. This is different from merely defining as a city any congested urban area. When urban areas are created on the basis of special needs, special local resources and industries, or the physical attractions of a given locality, it is doubtful if they can ever become true cities. By virtue of the *special* reasons for their existence they must have interdependent relationships with a host of other specialized urban areas. None of them is free, or able to make the maximum development of the human being their dominant concern. None is able to achieve on its own the coherence of a true city. This fact of interdependency is reflected in the inability of the contemporary metropolis to provide and finance the facilities and services necessary to its maintenance.

When the first 18th-century industrial centres made their appearance they too were not true cities. But some of them at least were economically self-sufficient. Their harbours, public utilities, and roadways had an intimate connection with local functions. As industrial centres expanded, the density of the web of interconnections tying them to the industrial order as a whole deprived the functions they performed of their original local autonomy. Each local industrial area found itself furnishing facilities and services for the entire industrial order. A port city which once thrived on the commerce flowing through it soon found that the channels, harbours, and docking facilities it maintained for an industrialized hinterland had become an unsupportable economic burden. While existing primarily to provide economic functions, they had themselves become uneconomic.

The streets, parking facilities, expressways, railways, and air facilities which encroached on cities and neighbourhoods grew until by mid-20th century they came to absorb up to 50 percent of their area. Much of this was to facilitate the movement of people and materials in transit. The metropolis is thereby forced to absorb invisible transfer costs it cannot recoup. Individuals may profit, but the metropolis loses. Too many exploit it for private advantage.

Prior to the development of the industrial metropolis the centre of the city contained its most beautiful precincts and its most desirable residences. On the outskirts one found its human and material refuse in slums and dumps. The industrial city reversed this pattern, depriving the central city of support from the very population which most profits from its existence, and replacing it with a slum population which not only could not contribute support but which itself became one of the city's most grievous burdens. The urban counterpart of the absentee landlord deprives the city of support and at the same time requires it to provide expensive commuting facilities and services. The city is unable to provide the needed mass service if forced to operate on the fees of its users.

This is but a partial catalog of contemporary metropolitan difficulties, but it is copious enough to reveal the general problem. The contemporary metropolis has no coherence. The sum of its parts is never quite able to produce a coherent entity. Each metropolis is itself more of a suburb of a larger community than it is an integral city. But a suburb of what?

At one time it might have been possible for the nation-state to assume the coherence and the integrative role appropriate to a true city. Socialism might have provided this impetus. But instead its aims became almost as narrowly economic as were those of the capitalist system it opposed. The welfare state of the 20th century was broadly conceived, but by the time it appeared the nation-state itself had become inadequate to assume the integrative role appropriate to a true city.

As the 20th century closes, one lesson of civic order stands out. Nothing less than a new kind of civic order will be adequate for the solution of the problems of organizing human functions and developing man's highest potentialities.

## On to Megalopolis

The term megalopolis is increasingly employed to describe the urban sprawl that links many once-distinct metropolitan areas into a large congested mass. The region which includes Boston, New York, Philadelphia, and Washington is the most familiar example. But the signs of megalopolis are appearing throughout the world. Los Angeles, Tokyo, London, Paris, Moscow, Shanghai, the industrial basin reaching from the lower Rhine to the North Sea, and the areas of congestion radiating out from Milan, Chicago, and Kiev are all taking on the sprawling aspects of megalopolis. These new monsters have even fewer of the attributes of civic order than did the industrial centres from which they grew.

Contemporary conurbations of connected suburbs are themselves but larger suburbs. This is coming to be as true of socialist regimes as of all others. But mere conglomeration will not satisfy the need for a true civic order, not even if megalopolis comes to look exactly the same the world over. To extend megalopolis to include the world might solve some of the financial and administrative problems of urban areas, but these are not the real problems. The deepest problems of Los Angeles and Bombay would still remain the same. These relate not to monetary but to cultural needs.

For the city in history has been not only the seedbed of civilization; it has been also the breeding ground of barbarism, of the base as well as the noble. The city is at once man's greatest achievement and his most abysmal failure. For the human being is in one sense the most inadequate of the social animals. He produces naturally an environment in which he cannot survive.

Every philosopher sagely repeats the maxim that man is a social animal. He is. But he is a deficient one. In one way he is the opposite of all other species. He is more shortsighted collectively than he is individually. Man produces his greatest cultural monuments in the city. But it is also the city that magnifies his tendencies toward cultural irresponsibility.

Men in nonurban environments cannot avoid appreciating the fact that the survival of the individual depends upon the well-being of the collectivity. Moreover, they see that the collectivity exists only to the extent that its concerns become an ingrained part of the behaviour of each individual. The institutions of nonurban cultures were rudimentary, but their function and meaning were never far removed from the awareness and involvement of each individual.

When man forms the city, and the complex institutions that go with it, he magnifies his power to achieve noble monuments, but the same maneuver also relieves each person of direct and immediate responsibility for the maintenance of the conditions that make civic order possible. This is the social cost of urbanization, just as smog is the social cost of the auto.

When the economist speaks of social costs he means those costs of a product which may not be charged directly against its manufacture but which must be borne in some way by the entire community. The community may be better off in some ways because of the presence of a factory but it also pays for having it. A coal-burning factory belches smoke into the air. The scenery is altered. Labourers are drawn to town and create problems of adjustment, education, and accommodation. The town must provide new streets and services. The air darkens with the smoke of the factory's ceaseless furnaces. Soot drifts down through the air, seeping relentlessly through the walls of houses and into the tender membranes of the lungs. When this is magnified to the scale of industrial London the social costs accumulate so sharply they sometimes seem to overwhelm the social benefits. For social costs are like excrement and no form of life can live on its own offal.

Counterparts of this problem permeate megalopolitan life. The most serious problem concerns the civilizing process itself. For the very urbanization which produces civilized conditions also produces their negation, in much the same way as does the coal-burning factory. The essence of urbanization is the creation of special institutions for the coordination of human effort and the resolution of conflicts. These take the place of the simpler and more direct collective processes of tribal and agrarian conditions. A system of courts and executive agencies run by experts supplants the informal and intimate processes of simpler societies. Education was formerly much the same for each child and was accomplished through rituals requiring the participation of the entire community. In an urban environment education becomes highly specialized and departmentalized. Different programs of education must be developed to serve the different needs of the community.

The distinctive benefit of organization is that it permits people who are unskilled to accomplish tasks that are beyond the capability of isolated individuals no matter how skilled they might be. By the same token, organization lowers the creative requirements of the functionaries and labourers, even though it makes higher educational demands on those in charge. The article on EDUCATION documents this dismal tale of how, ultimately, in a highly urbanized environment, the great majority of the population become destined for lowly functions. They require but correspondingly lowly or even negligible education. On the other hand, a relatively small minority may achieve educational and professional pinnacles previously unimaginable.

The very virtues of organization and urbanization sunder society into an elite which produces and embodies cultural excellence and a mass which becomes progressively decivilized. The masses may be relatively well provided for and even, in the most fortunate urban and industrial societies, affluent, and still remain essentially decivilized. For the level of civilization a man achieves is not automatically determined by his wealth or material possessions. It is not even determined by his level of formal or technical education.

An entire society might conceivably reach an extremely high level of formal schooling yet remain essentially uncivilized. For the type of schooling which characterizes complex societies tends to become highly specialized. A society of experts can also be a society of barbarians. A society may be quite affluent and at the same time devoid of civilization. Indeed, this has been the tendency of urbanization in general and of industrialization especially.

Specialization is the human condition that goes with urbanization just as the factory is the material associate of industrialization. The social costs of the former are even more grievous than are those of the latter. For to produce specialization among the elite and to treat the masses as if they were society's offal share one thing in common. They effectively decivilize both levels. A malevolent unseen hand guides an industrial order to the production of a population able to perform complex subsistence functions but unaware of the requirements for maintaining a high civilization and unable to provide for those requirements even if they knew them to be necessary to their own survival.

This has been the tragedy of urbanization. With rare exceptions, the cities of man have been like ancient Rome; the greater their size and opulence the more inexorable have become their forces of decivilization. Initially cities were made possible by the strength of primitive processes of acculturation. But the cities these powerful processes generated soon applied the logic of urbanization to the acculturation process itself. This left the civilizing of men to the newly formed urban institutions. There it was fragmented, specialized, given to some and withheld from others, and ultimately destroyed.

The one thing the industrial order never succeeded in perceiving was that its overriding purpose ought to have been the making of men rather than things. Men, in a narrow sense, may require for their survival the production of good things. But cities, in the most literal sense, require for their survival the production of good men. No high civilization has ever occurred outside the city, nor has any survived within it, for the human being has never learned how to live in the city. It is a lesson that obviously must be learned in a hurry, but it is one whose imperatives are revealed only through the architectonic approach to politics. The special mission history entrusts to today's new nations is the creation of a new kind of civic order with built-in safeguards against the decivilizing forces produced by every previous civic order man has developed.

But no matter how politically mature today's new nations ultimately become they are not likely to produce the same kinds of democratic institutions that appeared in the West during the 19th century. This is so for the same reason that we know their industries will never look like those of 19th-century Europe and America.

Today's new nations had to begin political development at the level of the contemporary West: professionalized administration and mass plebiscitary democracy. However, in one very important area their starting point was far in advance of the West. Their political systems implicitly assumed what the West had yet to recognize: the practicality and inevitability of world order. They could not have come into being without the United Nations. They cannot survive without world order. The new nations are autonomous, but not in the old way. They are more like the regional political parties of a world community than like old-fashioned sovereign states.

Potentially the new nations of today contain the seeds of history's most profound revolution. They have the opportunity of becoming the world's first political communities that do not require any form of imperialist despotism, internal or external, to achieve their development. Moreover, they can become the first communities to be organized from birth as integral members of a world order. These are the ingredients of a revolution. They are still remote from most nations of the West but they are already well under way in the leading new nations of Africa.

## Forces of Change

There are periods in history when the forces of change seem to overpower those of continuity. Plato and Aristotle lived in such times. So did St. Augustine in the 5th century A.D. The 17th century was another such period and so is the world of the mid-20th century. In all such times of change political institutions have been no exception. They are no exception today. Our investigation of these changes has led to an exploration of the apparent sacrifice of democracy to authoritarianism throughout the world. Diverse though the world's nations are, the political processes at work in them are remarkably similar. They are all part of the same world of political cause and effect. Tanzania in the 20th century may seem as underdeveloped as the European nations of the 16th century. Yet her new institutions are modern through and through. She is more like the advanced nations of her own day than like those of any simpler time. The problem of democracy today is by no means identical everywhere, but the local differences occur within the operation of large institutional forces that are everywhere comparable. The most pervasive of these is modern technology. Modern technology has been quite inhospitable to democracy.

In order for the democratic process to work, the problems posed to it must be the sort that can be resolved through the application of common prudence and wisdom. This is not because the masses are overly rich in the possession of prudential wisdom. On the contrary, prudence is a quality most sparingly distributed among men. But we have seen already that even the most soundly conceived democracy is frustrated when the problems it must solve become so highly technical and so complex as to defy the application of prudential wisdom. When science and technology invade politics democratic processes are undermined. This condition is most obvious in today's advanced industrial nations, but it is just as true of nations at simpler levels of development.

The problems appropriate to democratic processes are those that are at once the simplest and the most profound: the problems of the common good. Any problem that touches the common good raises issues of justice, equality, freedom, order, and so on. Such problems cannot be solved through mathematical formulas or by consulting experts and scientists. They yield only to prudence, wisdom, and deliberation. In relatively simple and uncongested societies, such as 6th-century Athens or 18th-century America, most problems were of this sort. But when advanced technologies and complex social conditions appear, they drive out prudence—putting science, expertise, and professionalism in its place. The result is to threaten democratic processes.

It is no solution to try to subject the complex problems of the sciences and the professions to the judgments of men of common prudence and wisdom. Not even great leaders, much less ordinary citizens, can bend the logic of science to that of practical reason. Not only matters of technology and science defy politics but so does justice, whose essence is prudence. In complex societies it also becomes highly technical in its administration. The story of the wise monarch dispensing justice to rich and poor under a great oak has been told of good kings from time immemorial. Shortly after James I became king of England in the early 17th century he thought that he too might dispense justice as had the kings of old. He was, after all, exceptionally learned, even for an enlightened monarch. But James's chief judges would have none of this. Already the dispensation of justice had become professionalized. The mysteries of the law

64

would no longer yield to common prudence and reason. England's professional lawyers had long since developed their own "artificial reason" for finding and applying rules of law. Only those trained in their special science could understand and utilize the artificial reason of the law. What happened to King James was only the culmination of the process that had begun long previously, when judges first expelled the common man from the common law by prohibiting jurors from ruling on questions of law.

This has been the history of modern politics. Issue after issue has become too complex for practical reason and hence for democracy. The simple and easy-to-understand problems of the local politics of the past have given way to the complex and highly technical problems of megalopolitan politics. The intricacies of air and water pollution, the organizational and financial problems of mass transportation and education, and the fiscal imbalances between central city and suburbs—all involve their own new and distinct kinds of "artificial reason," understood only by experts and professionals. The invasion of professionalism has reached to every level of politics: national economic planning, foreign trade, public health, and science policy. Even diplomacy, traditionally the exclusive province of practical wisdom, has been invaded by the mathematically trained experts who know how to program computers with complex problems of simulation and game theory. Not only the common man but the professional statesman and the experienced parliamentarian as well have been faced at every turn with the experience of King James I.

But this is only one side of the modern political equation. Democracy is like a balance scale. On one side is the active element of participational decision-making; on the other is the more passive element of mass consent. As the force of technology tips down the scale against popular decision-making it heightens by the same measure the indispensability of mass consent.

All societies require the habitual conformity and consent of their members. Societies that are relatively simple and static can operate fairly well if the consent is expressed through habitual conformity to hallowed traditions. But highly complex societies are dynamic. Novelty arises at every turn. Habit and tradition alone no longer suffice to keep such societies functioning. They must be supplemented by carefully designed laws and plans to organize, reorganize, and coordinate myriads of complex, specialized functions. Their members may have to change their occupations, and even their trades, several times in the course of their lives. They will almost certainly be required to change residences frequently. Each new generation witnesses a wave of innovations sweeping the culture, transforming factories, replacing machinery, renovating cities, and modernizing homes. Everyone and everything must be perpetually readjusted in response to changing conditions or unforeseen crises. Since habit and tradition no longer suffice to hold society together, something else must be substituted. The two basic alternatives are to manipulate people through terror, or to rule through the consent of the governed: despotism and democracy. But as we have seen above, the more complex the society the more limited the choice.

Terror is extremely expensive. It is also treacherous. It has a way of turning against those who would apply it to others. It works well for only the crudest, most unskilled operations. Except under the extreme emergencies of wars or revolutions it is not effective in complex technological societies. If any demonstration of this truth were needed, it emerged with tragic clarity from the concentration camps of Hitler and the forced labour camps of Stalin. By contrast, the efficacy of consent—the superiority of this aspect of democracy over despotism—was just as clearly revealed by the frontier kibbutzim of Israel.

The first Jewish refugees who escaped from Germany to wrest subsistence from the deserts of Palestine found living conditions little better than those they had fled. Despite their abysmal ignorance of farming they performed prodigious feats of agricultural development with furious speed. The Chinese Communists seem to have taken the same lessons to heart in their programs for organizing local communes and cooperatives. In Yugoslavia similar organizational principles worked miracles in large-scale industrial operations. Complex operations must be based on self-governing components if they are to be effective.

All this is relatively easy to understand on the level of individual firms and cooperative farms. But on the level of society as a whole the problem seems almost insoluble. There it appears that science and technology demand with one hand what they frustrate with the other. For while science and technology have produced the conditions of complexity that can work well only if affairs proceed according to democratic principles, they also have produced the expertise that displaces practical wisdom and democracy wherever it reaches. In the most advanced Western nations this has resulted in an upward flight of democracy. Each time technology and science displace the practical reason of democracy with the artificial reason of the expert, practical reason reacts by seeking the next higher level where its approaches may still be applicable.

Take an American example: The United States went through a period in the 19th century in which nearly all public offices were made elective: clerks, policemen, judges, treasurers, and so on. As technical complexity and professionalism spread, this was gradually abandoned. Democracy came to mean little more than the selection of the chief executives: mayors, governors, and only a few more. Indeed, the office of mayor was very nearly supplanted by a professional city manager. All Western nations have experienced this same steady upward drift to the point that democracy now finds its primary expression in a vast national plebiscite to name a chief executive with highly concentrated powers. Everything rests upon an intensive mass-media campaign between a few aspirants for the nation's highest office. The fewer the contestants the more intensive the campaign. When there is only one candidate, with no challenger allowed to compete with him for office, the campaign must elicit a frenzy of mass identification to insure the requisite level of popular consent.

## Government By Consent

The modern world's first taste of plebiscitary democracy was a bitter one. The Nazis and the Fascists corrupted democratic institutions into instruments of terrorism and mass manipulation. Since their overthrow following World War II, revolutionary dictatorships and counterrevolutionary militarism have spread through the world. In Haiti the Duvalier regime and in the Republic of South Africa the administration of apartheid were political abominations. Nothing quite so evil and corrupt as Nazism has reappeared. However, in making what was once reprehensible appear acceptable by comparison, Nazism is victorious in defeat.

The first historians of the Nazis and the Fascists tried to find special explanations for their appearance, explanations that would localize the disease to the sites of its outbreak. They delved into the strange doctrines of Germany's 19th-century philosophers and historians. They seized upon Hegel's absolutist philosophy of nationalism and upon the cult of the superman in Nietzsche. Psychologists dwelt upon the authoritarianism of the German family. A few observers claimed more general causes were at work: the decay of Christian faith, or what came to be called the "death of God." Some argued that the appearance of large bureaucratic organizations had made it impossible for people to exercise the individual responsibilities which must be upheld if democracy is to work. It was suggested that the Germans had resolved this contradiction between their old beliefs and their new realities by placing their trust in an all-powerful leader and embarking upon a mass "escape from freedom." But of course none of this was visible to the German people at the time. All they saw was that traditional democratic institutions appeared to have lost their relevance and their ability to cope with the complexities of the time. The German and Italian peoples merely followed the flight of democracy to the place where it still seemed applicable: a vast national plebiscite. This was not necessarily evil or corrupt in itself. What made it so was the despotic purpose to which the plebiscitary process was turned.

The clearest proof of this has been provided in France by De Gaulle. Parliamentary democracy was supplanted in France by a dynamic leader who claimed to embody in his own person the spirit of the nation. He surrounded himself with a carefully contrived aura of mystique, employing mass rallies and television to magnify and consolidate his personal prestige and authority. The forms were reminiscent of Hitler. It was the aims that were different. De Gaulle was forced to dissolve French imperialism, and instead of seeking an internal substitute for it he initiated a profound political reorganization. We have seen that the new nations are the first in history whose condition of birth is conducive to the ultimate development of a nondespotic foundation for politics. Among the older nations France could become the first to have made the same effort.

In the United States the trend toward plebiscitary democracy began with the emergency administration that Franklin Roosevelt devoted to curing the Great Depression. New, centralized federal agencies were needed and the President found it necessary to go directly to the people to mobilize support for them. Roosevelt's famous "fireside chats" provided a new departure in American politics. Succeeding presidents found it necessary to build on the Roosevelt precedent. They waged a steady campaign to see that the presidency monopolized the nation's attention. The potentialities of television were quickly exploited. News management, which became an openly acknowledged governmental policy under President Kennedy, was extended and rechristened as the "politics of consent" under President Johnson. The effect was to undermine intermediate political processes and concentrate the expression of democracy into the one overriding relationship between the President and the people.

In England, as always, events moved somewhat more hesitantly. Tradition had dictated that politics be based upon competing programs rather than personalities. But the logic of the mass media joined hands with that of the increasing complexity of government. Together they made the traditional deliberative processes of parliament obsolete. Science and technology favoured the expert over the politician, and television favoured the mystique of mass leadership over the mastery of parliamentary debate. In 1965 when the Conservatives chose their new leader they relied upon a public canvass to choose among the top three contestants. By 1966 Labour's prime minister, Harold Wilson, had moved away from the old principles of collective cabinet responsibility and emerged as a plebiscitary executive like those of France and America.

In the Soviet Union the starting point was authoritarian. There the force of technology had to overbalance the scales of dictatorship rather than democracy, but the result was surprisingly similar. Stalin's terrorist consolidation of power was dissolved into two functions, those of the technical expert and the master bureaucrat. The acquisition of political dominance was no longer determined solely within the closed confines of party councils. It required the consent of the military, the bureaucratic elite, and the top industrial managers—with the scientists and intellectuals in the wings impatient for inclusion in the power elite. Political leadership also required mastery of the art of mobilizing mass consent. And as we have seen, Cuba, Egypt, and Tanzania, to take three different types of developing countries, reveal the same processes. In the different countries there were many differences of detail and emphasis, but their overall similarities were unmistakable. Professional administration combined with plebiscitary democracy was beginning to characterize government throughout the world. The modern problem of government is symbolized by the United States and the U.S.S.R. Together they illustrate the emerging dilemma of democracy.

In the United States, as technology expelled common wisdom from issue after issue, it restricted the applicability of democracy, forcing democratic processes higher and higher up the scale of the common good until all democracy was concentrated at the pinnacles of executive authority. American society had become so complex and its problems so highly technical that the exercise of both democracy and practical wisdom remained meaningful only through a form of plebiscitary presidential democracy. It was far from satisfactory, however, for control can never be effective if it is exercised only at the top, if it is applied at the end rather than at the beginning of the political process. The more complex problems become, the more difficult they are to control from the top alone. Large bureaucratic institutions change and develop according to their own inner dynamics, making their ponderous procession through time like sand dunes inching across a desert. As they increase in technical complexity their ability to resist outside influences and controls also increases.

Now, however, the question asks itself whether this is democracy at all. It is in such remote remove from the people as to warrant vigorous skepticism. Democracy has assumed many different forms throughout history, but one element has always been present: direct and intimate involvement of the people with the issues of public policy. Is the world on the verge of leaving behind forever this crucial element of all the democracies known to history? If history itself is any guide the answer is certainly not. In the past it has been elitisms comparable to those of our day that have called forth democratic reforms. Democracy means figuring out how to counteract authoritarian government. The task of democracy is to combat professional government and plebiscitary manipulation. The new forces associated with the scientific revolution may help make self-government real.

Bureaucracies are like the chemist's large, complicated, heavy molecules. An intense and agitated Brownian movement may be going on within their borders, but nothing less than the elaborate statistical mechanics of the sociologist will detect the principles by which their massive structures change. Ministries of agriculture, departments of defense, and science planning agencies produce cumulative technical decisions impermeable to the influence of the nonspecialist, no matter how exalted his authority or how impressive his popular mandate. Bureaucracy seemed impervious to democracy. The only hope appeared to be an effort to outflank the bureaucracy through revitalized democracy in local communities. But looked at from yet another point of view, intractable bureaucracies are also islands of autonomy, bastions of resistance against despotism, allies of the rule of law, if not of democracy.

The forces generated by bureaucratization were one of the engines of reform in the U.S.S.R. The authoritarian methods that had successfully promoted rapid industrial development ended by creating a multitude of huge bureaucratic agencies. Each was a seedbed for the development of highly specialized technicians and professional experts. Each conducted its business in the only way bureaucracies can, through formal rules and procedures. They became collective "persons" possessing great power: the barons of the new industrial order, the agencies of accomplishment. Power was ineffective unless it went through their channels, and in order to do so, power had to accommodate itself to their special modes of operation. And while bureaucracies responded readily to law they were made impotent by terror.

The more intensely developed a country becomes the more it is necessary to govern according to rule-of-law principles. These were the principles that began to assert themselves in post-Stalin Russia.

The target of reform in Russia had no direct counterpart in America. However the forces of consent in Russia and the escalation of democracy in America led both countries from opposite directions to a similar result. This apparent trend toward similar organizational and political forms has given birth to a theory of cultural convergence. Its proponents state that of all the countries in the world those most alike are Russia and America, the two nations who were locked in a Cold War based on the belief that their societies operated on opposing principles. The theory of cultural convergence presents considerable difficulties. Its credibility rests in part upon the relative importance of institutions as against beliefs. This, in turn, is a matter about which scholars differ violently. If the perspective is broadened, however, the problem changes.

The United States and Russia are merely the two most prominent examples of a trend that reaches throughout the world. We have traced its effects not only in all the Western industrial nations but in the underdeveloped nations as well. If there is a process of convergence taking place it is worldwide. And this indeed seems to be the case. Modern government appears to be acquiring everywhere two dominant features: administration by highly trained professionals and the maintenance of popular cohesion and consent through plebiscitary democracy. Indeed, the best examples are found *outside* the opposing East-West powers, rather than in the two Cold War antagonists. For one must look at Russia and America in the light of developments in Gaullist France, Titoist Yugoslavia, Nyerere's Tanzania, Nasser's Egypt, post-Nkrumah Ghana, and Castro's Cuba. Then one sees that the process of convergence stems everywhere from similar causes and finds everywhere a roughly similar issue. In the light of this growing similarity we can speak of an emerging world political order. It is not self-conscious as yet, but the coming generation may well find that the converging forces for world integration will begin to overcome those of disunion, as happened earlier when internal forces of convergence led to the unified nation-state. The authoritarianism which seems to dominate politics in the closing decades of the 20th century may well be the passing mistress of a time of transition rather than the wedded helpmeet of a stable future.

Side by side with this underlying organizational and structural convergence were the persisting forces of disunity embodied in the Cold War. The Cold War drew its themes from 19th-century European ideologies: liberalism versus socialism. And yet, the real world was rapidly becoming both post-liberal and post-socialist. Curiously enough, the process of superseding the older ideologies was being speeded by the very Cold War dedicated to their defense. For it was the Cold War that accelerated the cultural convergence observable everywhere.

The older ideologies had been based upon a world in which labour and subsistence needs dominated every human concern. The promise of the postindustrial world was to render production labour obsolete and make subsistence the birthright of every human being. In a way, then, the Cold War was the last expression of creeds that had ceased to be relevant to immediate political and economic realities. And yet, merely being obsolete does not automatically insure that a belief will die. The graveyard of world civilizations is littered with the historical remains of cultures that found it impossible to respond creatively to novel challenges. One of the virtues of democracy has been its ability to cope with novelty and with challenge. We may now summarize the deeper relationships between the politics of development and democracy.

## The Inevitability of Democracy

In the most dynamic of today's new nations there is a more solid identification and a more intense communication between the people and their leaders than in any of the older established Western democracies. Moreover, as development progresses and as citizens come to make up a true political community, the deliberative institutions of a more mature democracy are certain to appear in the new nations. Such institutions are appearing already in the more fully developed nations of Yugoslavia, Poland, and Russia. Intellectual freedom is growing. The administration of justice is becoming more impartial. There is wider participation in the drafting of long-range plans. The demands of consumers are being accommodated. Ultimately similar improvements will appear in China, in Cuba, in Egypt, in Ghana, and elsewhere throughout the developing world in unison with the progress of their development. These propositions rest upon more than a pious hope. For there are specific reasons why democracy, in one form or another, must occur in all developing nations as their dynamism gathers momentum.

Democracy has always drawn its meaning from the stage of development at which it finds expression. For at each stage the form of despotism is different and so is the form of democracy. Accordingly, democracy's substantive ingredients change, and must change, from place to place with different stages of development, even though its inner logic remains the same. What is this abiding inner logic of democracy? There are three basic elements. One is scientific, one organizational, and one philosophic. Each one is irrefutable. Because of this, democracy will always be mankind's most valid political idea as well as the permanent reservoir from which its revolutionary impulses are drawn. What are these three basic, irrefutable elements?

The first is scientific and it is stated simply. The proposition that despotism has no basis in genetics is the shortest way to say it. The article on NATURE —*Man and the Cosmos*—shows that everything we know from genetics indicates that the stock of wisdom is distributed evenly throughout the human race. In fact, men have never discovered any infallible technique for either producing or transmitting wisdom. Wisdom does not appear to result from the formal development of brainpower through schools and colleges. It does not appear to be elicited by maintaining closed aristocratic castes in power, even though high cultural traditions have been maintained by a few of history's elites.

We have been talking about wisdom—what in common language is called common sense. It is something we can recognize more easily than describe. It is part integrity, part virtue, part justice, part self-confidence, part experience (though people who have it appear to get "experience" at a very early age), part intelligence, and a good measure of courage. Although we can't be much more exact about it than this, nonetheless we all know it when we see it. People in trouble are especially adept at nosing out those with common wisdom. Political systems depend for their survival on their ability to discover and utilize the talents of those with common wisdom, for common wisdom applied to politics is what we call statesmanship, and the larger and more complex a society becomes the greater is the need to put this talent to work throughout the political system. But inasmuch as it is a talent that is more or less randomly distributed throughout society, democracy is the only political device whose form is consonant with the principle on which practical wisdom is distributed. From this standpoint, Greek democracy, in which officials were selected by lot, is a perfectly defensible, if "conservative," solution of the problem of recruiting men of practical wisdom for political service. It is what today might be called a minimax solution, namely, one designed to minimize the possibilities of error by randomizing selection to correspond with the fact of randomized talent.

Representative democracy assumed that certain types of apprenticeship, combined with special forms of popular judgment, could improve on random selection. It is hard to say for certain whether or not this hope was ever borne out in practice. Moreover, a complicating situation arises which thwarts each of these forms of democracy. This is the situation described previously, namely, when societies become so complex that their proper administration requires expert technical knowledge in addition to practical wisdom. When this happens, there begins to appear what might be called a kind of informal technological despotism. The society is invisibly divided into those with the technological prerequisites to exercise political authority and those without them. For obvious reasons random selection can no longer be trusted. This was what led to the civil service movement in modern societies. But representative democracy also founders. For the same complexities that require experts in office by their nature also confound the average voter in his effort to discriminate the expert from the charlatan, just as most of us have no way of knowing whether $E=mc^2$ is true, or only mumbo jumbo, or whether the threat of inflation can be forestalled by an increase in taxes. Thus, even societies that are formally democratic become informally despotic as they become more complex. If, at the same time, it becomes more and more costly in time and money for individuals to offer themselves for political office, an "establishment" develops which in effect converts the forms of democracy into those of despotism. The tragedy is that this occurs precisely at the time when the growing complexity of the society requires for its survival the maintenance of democracy. This brings us to the second point, namely, the organizational foundation of democracy.

As with the proposition about science, the organizational basis for democracy is simply stated. The more complex a society becomes the more intricate are its functions and the more difficult is their coordination. This is exactly the condition aimed at by all developing nations. Everyone must learn to do his job correctly and at the right time. The work of the group or organization to which the individual belongs must fit just right with that of all others and the whole system must function in harmony. This means that in developing societies all the individual and organizational components of the system must understand and assent to the requirements of the system as a whole. The problems are those of motivation, consent, and integration. When organizations are relatively simple, and when the individual tasks to be performed require only rudimentary levels of skill and efficiency, then consent can be ignored and problems of motivation and coordination can be solved through slave systems. Highly developed slave systems produced monumental achievements in ancient Egypt and in pre-Columbian America, but they did not produce technical complexity. Terror, and the form of powerful motivation that was available in the factory under primitive capitalism, share the defect of slavery. With the growth of complexity these primitive methods no longer suffice. There are too many subordinate groups and organizations that can injure the operation of the whole by the withdrawal of consent and the exercise of an effective veto. Democracy has been the only solution mankind has found to this problem. No technically complex civilization has ever existed without some form of democracy: Greece, Rome, the great Renaissance city-states, the industrial nations, and the socialist regimes. This generating force for democracy operates the same way within the subordinate organizations of developing societies. The huge industrial enterprise, capitalist and socialist alike, must today obey roughly democratic principles in order to maintain its harmonious operation. Indeed, the most advanced socialist regimes are finding it necessary to introduce rudimentary democratic principles into their system of economic planning. Yugoslavia is a special case in point. However, decentralization and economic liberalization are occurring in Russia, Poland, and Hungary, as well. This is sometimes misinterpreted in the West to constitute a tacit admission of the validity of the free-enterprise market system. But the problem is the organizational and political problem of development rather than a purely economic problem. What is being felt is the operation of the same force that has been responsible for the introduction of democratic forms throughout history, when social functions have reached a stage of high developmental complexity.

The political philosopher Yves Simon once adduced a brilliantly compelling argument. He said that the need for government does not rest upon original sin or the imperfection of human nature. Even in a society of angels—even in heaven, argued Simon—there is a need for government merely in order to see that tasks are assigned and coordinated. To which it may be added that heaven's form of government must be a democratic one, assuming, that is, that the problem of running heaven is relatively complex. Whatever import this may have for the doctrine that God is dead, or at least democratically elected, is aside from the present problem. For right off it is apparent that not even a scientific utopia—or subtopia—could validly be nondemocratic—at least, not one for a complex society.

Let us assume that all the conditions for creating a manipulative society have been fulfilled. Statistics are of sufficient quantity and quality to permit accurate planning of every human function. Computers are big enough and sophisticated enough to devise and integrate actions right down to those of the most lowly functionary. Finally, behavioural drugs are available to make every human being completely suggestible. Under these conditions it might seem that the organizational argument for democracy falls. But there are several problems.

There could be no room for contingency or accident in such a society. Otherwise it would go to pieces as would a colony of bees in which some geneticist had altered the instinctual mechanism. Such a society would have to be absolutely static or it could not exist at all. But as a practical matter we can be certain that some accidents would occur. And the frequency with which they would occur would rise proportionately the closer the system came to being completely deterministic.

But why institute such a system? The individuals making up the system would have ceased to be human beings. They would certainly not decide to impose such a system on themselves. It could only appear through some dictatorial coup d'etat by a future scientocracy. But of course no such dictators would apply the system to themselves. There would be no point in instituting it if they were not to be exempt from its determinisms. But if anybody is exempt then to that extent there would occur the exercise of will. Accident, innovation, and contingency would then enter and by their entry foul the system. We can even imagine a time when the scientocracy, like the present regime in the U.S.S.R., would find it necessary to reintroduce free will, humanity, and consequently democracy. Not out of any humanitarian motive, and certainly not because of counterorganization from below, but for strictly organizational reasons. A freewill democratic system is simply more efficient for complex, highly integrated operations. Otherwise one of the instinctual orders of life would have long since taken over command of the planet.

Put it another way. The human being, as he stands, with all his fallibility, is still the best and cheapest computer available. What he lacks in digital functions he more than compensates for in analogue functions. It is simply cheaper, simpler, and more efficient to utilize these advantages through a system permitting a significant degree of organizational autonomy for each individual component than is conceivable for any possible system of determined behaviour. And as we have just seen, it is not feasible to supersede this with even the most sophisticated technical or scientific control devices that can be imagined. Consequently it must be concluded that there will always be a compelling organizational basis for the constant regeneration of democracy. By the same token, it appears that the human condition may incorporate a built-in cause for revolution. For when the scientific basis for democracy is added to the organizational it is apparent that precisely when democracy becomes indispensable for organizational reasons, it also becomes inhibited by the informal forces that produce despotic establishments and deprive wise men of political office. Just as the structure of revolution is political, so is its causation.

The third basis for democracy is philosophical. Again, it is simply stated. Politics is wedded to philosophy because of man's incomplete instinctual equipment. He must find compensations for this deficiency through the creation of values and purposes. The philosopher Stuart Hampshire has shown that this conclusion is inescapable even if one begins from deterministic assumptions.

Moreover, those instincts man does have are not completely trustworthy and, as in the case of food and sex, contain destructive as well as preservative potentials. Inasmuch as the establishment of values is a condition of human survival, the problem of how to discover and establish validity becomes crucial. Up to a certain level of social complexity the process of value creation may seem almost invisible and virtually automatic.

A series of institutions develops and human life becomes considerably better than is possible simply by grubbing for food in amorphous herds. The myths of all societies betray a primitive fear of the loss of their institutions and reversion to chaos. Societies guard against this through various types of functional norms and taboos. These are, in effect, ideals, or at least potential ideals, derived from the behaviour required of all if the institutions are to be preserved and chaos averted.

But with increasing complexity and with the appearance of literacy it becomes possible to write down what the norms and values are and to codify them. At this point values assume an existence of their own and philosophy is born. Not only is it then possible to explain and teach norms and values in a more reliable way, it is also possible to detect when they come into conflict with each other, and to judge between them. A society may preserve its family system by allowing the father to resort to arms in its protection, but it also preserves the society as a whole by prohibiting murder. One result of such conflicts may be the development of rules defining torts and crimes. Priest-judges may arise to safeguard and apply the society's norms and values, reinforcing them with the society's deepest religious beliefs. But if the society becomes successful and dynamic, as occurs when a great civilization develops, the pace of change and innovation breaks out of the confines of customary and traditional values and it is necessary to create new norms and values in addition to preserving those of the past. It is at this point that politics arise, namely, the formal process whereby new collective values and norms are created. Ultimately this raises the question of where the new values are to come from, the question of where value resides.

It is a question men attempt to evade as long as possible. They try to assimilate the new to the old through fictional analogies. A perennial problem is what to do about the subsidiary human groups and associations that appear—corporations, for example. What rules shall be applied to them? The Romans assimilated the corporation to their state-created religion and gave it the peculiar artificial citizenship of the priest-father. The English assimilated the corporation to the natural person and gave it an almost biological personality and existence. But ultimately analogical ingenuity fails and new values and purposes can no longer be robbed from customary institutions and beliefs. This is the political equivalent of the death of God. The problem of value creation must be met square on. This leads the mind directly into the deepest problems of political philosophy. For with the failure or discrediting of divinely sanctioned traditions there are only two sources of value, an elite or all of mankind: the problem of oligarchy versus democracy. The argument for oligarchy (or aristocracy) rests upon the proposition that a given minority possesses not merely more power but also higher ethical value than do the masses. Only on this basis can they justify their claim to the exclusive right to create values for the society as a whole. They can enforce this claim only so long as they can monopolize power. But it is the nature of dynamic civilizations that a traditional elite cannot do this very long. Some of their members become impoverished or discredited and sink to the lowest strata of society. Some members of the lower orders acquire wealth and power to rival that of the great lords. They occupy an arriviste position in their society like that of today's China in the world. Validity is formally withheld from them and their voices and desires are ignored, but the system cannot run without them. Ultimately, they must be recognized as equal, not only in power but also in validity, to the establishment. They must be allowed to participate in the creation of collective values and purposes. At that moment, the establishment loses its monopoly of value. The only remaining possibility is some form of democracy: the recognition that all members of the society are of equal value and must be accorded their rightful role in the political process through which collective values are established. This was the process through which collective values were established. This was the process through which the philosophy of democracy made its debut in Athens (Pericles), in Rome (Stoicism), in the Christian church (Protestantism), and in the modern democracies (Locke).

There is no way to disprove the philosophy of democracy, for there is no way to prove that some individuals possess higher ethical value than others. Once a society begins the developmental process and becomes dynamic it embarks unwittingly on a course destined to bring it to a philosophy of democracy. For once novel collective values must be created, there is no other valid source for them but the people as a whole. However, the philosophic course of democracy is dialectical rather than linear. To possess democracy is not like the possession of an art such as swimming, something to be retained forever once it is acquired. It is more like money. It is acquired and spent and then it must be acquired again. However, if we add together all three foregoing propositions it becomes apparent that democracy is neither a primitive nor an inaugural form of government. It is complex in itself. It is only called forth by cultural development and by complexity. It is the product of revolution. And with each fundamental, or systemic, change in the structure of society the conditions under which democracy may exist also change. The process of adjustment whereby the forces making for the resurgence of democracy assert themselves is what gives revolution its recurrent structure. The preservation of social dynamism implies a complementary preservation of the democratic revolution.

There are two conflicting processes in rapidly developing societies. One process is institutional and technological innovation, which always carries with it a despotic potential. Those who develop and control an innovation are in a position to capitalize on it politically. The other process is that of democracy. It is constantly being generated out of scientific, organizational, and philosophic foundations previously discussed. The result is a perpetually recurring dialectic of revolution. The world's future, far from being postrevolutionary, seems destined to produce a contrapuntal movement involving innovation, despotism, revolution, and democracy. This has always been the politics of development.

# *Chapter* 4   The Rise of Bureaucratic Cultures

TO CREATE AND MAINTAIN the state is not the only function of politics. It must also maintain the organization of life and work. Each function influences the other. During the Middle Ages the apex of politics was found in the assembly of the king, the lords temporal, and the lords spiritual in the realm's highest court. But most of the day-to-day politics of the time took place in the lower manorial courts. There the problems arising from the property system, the system of manorial service, and the rights and duties of the legally distinct social classes were all adjudicated and administered.

During the 18th and 19th centuries Western entrepreneurial capitalism was at its height. Politics in the large concerned the discharge of state functions. These were often distributed among the executive branch, the legislative branch, and the judiciary. The principle of representative democracy was provided for through competing political parties. The previous chapters have discussed the modern predicament of these 18th-century devices for organizing and maintaining states. But modern politics was also concerned with the internal characteristics of life: with rights of ownership, conditions of trade, civil rights, freedom of association, and freedom for associations. The state was expected to maintain these conditions of freedom so that individuals could organize economic and cultural affairs as they saw fit. Both sides of politics, that concerning the maintenance of individual freedoms and that concerning the role of the state, were embodied in the philosophy of liberalism whose chief tenets were individualism and the principle that "that government is best which governs least."

For the first time in the history of civilization, men tried to separate the organization of life and work from the direct concerns of the state. However, the goal was never completely realized and it was never unanimously accepted, not even in America. There were conservatives who continued to believe in aristocratic ideals of statesmanship guiding all departments of life. There were the various radical parties who wanted to submit economic and cultural institutions to public control. But these were the minorities of right and left. Proponents of liberalism remained in charge of Western politics until they were overcome, not by their political adversaries but by underlying changes in the organization of life and work.

79

What is sometimes called the organizational revolution, sometimes bureau-cratization, began to spread throughout the institutions of the West shortly after the opening of the 20th century. The rugged individualist celebrated by lib-eralism was replaced by the organization man. The effect on politics was pro-found. The state was confronted with new problems, alien to the beliefs and confounding to the politics of liberalism. Men were faced with new threats to individual freedoms. In the space of a few decades a silent revolution had oc-curred. Liberal culture was replaced by bureaucratic culture.

At this point a qualification is in order. Just as the tenets of liberalism were never completely realized in practice, so also with those of bureaucratization. We are confronted with a pervasive and dominating influence rather than with total inundation. Moreover, the closest operational approximation to liberal-ism's ideals came during the 19th century. Now it lives on primarily as a nostal-gic ideology. Today the operational fact is bureaucratization. This means that the dispute between liberalism and bureaucratic culture is one between a creed and a condition. This makes for some confusion. In contrasting the two we imply that at one time the Western world actually operated according to the tenets of liberalism. Yet some historians deny that 19th-century conditions ever con-formed to liberal ideals. However, this historical debate is outside the scope of this essay. This is an essay on contemporary conditions—whether or not they are discordant with the ideals of liberalism. This requires a preliminary discussion of liberalism, its origins, its growth, and its principles.

## Origins of Liberalism

In the early 17th century, independently of each other, vigorous religious protest movements sprang to life in three or four separate lands bordering the North Sea. Those early Protestants were unlikely libertarians. They seemed more opposed to established dogmas than to dogmatism itself. But in order to claim freedom to ignore established religion they had to tolerate an equal free-dom for those (excepting Jews and Catholics) whose beliefs they abhorred.

In 17th-century England the Protestant movement was swelled by dispos-sessed small farmers, tradesmen, and craftsmen—those whose descendants were to become the libertarian middle classes. But at first their programs were reactionary rather than forward looking. They wanted a return to the good old times their fathers had known under the 16th-century Tudors.

By the middle of the 16th century the small farmers had ceased to be the fa-vourites of the Crown and instead became victims of a long period of inflation. Their selling prices were held constant while the new market-minded magnates raised rents against them. Depressions, plagues, and famines haunted them. The new landowners turned their farms into wool factories. They abandoned grain farming for sheepherding and pushed the small farmers off the land to do so. The 16th-century yeoman reacted the way small farmers have reacted ever since. He wanted secure land tenure and guaranteed prices. He was the spiritual brother to all the populist and Greenback insurgents who have ever lived.

These early yeomen were not paupers, but hardworking, comparatively well-to-do people who had fallen on hard times. Many, surprisingly many, were literate. Literacy was a requirement of two rising forces: Protestantism and trade. Both were spreading through the people, silently changing their natures, as catalytic agents spread chemical reactions through a previously stable solution. One result was the appearance of a new group of "mechanic-preachers." Victims of depression and technological unemployment, they were free to wander the land, carrying the message of protest. Unemployed scriveners rushed to supply a growing demand for ideological novels and epics that told of the struggles of virtuous peasants and craftsmen against oppressive aristocrats and officials.

Sporadic local uprisings produced manifestos and even revolutionary banners, some of which were remarkable precursors of the Communist hammer and sickle. Libertarian, radical, dogmatic, and reactionary all at once, these movements sometimes blossomed into near-totalitarian regimes like that of Cromwell in England and those of the Puritan theocrats in the New World. True, their spokesmen often wrote movingly of a utopian future of liberty, but speculative onlookers remained doubtful that liberty could ever survive in such inhospitable surroundings.

History proved the poets to be more prescient than the politicians. The protest movements matured gradually into what later was called middle-class liberalism. Liberalism became so well established and it so dominated the thinking of the West that by the 19th century it had even inspired its own new model left-wing working-class protestants. In numerous ways they were startlingly reminiscent of liberalism's own 17th-century forebears in social origin, ideology, and authoritarian impulses.

Now that it has receded from us a little in time, we can discern more clearly the broad tenets of liberal culture. Its dominant principle was that value resided in the part rather than the whole. This is most familiar from doctrines of individualism. The state was seen as a collection of rational, autonomous individuals who freely contracted together to provide security for their persons and property. One did not look first at an organized community or corporate group and seek to discover the collective needs of the community. Rather, one gave sovereign power to its members, who, raising issues for joint consideration as they saw fit, found in their own agreements the only valid source of justice and authority.

This was the political counterpart of Protestantism, which had proclaimed

81

the religious sovereignty of the individual believer. In economics, liberalism claimed that sovereignty lay with the individual entrepreneur. Here, as in politics, self-interest and individual wealth, rather than justice, was the goal. Conflicting interests would be automatically harmonized by free, competitive markets. International politics was no different. Sovereign states in free competition, following their national interest and relying upon war as their ultimate arbiter, would recombine in a perpetual balance-of-power struggle which would automatically produce world harmony. The world of matter—planets as well as atoms—functioned according to the same principles of mechanics and automatically produced similar equations of harmony.

The method of science obeyed the nature of its matter. Autonomous investigators, patiently seeking information about the individual components of the world, would find revealed in the collection of data the laws nature automatically obeyed. Philosophers were of the same mind as scientists. They held that a naturally beneficent providential hand would guide men's minds to the deeper truths of philosophy and morals if they would maintain for the world of ideas the same free-market principles they applied to the world of business. Falsehood was to philosophy as avarice was to supply and demand; truth needed error to show it off. The world of biology was just as "liberal" as was everything else. Forms of life from amoeba to man exhibited the same competitive struggle, with the same naturally harmonious and beneficent result as obtained everywhere else in the liberal world view.

It followed that what was true of man in nature must be equally applicable to man in society. If misguided humanitarian impulses could be restrained, and the social struggle for survival permitted to proceed freely, the same self-regulating principles that applied to prices in the marketplace and to the survival of the fittest in nature would automatically produce the best possible social system. History itself was no different. It was just as subservient to the guidance of a providential unseen hand as were all other departments in liberal culture. This was expressed in the doctrine of progress. Progress was assured so long as it was not sought. Human history would climb unerringly onward and upward in a straight and narrow line, better and better every day in every way.

## The Irony of Individualism

Such was the all-prevading pattern of the liberal world view. The pungent aroma of the 19th century permeated each of its parts. It was surely one of the most bizarre episodes in the history of human thought. Parts of it would never die. Like the immortal contributions bequeathed to civilization by the Greeks, the Romans, and the Chinese, liberal ideals of freedom and constitutionalism were certain to make a permanent addition to the cultural baggage mankind will still be carrying centuries hence. But the farther liberalism recedes into the past the harder it becomes to believe that such cultural ideals could have existed at all, much less flourished. None of the ancient fathers of political philosophy would have dreamed that anyone in his right mind could possibly believe the good life might be produced automatically, without the conscious application of wisdom and without subordinating private desires to the common good. Indeed, liberalism revealed self-destructive tendencies from the start. They were detected, not so much by critics from the left but, initially at least, by skeptics from the right, lamenting the demise of aristocratic institutions.

The young Alexis de Tocqueville, anxious for a preview of the future, rushed to study early 19th-century America. If the view from a valley reveals only hills, from a pinnacle one sees only the flatlands below. Looking down upon infant American democracy with the eyes of a French aristocrat, Tocqueville saw only bland equality: men who were nearly equal in rights, education, fortune, social condition, wants, habits, and taste. With remarkable accuracy he foresaw the arising of a mass society of atomized individuals, constantly swayed by the changing currents of public opinion. And in truth, individualist liberalism, simply in being itself, changed into a mass culture that made individualism archaic.

As societies dominated by liberal beliefs matured, they achieved spectacular feats of mass production and mass distribution. Mass production of items of daily use such as nails and cloth were quickly followed by nearly everything that can be used or consumed. Standardized design and centralized production swept from commodities to styles, from motorcars to newspapers, from business to politics. Liberalism's unceasing drive for the economies of scale was its ultimate undoing. Social systems that had been born under the emblem of liberty and individualism found their ultimate realization in cultures of mass standardization and conformity. Liberalism's characteristic mode of operation, its business system, systematically subverted its original reason for being. By the 20th century, liberal culture merely in seeking its highest realization converted itself unwittingly into bureaucratic culture. But while the underlying facts of social organization had changed there was no corresponding change in the realm of ideas.

Bureaucratization is in great part a function of size and complexity. When any operation gets so large as to employ thousands of human beings to achieve a complex goal, then the individuals involved, whether they are file clerks or machine operators, must be organized and integrated into an intricate series of specialized, subdivided, standardized, repetitive, and interchangeable functions which call for the exercise of little or no discretion. While bureaucracy is often identified with governmental agencies alone, we have seen that one paradoxical result of liberalism was to make bureaucratic principles applicable to other operations as well. Business, religion, and science all became bureaucratized. The irony was that the function of the individual was eliminated in the name of individualism.

Bureaucracy, like liberalism, has its own ideology. It teaches that large-scale organizations cannot operate if they are dependent upon the unique talents or personalities of their individual members. This would mean that sickness, personal whim, promotion, or accident would perpetually interrupt operations. In order that no man be indispensable the job of every man must be depersonalized and converted into a series of rationally organized routines capable of being learned quickly by a ready alternate. Instead of doing what is the uniquely desirable thing from the standpoint of his own judgment or desire, each man must perform only those functions called for by his job specifications.

Bureaucratization is accomplished by substituting functions for people wherever possible. Ideally, it is not people at all who do things in a bureaucracy, but functions. People are needed to carry out the functions, but the same functions must be carried out regardless of the unique personalities of those who discharge them. In theory a bureaucracy is an intricate network of rules and roles like those governing the performance of an elaborate ceremonial ritual. The role players arrive each day. They see that the roles assigned to them proceed at the right cadence. At night they leave their roles frozen and ready for reincarnation the next day.

It is because bureaucracies are theoretically composed of functions rather than persons that computers can be programmed to displace the people whose ineradicable humanness becomes more and more troublesome the higher the degree of bureaucratization. The theory of bureaucratization nowhere works perfectly, but the spread of its principles has been so pervasive that the conditions of life everywhere have become profoundly altered.

The inhabitants of all bureaucratic cultures share the same conditions:

1. They are employed in huge organizations that are administered by distant, impersonal authorities.

2. Their job functions are depersonalized and routinized. Functions are determined by the needs of goals so remote that the reason for the immediate tasks to be done often evades the understanding of those doing them.

3. Bureaucrats, and this includes production workers as well as those in clerical, sales, and personal service jobs, tend to receive salaries determined by general rules rather than individual performance. Promotions, vacation allowances, and pensions vary with seniority, making bureaucrats increasingly dependent upon their bureaucracies.

4. Residence tends to be in huge satellite suburbs in homes as standardized and bureaucratically organized as are the jobs performed by their inhabitants.

5. Mobility is bureaucratically enforced. Jobholders must be reshuffled fre-

quently to increase flexibility and decrease indispensability. Bureaucracies have branch operations everywhere; their employees have no home towns. They must change to new residential communities with changes in bureaucratic status.

6. Bureaucracies require high levels of formal education. Educational level determines the level at which employees initially enter bureaucracies; the level of initial entry determines the lifetime career.

7. Family units must be small and mobile. Children, formerly assets in agrarian and entrepreneurial societies, become liabilities in bureaucratic societies. They require high levels of expensive formal education and they produce no family income.

8. All consumption items, food, clothing, shelter, home furnishings, education, amusements, styles, opinions, are produced by huge bureaucratic structures. Bureaucratic men are not able to control by their own efforts any of the things that are necessary to life, liberty, and the pursuit of happiness.

The conditions of life in bureaucratic cultures are almost the opposite of those associated with liberal cultures.

*Problems of Bureaucracy*

Bureaucratic cultures, both East and West, produce a series of characteristic problems:

1. At the heart of liberalism was a principle of mechanics. It was assumed that people and associations would add up to a harmonious society even if the component parts behaved irrationally. It would never be necessary to take thought for how everything should fit together; coordination and synthesis were produced automatically. The architectonic function of politics was unnecessary. Bureaucratic society reverses this principle, as it does with most of the principles of liberalism.

Bureaucracies are institutionalized reason. They separate complex tasks into logical components and provide for their cooperative achievement. But the more complex and expansive bureaucracies become the more difficult they are to control. Reason in the individual bureaucratic operation tends to produce unreason in the collection of bureaucracies as a whole, for there is no longer the safety in numbers relied upon by liberalism. The component parts of bureaucratic societies are large in size but few in number. When forty auto companies are all competing for small shares of a small market nobody is hurt very much if any one company makes a serious mistake and fails. But in a bureaucratic society a relatively small error at the point of origin can cast a large dislocation at the point of impact.

Bureaucratized socialist regimes are no different from their nonsocialist bureaucratic brethren in this regard. Under socialism bureaucratic error results in pockets of unemployed resources even if people are kept fully employed. In each of the advanced industrial countries the market for basic commodities such as machine tools and automobile products is dominated by a few huge producers. If for some reason any one of them had to suspend operations, either unemployment would skyrocket or unusable products would clog the industrial system, threatening economic thrombosis. Adversity would hit steel, rubber, glass, plastics, chemicals, and transportation immediately. Rapidly spreading secondary effects would disrupt the entire society. The very rationality which permits large bureaucratic units to come into being also permits the occurrence of the bureaucratic counterpart of the old-fashioned market depression: sporadic crises resulting from unavoidable bottlenecks and failures of coordination.

2. Bureaucratic organizations have extremely difficult problems of accounting, allocation, integration, quality control, and administration of their complex human and material resources. To solve these problems, an ever larger army of programmers, engineers, planners, and scientists is required. These are the middlemen of bureaucracies. Their functions are comparable to those of the entrepreneurial middlemen of market economies: they are the brokers of bureaucratic affairs.

The brokerage system required by a nation of entrepreneurs was relatively simple. Buyers were brought together with sellers, small lots were pooled and large ones factored. It was a function more personal than technical. The requirements of such a brokerage function emerged simply and with clarity from the nature of a market system. Its imperatives were inherent in its own processes. Anyone could look at the output of a factory and see that middlemen were required to break large quantities into small ones for distribution to small users. The opposite is true of a bureaucratic culture. Its brokerage functions are highly technical, requiring the synthesis of complex, potentially discordant systems.

One of the chief differences between bureaucratic cultures and those of the past is that the order of synthesis needed to solve problems is not inherent in the situation producing the problem. It must be specially invented and imposed from the outside. Multiple, indigenous self-direction and self-indulgence is not sufficient to connect and disconnect the infinitely ramified and perpetually shifting vertices of bureaucratic interaction. Some of them are potentially complementary, some contradictory, others redundant, but few of them are automatically self-regulating. One reason is that bureaucracies almost never die, even when they fail. They cannot be allowed to die. Too much is involved.

Ultimately the computer would provide the answer. In one direction it would make miniaturized and more easily manageable bureaucracies technically possible. In the other direction it would facilitate the complex planning and synthesizing operations necessary to rationalize the overall operation of bureaucratic societies.

3. In human societies, as in those of insects, what their members do and produce influences the environment in which they live. Ancient men lived as actors in a cosmic drama. At any moment their roles might be revised by the Olympian scenarists who gave fitful management to human affairs from offstage. The medieval world was inhabited by a host of spirits assigned to every department of nature and society; from those who made milk curdle to those who brought pestilence and famine. The inhabitants of liberal societies lived in a world in which all spirits were dethroned and their places taken by autonomous forces observing the principles of mechanics. The inhabitants of classical China lived in an environment similar to our own bureaucratic times. Elaborate codes of propriety were applied to the conduct of everything in the universe and each person's life was spent treading his way carefully through fate's labyrinthine ways.

During the 20th century a change occurred in the nature of man's environment. The familiar world of separate, mechanistic fields of force was transformed into one composed of spheres of interconnected lawfulness. These have been projected onto a universe mindlessly indifferent to the successive legal orders with which man visited it. This brought a second change. The way one deals with forces is through technologies. Techniques for converting force into power abounded throughout the liberal era, making it the age of technology. There were separate techniques for everything: conversion techniques for changing fuel into power, machine techniques for converting matter into commodities, entrepreneurial techniques for converting the forces of supply and demand into profits, constitutional techniques for converting local political forces into national power.

In bureaucratic societies all of these separate technologies became so elaborately developed and interconnected that new architectonic technologies were required. Separate technical processes had to be integrated and coordinated through sophisticated new control systems employing exotic new analyzing, programming, and calculating methods. The new languages of architectonic control, such as mathematics, graph theory, symbolic logic, operations research, and linear programming, became superimposed on the old technologies of power. But these sophisticated new analytical and theoretical control systems imply a profound revolution. They take their model from politics rather than mechanics. They require theoreticians rather than technicians. It is like the transformation that occurred when the architect assumed dominance over the carpenter. Practice yields to theory; techniques yield to symbolic calculations.

As technique gives way before symbol, the environment of the inhabitants of bureaucratic culture becomes characterized by the systems of rules and laws which envelop each of its component parts. The universe itself assumes the characteristics of a vast bureaucracy much like that in which human beings live and function. The critical factors which impinge upon human beings, influencing and determining their actions and their careers, cease to be primarily material and physical and instead become symbols, rules, norms, plans, and laws. Bureaucratic life takes place in an environment different from any previously known to man. This difference is observable in everything bureaucratic man does. It makes both conformity and rebellion assume novel aspects.

4. All societies produce conformity, and so did liberalism. But it was not imposed through political authority. Liberal conformity was viewed as the harmonious pattern which resulted from myriads of individuals reacting autonomously and rationally to an impersonal world of objective forces. The conformity of bureaucratic cultures is explicitly man-made. It is produced by an artificial environment of conformity-inducing patterns and rules. Bureaucrats must always follow their preestablished rules and roles even though they need not become personally identified with them.

Separation between person and function was completely foreign to the liberal way of life. A man *was* his job. If he became impersonal toward it he failed. If he completely separated his personality from his life role he was regarded as being mentally ill and given treatment for paranoia to recement the essential liberal nexus between person and function. But an almost paranoid separation of the person from his functions is the ideal at which bureaucratic culture aims. Only then is it possible to realize the special type of conformity required by a bureaucratic culture. This presents men with a new series of stresses, comparable to those which confronted the people who lived during the transition from feudal to industrial conditions.

But if bureaucratic functions required the separation of person from job in a technical sense, it followed this with a requirement that the bureaucrat identify himself with his bureaucracy more intimately than he was required to do with liberalism's characteristic firms and organizations. This was the message conveyed by sociologists who wrote of "organization man," the "organization wife," and the age of mass conformity that accompanied bureaucratization. Liberalism's conformity had been enforced through the social institutions of church, town, and neighbourhood. Bureaucratization virtually transformed these institutions out of existence and substituted its own processes of conformity.

Bureaucratic culture introduces strange new coercions, but they arrive bearing the seeds of strange new freedoms as well. For the freedom to treat a bureaucratically demanded function as an impersonal chore, rather than being forced to treat it as the essence of one's being, may reserve that being for greater private fulfillment. There is the prospect of a glorious future that beckons to bureaucratic man, or perhaps it would be better to say postbureaucratic man, but it cannot be allowed to befog a grievous problem of the present.

5. The jurisprudence and the constitutionalism of liberalism rested upon the personal responsibility of each individual for all his acts regardless of whether they were committed on his own initiative or at the behest of some higher authority. There was always a perplexing problem when a soldier, in time of war, was ordered by his superiors to commit a heinous crime. If he refused he might be shot on the spot. If he complied he might be convicted for it later. And in any case, the soldier could not rid himself of the sense of guilt, no matter how irresistible the order. This problem, formerly an aberrant ethical curiosity, was moved to the forefront of jurisprudence with the appearance of mature bureaucratic cultures. With the advent of the completely bureaucratized warfare of World War II it could no longer be avoided. Nazi war crimes provided the most familiar example, but others began to crop up everywhere.

Much earlier in history the seeds of a similar problem had been planted when the Roman Catholic Church announced the doctrine of infallibility in matters of faith and morals. Later a counterpart arose in the great Moscow purge trials of the old Bolsheviks who had opposed bureaucratically established Communist Party directives. Some of the American fliers who participated in the atomic raids on Nagasaki and Hiroshima faced a similar problem. But these were only the most dramatic instances of a feature which characterized all bureaucracies.

By his nature the bureaucratic functionary is a man who must perform each of his allotted roles with impersonal detachment. His concern is not substance but process, not matter but form, not essential justice but legal authority. He may be required daily to engage in behaviour whose effects he regards as completely reprehensible. Yet so remote are they from his own personal responsibility as to absolve his conscience from guilt and enlist his willing compliance. It is even possible that every single member of an organization, from chief executive to lowest functionary, may be morally opposed to what he must do and yet do it with utmost dispatch and detachment.

Organizations whose function it is to produce television programs—whether at the behest of public or private authorities—turn readily and efficaciously to the self-conscious portrayal of untruths and distortions about politics. They become factories efficiently turning out the calculated sensationalism and immorality deemed necessary to motivate the masses. The result is a series of bureaucratic crimes against humanity for which responsibility is impossible to assign. There is little difference in principle between this and the more colossal crimes against humanity of which efficient Nazi bureaucrats like Adolf Eichmann were guilty. Society will not be proof against the reappearance of the horrors of Nazism until it has mastered the constitutional principles for preventing the low-grade bureaucratized immorality of the clerk who performs evil deeds with impersonal detachment.

Liberal culture had a comparable problem, that of insuring financial integrity. A special jurisprudence of business ethics developed to insure the inviolability of private property. Bureaucratic culture requires a special jurisprudence of organizational ethics to insure a correspondence between the impersonal collective ends of bureaucratic policy with the dictates of personal morality. For the case of the Nazi death camps is merely an extreme illustration of a form of corruption peculiar to all bureaucratic organization.

6. The type of conformity induced by a social system will affect the type of rebellion it generates. Rebellions have occurred in every historical epoch. Revolution, however, is a term usually reserved for the great social upheavals that were sprinkled through the 17th, 18th, and 19th centuries. These were quite special affairs. It may be that men had never before envisioned the possibility of supplanting one social system with a completely different one. The modern revolution thrived under a libertarian creed suited to the needs of the rising middle classes. Their revolutions were devices for destroying feudal regimes and putting in their stead modern industrial nation-states. Very few modern states were created without this modern kind of revolution, and even the perplexing pseudostates now undergoing development throughout Africa and Asia have been born in a way reminiscent of the revolutions that opened the Western industrial era. But once the revolution was consolidated and the modern nation-state was firmly established they have been seemingly impervious to the instrument of their own creation. Some sociologists even proclaim that the age of revolution is over. But it is merely that the revolutionary style of the 18th century has ceased to be applicable to contemporary revolutionary needs.

Fascist and Nazi successes in Italy and Germany carried some of the marks of revolution, but they were really coups d'etat—maneuvers for stealing the machinery of a state intact—instituted by legally organized parties. The coup d'etat has occurred quite frequently in the modern nation-states, but 18th-century type revolutions have not. And it must be remembered that while bureaucratization has profoundly transformed modern societies, it has done so without any kind of formal revolutionary expression or recognition. We have already seen that bureaucratization grew naturally and surreptitiously out of the impulses liberalism itself had set in motion.

We also speak of the "revolution in warfare" and the "scientific revolution." They will be referred to in succeeding chapters and there we will see that their transformations are like those that characterized the emergence of bureaucratic culture out of liberal culture: evolutionary rather than revolutionary. The struggle for world order is also commonly referred to as involving a revolution. Here, indeed, we are in a problem different from those of bureaucracy, warfare, and science. One cannot well see how world order might evolve naturally out of the present system of autonomous nation-states. The struggle for world order is one foreseeable occurrence that may be capable of producing a revolutionary movement comparable to those that accompanied the creation of the nation-state in the past.

But even though revolution may have departed from the nation-state with its founding, rebellion, as we have seen, did not. And the very conformity that has become the hallmark of bureaucratic cultures also became at once the source of their vulnerability and the stimulus for eliciting opposition. Those who were driven to frustration by the anonymous inexorability of bureaucratic forces found ways to humble seemingly invincible organizational monsters by simple acts of nonconformity. A few Russian poets with access to a mimeograph machine could stun the commissars in charge of the writer's union. A few demonstrating students at the world's most bureaucratized university in California could defy the august heads of business, politics, and education who made up its board of trustees. A few scientists making a concerted push at professional and mass-media pressure points could bring thermonuclear testing to a halt. Negroes constituted little over 11 percent of the American population. Yet a small minority of them were able to align themselves effectively with the world independence movement of the coloured races through simple acts of domestic nonconformance. A relatively small band of guerrillas in a remote peasant land could stand off the world's most scientific and highly bureaucratized army.

Liberal cultures were produced out of revolution. They proclaimed the right of revolution to be an inalienable right. This does not hold for bureaucratic cultures. But even bureaucratic cultures are vulnerable to determined acts of nonconformance. It is only necessary to recall the examples of Nazi Germany and Stalinist Russia to realize, however, that nonconformance alone is not enough. Revolution, after all, is the chief way fundamental political changes have been made. A society in which revolution is impossible must find some substitute or stagnate. What is needed is a bureaucratic alternative to revolution and along with it a supporting doctrine comparable to the liberal tenet of the right to revolution. Perhaps the direct-action, pressure-point tactics of the protest movements and the mass demonstrations of the West will provide the answer. If so, they will require new developments in jurisprudence and constitutionalism so that acts of nonconformance can be endowed with the same protections that labour unions acquired for the freedom to strike.

7. Pent-up mass frustrations can vent themselves on segments of the population even more easily than on the centres of power. This is the second face of the problem of rebellion in bureaucratic cultures. The inhabitants of preindustrial cultures viewed their physical environment as a vast and frightening arena

in which the willful forces and spirits of nature contended against each other in a perpetual struggle whose outcome was in doubt from moment to moment. Violence or chaos might break out at any time, bringing catastrophe, pestilence, war, and famine down upon the heads of man. Accordingly, nature was often seen as subject to the whim of demons, good and bad, and men had to try to enlist on their side the good ones and frustrate the machinations of the bad ones in order to survive. One of the functions of kings and priests was to administer appropriate codes of demonology to regulate the unseen world.

Modern science changed all this. Nature became an arena of order and predictability. It was the social order, in modern cultures, that became the unpredictable source of danger and chaos. This was aggravated by bureaucratization, with the separation between the person and his functions. As it became increasingly difficult for the individual to perceive the connection between his own functions and the larger needs of his culture, the cultural order itself became incomprehensible. The situation was in some sense the opposite of that which had faced preindustrial men. The more the environment of bureaucratic man came to be dominated by a seemingly chaotic network of rules, laws, and functional norms, the more incomprehensible it appeared. Daily life was characterized by a condition of low-grade terror cropping out without warning from the treacherous thickets of rules and regulations in which bureaucratic man had to forage each day of his life.

Bureaucratic man reacted in much the same way as his preindustrial predecessor. He fell naturally into a demonological frame of mind. He attributed to internal subversives and conspirators responsibility for the rude forces of society that seemed to buffet him about. The result was a social terrain naturally conducive to the spontaneous generation of cultural demonologies. Revolution might have ceased to be possible and sociologists might argue that the world had come to an end of ideologies; nonetheless, these were the twin spectres that haunted men's minds.

From this soil a new breed of bureaucratic despot arose. He acquired power through his ability to foster and give charismatic direction to these indigenous tendencies. He assuaged the frustrations of the people with scapegoats drawn from their own midst. Whether or not such forces could ever again provide power for a man like Hitler they would remain smouldering deep inside bureaucratic cultures, like the gathering subterranean forces of a dormant volcano. Their antidote would only be found in a new politics able to bring to the people a sense of social coherence, of understanding, and of political competence.

8. A previous section was devoted to the enhanced role of the executive in contemporary societies. American democratic leadership—such as that of President Lincoln—was described in a setting of contending political forces and was contrasted to the authority-magnifying environment of the 20th-century

world. Lincoln was immersed in the grass roots of politics as was the dirt farmer in his land. His dominance grew out of and was a part of the autonomous political forces surrounding him. A leader like De Gaulle was almost the opposite. He was distant, unapproachable, and almost godlike. He appeared to impose his own autonomous will on a permissive political environment. But for all his charisma and mystique, his actual authority was exercised through a highly bureaucratized structure. Nor was De Gaulle unusual for his time.

The world of the 1960s witnessed a host of leaders who sat at the pinnacle of large bureaucracies and yet exercised a seemingly personal authority. Mao Tse-tung, Khrushchev, Adenauer, Nasser, Johnson, Tito, Castro, and Nehru were familiar examples. They were also the heads of political parties mostly without effective opposition. This permitted them to represent in their own persons the popular will as well as the executive authority of their nations. Each factor reinforced the other. The bureaucratic apparatus could be employed to project to the people the image of a leader with near-miraculous power; the popular adulation which resulted could be used to mobilize the contending bureaucracies which would otherwise become divisive and recalcitrant.

Bureaucratic cultures made possible the appearance of a new kind of leader who combined features previously thought to be mutually exclusive: the mesmerizing personal power of the charismatic prophet who claims an almost godlike power, and the impersonal administrative authority through which vast bureaucracies organize the behaviour of their functionaries. New as this was to the modern world, it had been long familiar to Romans, old and new. It was the contemporary counterpart, magnified several times, of the combined charismatic-bureaucratic authority of the Roman emperors and the Roman Catholic popes. The charismatic component of this power-producing pair was discussed earlier. The bureaucratic element in contemporary leadership contains novel dimensions with far-reaching implications.

## Bureaucratic Decision-Making

Magical, unquestioned, autocratic power undoubtedly has been the possession of some of history's most miraculous leaders. However, as soon as it is approached closely in one case it darts elusively to another farther away. The historian of Rome, knowing the web of political forces that surrounded Caesar, may think of Napoleon as the epitome of an autocratic leader. Here the historian is like the harassed executive who, no matter how high is his own position, sees in it only the countless ways his will is frustrated and looks above himself to a fancied executive paradise of pure unsubordinated command.

Much of what we know about leadership comes from the memoirs of retired statesmen staking their claims to historical immortality. They reconstruct a story of the past in terms of their own leadership. They explain that the bad they did was forced upon them by irresistible forces, whereas good acts were those in which they bent a recalcitrant environment to their indomitable wills. But of course, they differ wildly among themselves about which is which. One man's imposition of will is seen by others as determined or accidental.

No matter how we qualify the role of the executive, will is exercised and decisions are made, but they vary in relation to the environment in which they arise. Decision-making in the liberal world of countervailing autonomous forces and rationally competitive individuals was qualitatively different from decision-making in the densely intertwined network of formal regulations, depersonalized functions, and organizational forces which comprise the environment of bureaucratic cultures. One thinks of the difference between an autonomous captain of industry like Henry Ford and the bureaucratic papacy of a man like Robert S. McNamara, the man "computers would like to emulate." Each achieved enormous personal power (authority rather than power seems to be the proper word for McNamara) and each was the most celebrated executive of his time.

A great change occurs in the decision-making process when organizations become bureaucratized and explode into concatenated galactic congeries of formal structures and functions. Bureaucratization converts the hunches and intuitions of the dynamic personal leader into routinized staff procedures for gathering, processing, and analyzing information. Bureaucratic leaders are provided with elaborate display models of the range of possible actions. Their computers project the consequences associated with each alternative. They assign probabilities, articulate, and give a preference order to the range of desired goals and their foreseeable consequences. All such calculations can be brought together in a decision-making display capable of revealing to the executive which decision is most likely to bring the maximum results with the minimum risk of failure; which will involve the least effort and the lowest cost.

Contrast this with the accepted image of the great industrial moguls and military generals of the past: the personal leadership of an Admiral Nelson, with the computerized decision-making of his bureaucratic successor. When asked about the great decisions he had made, the American admiral Arthur William Radford demurred that he had seldom made any decisions at all. A decision, he explained, was what was done when the solution to a problem was not implicit in the facts. Bureaucratic leaders don't "make" decisions, they find the minimax solutions to decision-making problems. In theory, any other leader, confronted with the same situation, would arrive at the same solution. So might a sufficiently sophisticated computer.

General Eisenhower had a public reputation for charm, friendliness, and informality. He had been known as the soldier's general and his homely, ungrammatical inarticulateness established immediate rapport with the American masses. He was the nation's greatest war hero, but he was also an unambiguous image of fatherly kindness and justice. What was *not* so apparent to the television audiences was the spit-and-polish orderly room discipline with which President Eisenhower's White House staff was organized. For General Eisenhower was also the model of the bureaucratic decision-maker, and he carried the decision-making methods of vast military bureaucracies directly into the American presidency. So effective was the staff analysis system he organized that the presidency seemed to run just about the same during his three crippling illnesses as it did when he was in active personal control of the presidency. Even to the very highest level of leadership bureaucracy carries its depersonalizing effects, diminishing wherever it goes the unique significance of any individual decision-maker at the same time that it enhances the role of the plebiscitary leader of the masses. The same process is at work in all the great bureaucratic cultures.

The decision-making processes that produced the "Walking on Two Legs" program of interwoven agricultural and industrial development in China, that produced the American "Great Society" program, and that produced the program ratified by the Soviets at the 22nd Party Congress were all the result of similar bureaucratic processes. Indeed, the deposition of Premier Khrushchev, one of the last of the old Bolsheviki, was primarily due to his inability to function properly in a bureaucratized decision-making environment.

A world dominated by bureaucratized decision making exhibits its own distinct characteristics. Personal responsibility disappears along with personal power. One implication of this has already received attention. Another is that the redress of wrongs and grievances ceases to be a personal power. There is no one, no matter how high his office, personally able to countermand a bureaucratic directive or to reverse its determinations. Bureaucratic actions are elaborate and ponderous in their generation. They can only be truly corrected by the same processes through which they were made: bureaucratically. To do otherwise is to flail ineffectually at insensible windmills.

If one seeks to influence the decision-making process in a world of bureaucratic leaders as if it were a world peopled by men of personal power, the initial result is a feeling of complete helplessness. This was the feeling that haunted the millions whose lot it was to form the first-generation inhabitants of bureaucratic culture. This lost and anonymous feeling is in large part a result of projecting the values and habits of the past into the ways of the present. But it is also due to the fact that bureaucratic man has yet to perfect instruments to control, correct, and countermand complex, bureaucratically derived decisions.

The means of control must be as sophisticated as its object. The Russians developed a system of commissars, and while their original object was to enforce ideological conformity, an adaptation may be useful against general bureaucratic incorrigibility. The French *conseil d'etat* and the Scandinavian *ombudsman* hold similar promise, as does the office of inspector general, familiar from the armed forces. Whatever the solution, the need is clear. Bureaucratic cultures require the institution of permanent, independent organs of inspection and criticism, accessible to the public, with processes as sophisticated and authority as high as the bureaucratic organizations to be brought under surveillance.

9. A second feature of bureaucratic decision making derives from its close ties with the processing of information. All relevant facts must be known and they must be known immediately. As a result, an environment choked up with information surrounds every bureaucratic decision-making centre. Contrast this with the situation that obtained a half century ago. In foreign relations, for example, 19th-century diplomats had much more authority than do their contemporary counterparts for they held down outposts of ignorance and isolation. The facts about an inflammatory incident might reach a diplomat long after it occurred and even then the authenticity of the information was always suspect. Battles were fought after wars had ended and truces were celebrated for wars that had not. An informational famine surrounded every event, and national leaders stood as sentries in darkness, unaware of what information was true and distraught by fear that all reports might be false.

When facts are like Cheshire cats the wisest course is to ignore them for they'll shortly disappear. This was the other side of the dynamic personal leader of old. He had less to lead about and less awareness of the true state of affairs when he did. As a result, any first counsel of leadership had to be, and appropriately was, inaction. Tolstoi's *War and Peace* makes this the basic explanation of the victorious war against Napoleon. His General Kutuzov was the symbol of inaction as a principle of strategy.

One's actions cannot be more definite than are the occasions for their exercise. A reported crisis might not exist at all, and even if it did, because of the communications lag it might have disappeared of its own accord long before actions designed to correct it could be executed. Leadership took place at arm's length from the objects of its concern. When crisis did arise, it had to be resolved on the spot if at all possible. A shop breakdown in a factory was like a border incident at a remote outpost. The foreman was like the diplomat. All manner of crises were smoothed over on the spot with top leadership none the wiser. Actual events might jerk through time by fits and starts but the picture of them reported topside would be one of steady calm and progress.

All this changed when information became complete and instantaneous. Every crisis, no matter how small and no matter how remote, was referred immediately to the highest executive echelons for resolution. No one at any lower level had sufficient information. Minor executives were converted into the telemetering components of an automated decision-making process even before the advent of the computer. In 1965 when President Johnson decided to begin the bombing of North Vietnam his information system was so instantaneous that each raid could be directed and postaudited from the White House.

This novel inundation of information surrounding the decision-making situation is complemented by a previously noted factor. The intricate intermeshing of functions and the problems of coordination in bureaucratic systems tend to produce bottlenecks and disjunctions, that is, crises, in far greater number than occur in social systems characterized by the autonomy and self-sufficiency of numerous small components. Not only is crisis magnified but so is the executive awareness of crisis.

The executive is confronted instantaneously with nearly every crisis in his system and called upon to resolve it equally instantaneously. Every morning each of the world's great leaders is served up along with his breakfast the world's crisis roster. At the least he must make some public pronouncement to still the voracious appetites of the mass media. The mass media feed on the novel rather than the ordinary. Consequently they have the effect on crisis of magnifying what is small or inventing crisis where none exists.

The result of all these forces is for bureaucratic cultures to become crisis-producing social systems. And while it is true that the immediate revelation of small problems may prevent them from festering into large cataclysmic ones, this benefit is purchased at a fearsome cost. For it requires learning to live in a social environment of perpetual crisis.

10. Bureaucracies must deal with crisis after their own fashion and through their established decision-making processes. From the start the information-processing system must visualize and account for the possibility of accident and crisis. Accordingly, a new profession of specialists in bureaucratic systems was called into being. Systems engineers employing sophisticated mathematical and electronic tools were enlisted in a frontal attack on crisis. Each possible source of breakdown was identified and reinforced with a duplicate, backup system able to take over in the event of crisis. Redundancy, that is, mirror-image duplication, which had been the gravest evil of previous modes of organization, became the hallmark of efficacy and crisis-prevention in bureaucratic systems.

Redundancy as a fail-safe principle of control found its counterpart in decisions themselves. For the more single-minded and irrevocable a decision the more it was subject to frustration and contradiction. Bureaucratic decisions tended to incorporate within themselves principles of their own negation, available for use in the event of crisis. This ambivalence came not only as a safety valve to help dissipate crisis but also as a result of the composite nature of bureaucratic structures.

11. A bureaucracy by its nature is a confederate organization composed of a network of component bureaus. These separate departments and bureaus are the source of its ability to control complex operations. They are the instruments through which bureaucratic action is accomplished. Consequently they are also the primary producers of the raw information essential to upper-echelon decision-making. Bureaus are the specialized tools by which bureaucracies achieve their purposes.

Like all tools, bureaus impose their own requirements on their would-be users. One cannot reap the full benefits of departments of accounting, procurement, or operations unless one submits to the conditions which maximize their effectiveness. Otherwise a host of barely visible resistances spring up all down the line. Bureau chiefs drag their feet. They raise interminable technical questions. They bury the projects they oppose in a dense thicket of staff procedures. Morale crumbles and instruments of accomplishment turn into agencies of frustration. By virtue of their effectual veto power the leading departments of every bureaucracy must be accorded a creative role in bureaucratic decision-making. Consequently, the decisions produced by large bureaucracies are not single-minded. They are as pluralistic as are the decisive units that must participate in their creation and execution.

Bureaucratic decisions are arrived at through a process quite similar to the budget-making and law-making that takes place in parliamentary institutions. This is apparent in the policies produced by any large organization: the foreign policies produced by modern states, as well as the pricing policies produced by large corporations and trusts. The same thing is true of manufactured products. A careful inspection of the items produced by any large manufacturing firm will reveal the participational role of the chief departments who participated in their design, financing, construction, and distribution. The same process applies to the policies produced by the agricultural, defense, and economic agencies of bureaucratic states.

The federated decisions, products, and policies produced by large bureaucracies reveal not only compromise but also contradiction. A committee report or a joint judicial decision may be free to reveal the conflicts of its members or its component groups by appending minority dissents at the end. Not so with a bureaucratic decision or a product. It must appear integrated even though it actually possesses the same discordant characteristics as a committee report. The position of the majority will establish the major theme of announced policy, but there will also be the contrapuntal theme of powerful dissenters interwoven in the statement.

In every contemporary nation the makers of foreign policy are divided into those who favour international conciliation, negotiation, and cooperation and those who favour adopting a more independent and belligerent stance. Rarely do the two sides come to a single mind on any great international issue. The public statement of policy that results from their deliberations may carry the dominant voice of one faction, but the veto power of the other will be revealed in an undertone of ambiguity, equivocation, and even the hint of possible reversal with the passage of time or the change of conditions.

Following World War II the American foreign policy of containment was stated in terms of belligerency and uncompromising opposition to Communism. Yet it also expressed the conviction that Communism would someday change into a form of government that would make world peace possible. On the other side the Russians attributed the evils of the world to capitalism. While constantly vowing to help speed its overthrow, they proclaimed at the same time the necessity for peaceful coexistence. The perfect example, however, came with the Russo-American conflict over Cuba during the early days of President Kennedy's administration. The Bay of Pigs invasion was a classic instance of the self-contradictory nature of bureaucratic decision-making. It was an engagement that contained within itself an action set to counteract every action it set to achieve. Later revelations documented the fact that this was a direct result of the internal civil war that divided President Kennedy's advisers.

An example of how this process applies to commodities is seen in the mass-circulation newspaper. The British daily tabloid is rife with sensationalism and blatant appeals to the baser instincts. At the same time it is produced with a lively concern for truth and professional craftsmanship whose purposes can only be realized by a journalism which aims at man's higher rational faculties. Again, there is the American auto, a never ending source of fascination and puzzlement. It is the industrial counterpart of the British tabloid. Its speed, comfort, size, and appearance are pure sensationalism; its engineering, reliability, production processes, and price are marvels of rationality and technical achievement.

12. The internal forces out of which bureaucracies produce schizophrenic products and policies are reinforced by external uncertainty. Forces from without that are beyond control may thwart even the best, the most carefully designed, and the most unambiguous foreign policy. Overnight it can be outmoded by a Latin-American coup d'etat, an African assassination, a border incident in India, a technological triumph in China, a farm crisis in the Soviet Union, or an unemployment crisis in the United States. Decision makers must try to find policies which cannot completely be outmoded by such unforeseeable adversities. The typical solution again is to adopt policies that are designedly ambiguous. External unpredictability joins hands with warring internal power factions to produce the ambiguity of program and product characteristic of all bureaucracies.

A bureaucracy is a vast organism with an assortment of specialized, departmentalized tentacles for coping with the different kinds of reality it may encounter. The presumed nature of the outside world together with the shifting balances of power within the bureaucracy issue in the adoption of a policy whose ingredients are the result of estimates about how best to cope with reality: which group of tentacles are to be put forward and which to be held in reserve. But both groups are there and both represent not only different possible states of the world but also different power constellations inside the bureaucracy. The result is that when a crisis occurs it tends to discredit the established factional balance of power. From crisis to crisis there takes place a perpetual reshuffling of the dominant power constellation within the bureaucracy. As this happens the official definition of the external world confronting the bureaucracy changes in mutual correspondence. Either may cause an alteration in the other.

Flexibility to cope with such indeterminacy and at the same time provide for the stability and continuity required to maintain levels of operation is facilitated by incorporating contradictory principles into decisions and programs. Entrepreneurial firms once found a comparable flexibility through fluctuations in the market. Changes in prices and demand changed their outside world and also led to internal changes of policy. Democratic governments achieved a similar result through elections in which the party in power was displaced by a new one. Neither of these devices work well under bureaucratic conditions. For one thing, they required the demise of the firm or the administration that failed. But under bureaucratic conditions firms, trusts, bureaus, and political establishments have become impervious to displacement for reason of crisis or failure. The bureaucratic solution to the problem of flexibility is accomplished through fluctuations in the federative amalgams of bureaucratic factions and their associated policy positions.

## A New Politics

In a comment on *1984* George Orwell explained that his fantasy was really written about English socialism in 1948. One of the most arresting features of his book was its discussion of "doublethink," the tendency of bureaucratic pronouncements to be phrased in terms that were internally contradictory. His portrayal may have been highly exaggerated, it may have been overburdened with liberal prejudices, but Orwell had put his finger upon an integral feature of life in bureaucratic cultures. The society described in his novel took on the aspects of a totalitarian and terroristic nightmare.

Back in the 18th century the first of the visionary liberals like Adam Smith were also derided. The Orwells of that day claimed that nothing but chaos and avarice would be possible in a liberal utopia. They, like their contemporary counterparts, were not completely wrong. On the contrary, they alerted men to new forms of insecurity and unpredictability that would govern the liberal future.

Bureaucratic societies replace the indeterminism and flexibility of the market with a new indeterminism built into their policies and products. Confusion, ambiguity, and inconsistency are devices for insuring flexibility under bureaucratic conditions. Market contradictions tended to become aggravated into trade cycles and depressions. Bureaucratic contradictions tend to build up and produce contradictions so severe that policies become fraught with stalemate and indecision. They then become impossible to administer: inadministrability is the bureaucratic counterpart of market depression. Just as it became necessary for politics to intervene in the market process to alleviate depression, one of the tasks of the politics of the future will be to discover how to alleviate the inadministrability which tends to beset bureaucracies.

A dominant theme emerges from the characteristics of bureaucratic culture. Its people and its organizations share in common the fact that they must resort to an architectonic politics to solve all of their most grievous problems. Individuals who are buffeted about from every side by huge and impersonal bureaucratic forces can protect themselves only through resort to the superior power of politics. And the bureaucracies themselves are in the same position as are people. The synthesizing talent required to compose their mutual discords requires applying a modern counterpart of the architectonic science that the ancients regarded as the essence of politics.

Liberal culture had regarded politics and government as being inherently bad. It was something to be avoided and restricted in all possible ways. Its well-known maxims—that man's corruptible nature made him unfit for the exercise of political power and the familiar corollary that the best government was that which governed least—were the axiomatic political principles of a society of individualistic power-seekers. But the nature of bureaucratization is to depersonalize power. Despotism, if anything, has become a more serious threat. But it has also become impervious to the archaic maxims of the fathers of liberalism. It can be rendered politically accountable only through an augmented, rather than a diminished, politics. But augmentation alone is insufficient. Bureaucratic societies are so different from their predecessors that more is required than merely expanding traditional political institutions. A new politics and a new constitutionalism will be required to cope with the novel problems raised by bureaucratization.

# *Chapter* 5   The Scientific Revolution

SCIENTIST, MATHEMATICIAN: these are names that rocket through the imagination. They combine the romance and excitement of space exploration with the awesomeness of a life spent at the frontiers of human knowledge. Not long ago in the West quite different names would have evoked this level of excitement: industrialist, financier. These changes in esteem symbolize the industrial and the scientific revolutions. One need only compare adjacent generations of scientists to savour the essence of the scientific revolution of our own times.

Albert Einstein was a respected scientist—especially in his old age—but he lived when scientists in general were regarded as secular monks. For all his genius Einstein spent his life shunted off onto the cultural side roads that Western societies in his generation reserved for scientists. In the following generation a physicist like Edward Teller would travel the superhighways of social prestige. During the Einstein era to choose to be an astronomer or a mathematician was to select what were very nearly the most impractical of all vocations. An Alfred North Whitehead and a Bertrand Russell could progress from mathematics only to the even more ethereal world of philosophy. Not their students, however.

The mathematicians of John von Neumann's generation were more at home in the corridors of power than in the graduate seminar. The names of leading scientists became household words. Their doings, in politics as well as in science, became front-page news. They had laid the foundations for one new world with the physics that could release energy from atoms and focus it in lasers. They promised to produce others even more astounding out of the molecular biology that could plumb cells to the threshold of life and refabricate them into miracles of synthetic matter. They stirred us with visions of a new technological paradise in which mathematical logic would have cracked the secret of thought processes and installed it in machines that would know the answer to any question that could be asked, providing incidental services, like running the economy, in their spare time.

The university itself, until quite recently, was regarded as a monastic ivory tower peopled by priestly scholars in lofty remove from worldly affairs. Now the university was the rival of the bourse. In the past new enterprises sprang only from financial centres like New York's Wall Street—one thinks of the birth of RCA in the 1920s. Today they are spawned by the great research and development centres. This is the way Ramo Wooldridge (later to blossom into Thompson Ramo Wooldridge) emerged from the California Institute of Technology. M.I.T. boasted that by 1964 over 70 firms had been founded by its science and engineering graduates. The generation that came to power after World War II drew on the university's fund of intellectual capital as its fathers had done at banks. This was the public face put forward by the scientific revolution. But its covert effect on the fabric of society was fully as great.

How did it all begin? It is almost like asking how medieval feudalism or modern bureaucratization began. There was no inauguration ceremony to set the scientific revolution in motion. If a single birthdate must be chosen it was that secret day in 1942 at the University of Chicago when a small group of Promethean scientists nervously kindled the awesome atomic fire whose secret they had stolen from the sun. Considered solely as a weapon, the atom bomb wrought a revolution. It transformed warfare, diplomacy, and the Western state system—and then made them all obsolete. As a new source of energy it inaugurated a second revolution. But its mode of creation symbolized an even deeper revolution.

In principle the problem of designing and building a new weapons system may seem little different from that of designing and building great ship canals like the Suez and the Panama, or a regional system of hydroelectric dams for controlling and utilizing all the powers of water. In the United States the Tennessee Valley Authority had represented the most massive governmental undertaking prior to the creation of the atom bomb. But the differences between the TVA and the Manhattan Project, as the atom bomb program was called, illustrates the differences encompassed in the Scientific Revolution.

TVA was a vast undertaking of great technical complexity. However, it was an idea that was produced from the operation of the common wisdom reflecting the needs of the body politic. Moreover, it did not require novel scientific discoveries for its accomplishment. Carrying it out was an exercise in basic engineering rather than in basic science. TVA was the sort of thing ordinary men could dream up and then realize by employing engineers and contractors. The fathers of TVA drafted their proposals in the manner traditional to politics. They organized popular and legislative support no differently than they would have done for any other legislative proposals.

## The New Concept

With the atomic bomb, from conception to realization, everything was different. These differences were not due merely to the need for secrecy imposed by the war. Had there been no war the process would have been much the

103

same. Indeed, the famous letter in which the atom bomb project was proposed to President Roosevelt was dated August 2, 1939, long before the United States went to war.

What were these differences? In the first place, the idea itself could not have been conceived except by scientists, and only by a handful of the world's leading physicists at that. Only a few more could really understand it once the conception was explained. One or two ingenious nonscientists—H. G. Wells was among them—had written imaginatively of unleashing the energy of the atom. But when such speculation is produced by nonscientists it is always science fiction by definition. No one but a certified scientist has a right to be taken seriously with respect to a scientific project. And not just any scientist. Only one who specializes in the matter at issue. Politicians, along with all other nonscientists and all other types of scientists, are incompetent when it comes to making decisions about specific scientific projects. The article on NATURE in this series explains the role played by scientists at each of the critical stages in the creation of the A-bomb, from its first conception to its ultimate utilization. It is a story that illustrates the fundamental revolution that was prefigured in the creation of the A-bomb: a revolution in morality and politics, as well as in technology and industry.

In other cultures at other times intellectuals, philosophers, priests, and physicians have played dominant roles in decision-making. The Hebraic priest-judges, the Mandarin scholar-administrators, and the philosopher-statesmen of ancient Greece are examples that come quickly to mind. In the earliest times science and technology were not so complex as to defy the comprehension of princes and statesmen. The parting of company between science and statesmanship did not occur until quite recently, not until the early 19th century. Prior to that time the conception of politics as queen of the sciences retained currency even among proponents of radical democracy such as Rousseau. The ideal leader was one who followed Francis Bacon's prescription and took not only politics but also knowledge for his province.

Remember that Alexander the Great had been the pupil of Aristotle. The great Roman statesmen, Cicero and Marcus Aurelius, were leading natural philosophers of their time. King James I and his lord chancellor, Francis Bacon, were exemplary men of knowledge and science. Science and philosophy flourished among the American Founding Fathers. Jefferson and Franklin were especially illustrious representatives of the ideal men of the age of reason. Both regarded the arts and sciences as accessible to their talents as was politics. These were all admittedly exceptional men. The average rulers and statesmen of history fell far short of their mark. Yet the ideal they represented was shared by all cultures. It was imperishably enshrined in the tales they told of their epic heroes and in the dreams they told of their ideal utopias.

The traditional utopia was inaugurated by Plato. But it descended in a direct line from the older heroic epics. Both epic and utopia relied upon wise men to bring good government. During the Middle Ages this tradition issued in a special series of training manuals for rulers known as the "mirror of princes" literature. These tried to describe the rounded education in politics, science, and morals required to produce a wise and virtuous ruler. Similar manuals are found in ancient India and China. Strange though it may seem to the industrial world, the Platonic ideal of politics wedded to science and virtue really represents the dominant tradition of political philosophy found throughout the history of civilization. Bacon's *New Atlantis* was a utopia, but it was also intended as a practical handbook for bringing about a marriage between science and government. The highest levels of science, education, wisdom, and statesmanship were brought together in an imaginary institution that finds neither precedent nor progeny in history or literature. But Salomon's House was not pure invention. It was patterned on two institutions Bacon knew intimately, England's Chancery and the Inns of Court. As lord chancellor, Bacon was not only England's chief judge in equity, he was also head of her mercantilist bureaucracy. The Chancery was a fountain of justice, a planning agency, and an administrative organ. The Inns of Court had provided the seedbed for the rapidly maturing English common law. They combined the elements of a medieval guild, a college, and today's research and development institute. Britain's Royal Society, instituted in the 17th century, was inspired by Salomon's House in Bacon's *New Atlantis*. But it was never more than a pale imitation of what he had in mind. Only in our own day are governments feeling their way unawares toward the same institutional solution Bacon designed.

Salomon's House was a cabinet, a supreme court, an administrative headquarters, a legislature, a planning bureau, a university, a research laboratory, a central information bureau, and a policy institute all at once. History has visited Bacon with a curious fate. It so closely identified him with the industrial revolution that his relevance was assumed to wane precisely when the scientific revolution he envisioned burgeoned.

The industrial revolution brought liberal democracy and with it a reversal of the relations that had previously existed between science and politics. The closest approximation to the classical scientist-ruler became the lawyer-agent. His training fitted him perfectly for the job of maintenance engineer for the new legal mechanisms. He was by profession an agent rather than a principal. His craft consisted in the operation and maintenance of legal machinery. This was all that was required. Falling bodies don't need scientists to tell them their proper rates of acceleration. The same was now deemed true of government. Not only was it freed from dependency upon men of wisdom and reason, it was threatened by them. They threatened the operational self-sufficiency of the constitutional machinery, the political self-sufficiency of the people, and the technical self-sufficiency of the lawyer.

From time to time, especially in national emergencies, science was called upon for special tasks. But even then it was science with second-class citizenship. Like the good servant, it was supposed to know its inferior station and keep it. This was true not only in politics but also in industry. The industrial executive was rarely a scientist. Sometimes, like Thomas Edison, he was an "inventor." At the most this was the exploitation of science but by no means its enthronement. Just as prospectors used science to find valuable mineral deposits, the industrialist used principles of engineering and science to invade the market with new or cheaper products. Bacon's vision of science serving the dictates of the common good lay fallow and virtually ignored for over three centuries. In the interval science remained on tap rather than on top, and too infrequently tapped at that.

Liberal democracy fostered the general spread of intelligence, but it was hostile to intellectuals. It stood for the claim that no special expertise was needed to cope with political problems. It maintained that the common good could best be determined by consulting the common wisdom of the common man, not the expert, the bureaucrat, or the aristocrat. The elaborate schemes of representation and parliamentary organization that the liberal democracies created were designed to see that ultimate decision-making authority—sovereignty—resided with the people.

## The New Practice

Political discrimination against the expert and the man of knowledge was carried further in the United States than anywhere else. Americans were fiercely practical. They were skeptical of all theorizing and distrustful of the intellectual. The very term was one of reproach. America's lawyers and doctors did not require university training of their practitioners until late in the 19th century. Accordingly, they fared better than did her scientists and professors. As late as 1950 public opinion surveys showed that American university professors ranked just below airline pilots in social prestige. Their average annual income was then but slightly higher than the average for the nation as a whole. It was almost un-American to have too much "school learning." Yet it was precisely in America, after World War II, that the scientist gravitated most quickly to power.

The abruptness of the change was disturbing for all. Resurgent anti-intellectualism ebbed and flowed in unison with periodic national crises, but the change was irreversible. Atomic physicists were needed to control thermonuclear power. Astrophysicists were needed to design the space program. Mathematicians were needed to install and maintain automation. Governments and corporations built exotic science centres to help themselves solve practical decision-making problems. Policy research institutes mushroomed until nearly every firm or bureau and virtually every community had one all to itself.

The process by which the A-bomb was conceived and created reveals the inner logic of the scientific revolution. It also reveals the corrosive impact of that revolution upon traditional liberal democratic dogmas and practices. The bomb demonstrated once and for all that neither the people, nor their elected representatives, nor even bureaucratic experts were competent to "legislate" about scientific programs and issues. This was the negative side of the scientific revolution, the element in traditional politics it vetoed. It appeared to undercut the common sense and the deliberative processes upon which liberal democracy had rested.

But there was also a positive side. For the basic decisions taken in science were beginning to furnish the foundation on which the future shape of society would be built. It had been true always that important scientific discoveries wrought profound social changes. But so long as discoveries occurred infrequently and without conscious anticipation, much less design, one could not say that they were produced politically. However, with the maturity of the sciences Bacon's vision in the *New Atlantis* became a description of reality. The time had arrived when it was possible to "legislate" the confines within which scientific advances and innovations might occur.

At this point civilization embarked on a new stage and politics shifted to a new plane. Those who had brought about the atom bomb were appropriately the first to see that they had wrought not only a scientific but also a political revolution. Their actual product might turn out to be less important for history than the political implications of the process by which it was born. Legislatures might continue to operate in their accustomed fashion. Representatives and even chief executives might continue to campaign for political office as of old. But those who were in fact busily legislating the outlines of the future were the scientists rather than the politicians.

## The Revolutionary Result

But here we must stop short for a moment. The idea of revolution is controversial enough by itself. To speak of a "scientific" revolution seems either too prosaic or too fanciful. Historians have long referred to the 17th-century advent of modern science as "the scientific revolution." But properly speaking they meant the revolution *in* science associated with the names Descartes, Bacon, Newton, and so on. The meaning of scientific revolution intended here is more like what is meant when the industrial revolution or the capitalist revolution is referred to. To speak in this way of the contemporary scientific revolution, a revolution still largely in the future, verges upon the cavalier. We stand here at one ambiguous moment in time and imperiously marshal the future into a speculative revolutionary pattern as if coming events were but so many lead soldiers to be deployed at will.

The answering plea is "guilty." The indictment is just. Indeed, the bill of particulars can be lengthened. Revolution is not used here merely as a figure of speech, as when one speaks of the revolutionary treatment of hemlines by the season's most daring fashion designers. No, here the intention, if not the accomplishment, runs somewhat deeper. Revolution is used here in contrast to reform. Reform is the treatment called for when some relatively minor function needs adjustment. When the difficulty does not run so deep as to defy correction by alleviatory or remedial devices, reform is appropriate.

But there are conditions that defy reform. The physician has a useful way of making the distinction we are after. He distinguishes between diseases arising from local causes or disturbances, and those that can be called systemic. Systemic diseases trace to some fundamental disability of the organism as a whole. Its entire principle of operation is being interfered with. To be effective the corrective treatment must be as profound as the scope of the disorder. Certain drugs, hormones, for example, have systemic effects. Others, like mercurochrome, have local effects. Social systems can be spoken of in the same way. Sometimes a malfunctioning is systemic. For example, medieval kingship was incapable of providing the fiscal base required by government in industrial societies.

The chief elements that characterize the rise of the modern world were the autonomous, centralized nation-state, the mass national army, a commercial social order, and a machine technology and liberal democracy. Each component was revolutionary because it represented an entirely new system of relationships. More significant is the fact that each implied the others. This seems to be always the case. A revolutionary, or systemic, change in one of society's major institutions portends comparable changes in the others.

Now that this revolutionary turmoil is safely in the past we can look upon it with a certain amount of serenity and detachment. Not so for those who were alive at the time. A great deal of violence accompanied every phase. Actual wars were required to consolidate kingdoms against the divisive power of feudal barons. Wars of liberation accompanied the assertion of national independence. Civil wars accompanied the reorganization of the state and the liberalization of the class system. The introduction of the factory system occasioned a long history of industrial strife and violence. It is partly because of these experiences that the prospect of revolution instills fear.

What if we could be assured that physical violence would not accompany a future revolution? Would this make any difference in our attitudes toward it? It seems doubtful. Violence is not really the culprit. International wars have become far more violent than any conceivable revolution. The violence of war is constantly bemoaned, but its prospect does not seem to deter nations from either advocating or fighting wars in pursuit of their goals. There is more than physical violence at issue in a revolution. It carries the deeper and more frightening prospect of overturning vested interests and thwarting traditional expectations.

Our forefathers had hoped that constitutional democracy might bring about nonviolent revolutions. This hope was based upon the rationalistic belief that once democracy had made physical violence unnecessary men would engage periodically in bloodless revolutions. But in point of fact the constitutional democracies have been at least as impermeable to fundamental change as have any of the other political orders known to history. The world's socialist countries present a somewhat different problem. Their dictatorial parties are committed to guide their countries through several revolutionary stages. But the stages envisaged are those associated with the West's familiar industrial revolution. What about the new forces of change associated with the scientific revolution? Will the party cadres of socialist regimes prove to be more, or less, amenable to revolution than their Western counterparts?

These are the kinds of thoughts that are bound to fill the mind as the gathering forces of the scientific revolution are pondered. In the first place its sway is systemic rather than local or isolated. It implies changes in society's operation and organization as profound as those that accompanied the supersession of agricultural production by the industrial revolution. Moreover, the scientific revolution also seems comparable to the industrial revolution in other ways. It implies the introduction of widespread planning—not only economic planning but also the planning of cultural institutions and of scientific development itself. It implies the need for the political integration of the world into some form of world order. It implies a change in the world's conception of work and the proper occupation of man. The organization of human culture and of world interrelationships is in for a fundamental change. The factors that determine who shall assume leadership and exercise power are undergoing change. The mere summary of such matters underscores the fact that, like all fundamental revolutions, the scientific revolution is truly systemic.

This raises an important preliminary question. Are revolutions such as this inevitable? The historians who explain previous revolutions to us tend to write as if it would have been impossible to forestall them. We are familiar with statements that the times were ripe for the rise of the middle classes or the introduction of the steam engine, and so on. Historians of Rome prove to us that she had no choice but to succumb to the Christian revolution. Europe is portrayed as lying similarly helpless before the forces of the industrial revolution. At one time questions such as these carried the heavy odour of the scholar's archives and held little interest outside the seminar. Today they have become highly practical issues demanding immediate attention. What to do about the scientific revolution is one of the most pressing problems facing the world. Is it truly inevitable? Can it be avoided entirely? If not, can it be controlled and shaped to humanitarian ends? Academic debates about historical determinism that were formerly of interest only to scholars have become matters of lively and pressing concern to all. Again we seek enlightenment from the industrial revolution. Two questions are especially relevant: Did it require a capitalist, a laissez-faire economic system? And, in what sense was it inevitable?

The first question was actually the matter of considerable debate during the 17th and 18th centuries, especially in England. The traditional governmental approach to economic questions was known as mercantilism, and this form of economic organization was discussed in an earlier chapter. Mercantilism's principles were applied throughout the monarchies of Europe. It was a system that provided for the central direction and control of economic policy. Basic areas of capital investment were introduced according to a government plan. Prices for major commodities were officially established and regulated. Even the United States was a typical mercantilist state until after the Civil War, and, although most economic regulation was accomplished by the individual states, it had been Hamilton's dream that the new federal government would take their place and assume explicit direction of the economy. Hamilton's plan never succeeded. Indeed, the U.S. Supreme Court gradually dismantled mercantilism on the state level in favour of *laissez faire*.

England experienced a similar development, as did France. But when one looks beyond these countries the story changes. Mercantilism was never quite dismantled in Germany, Japan, or Russia—not, indeed, in any country that industrialized after the mid-19th century. One can go even further. It appears that except for one or two historical accidents, laissez-faire capitalism might never have flourished anywhere. If King James I had died before he could take the English throne in 1603 and inaugurate the Stuart dynasty, England might well have entered modern history with the efficiently planned mercantilist economy started by the Tudors rather than with one committed to *laissez faire*. The same thing might have been true in America had Hamilton's proposals prospered; perhaps if he himself had lived longer, or if the country had not adopted the federal structure. It was federalism that furnished the U.S. Supreme Court with its occasion for invalidating mercantilism on the state level.

If one views the long sweep of the history of industrialization as a whole, a history that is still working itself out in contemporary Africa and Asia, the capitalist, laissez-faire approach assumes reduced significance. It has been the atypical mode of industrialization. The typical mode has been mercantilism. A broad view of economic history seems to teach that it would have been possible for capitalism never to have developed anywhere in the world. In this light, and keeping in mind its limited appearance in a few Western countries, capitalism begins to appear as something of a historical anomaly.

The second question we posed was whether or not the industrial revolution might have been completely forestalled. It seems preposterous at first blush, and we would not even consider it were it not for the appearance of comparable revolutionary forces in today's world, and our desire to know if we must stand helpless before them. But in point of fact, the prospect of a modern nation committing itself to a full-scale counterrevolution against the scientific revolution is not fanciful after all. Recall that early in the 19th century Japan's feudal ruling classes had become well acquainted with the nature of the industrial revolution then under way in the West. They resolutely barred the doors of Japan against the inroads of the industrial revolution. Later, toward the end of the 19th century, when Japan changed her mind, industrialization was introduced, but only under careful political guidance and control.

An even more impressive example of a successful counterrevolution is provided by the case of 16th-century Spain. Renaissance Spain had been the "America" of her day. She was the world's wealthiest nation. She was far and away the world's leading imperial power. By the standards of those times Spain's formidable military establishment appeared to be absolutely invincible on land and sea. She was convinced that her own way of life, her ideals, and her beliefs were appropriate for all mankind and would remain valid for all times. Into her colonies, along with her invading conquerors, she sent a corps of highly competent clerical commissars to save the souls and organize the efforts of the pagan peoples of the New World. They were the most efficient administrators the world had seen since the time of the Romans.

These Spanish glories must be ranked alongside the greatest splendours mankind has known. As a result, the cultural system that produced them continued to hold the people of Spain as helpless hostages long centuries after its prime was past. Spain's glories had disappeared, her military had been humbled, she was shorn of power and wealth. Yet she doggedly retained her obsolete cultural system. One might have thought that of all the European countries, Spain was the most favourably situated to exploit the forces of the industrial revolution. Logically this was true. Her imperial ventures had produced an enormous reservoir of organizational and administrative know-how. She had only to apply this expertise to the new organizational problems of industrialization. But Spain made the opposite decision. She turned her powers of organization and control in the other direction and set them to the task of warding off the industrial revolution. She preferred the ways of the past to the wave of the future.

Spain is by no means a special case in history. Indeed, Arnold Toynbee concluded that something like the Spanish pattern has been repeated over and over again throughout human history. On this evidence it seems probable that somewhere in the contemporary world some nation will make a counterrevolutionary stand against the scientific revolution. Spain's example indicates that the effort will succeed where people are willing to pay the price of cultural stagnation and eclipse. In the light of fuller knowledge about the consequences of industry and machine technology Spain's decision may seem more defensible. At least, her example makes it clear that industrialization was not an inexorable, deterministic force irrevocably bound to stamp everything with a single image. It could be resisted entirely, and, as the case of Japan indicates, it also could be controlled. These are precisely the questions the world must now ask about the scientific revolution: Can it be prevented entirely? Or failing that, can it be regulated? These problems resolve themselves into three different issues: philosophical, political, and practical.

## Science and Philosophy

The philosophical issue turns on a very old argument about science; it is as old as the temptation of Adam and Eve, the curiosity of Pandora, Prometheus' defiance of the gods; it is as old as human thought itself. The issue came to a head in the 4th century A.D. in a famous debate between a young convert to Christianity, Aurelius Augustinus, and Dr. Faustus, a great magus and the leading Manichaean of the day. The young Christian was, of course, the future St. Augustine. The story of his debate matured over the centuries into the medieval myth of Dr. Faustus. This was the fabled story of the scientist who sold his soul to the devil in return for earthly knowledge and power. It embodied the essential ethic of medieval science, a science which, like everything else in the medieval world, maintained intimate connections with the supernatural. Everyone believed in the power of science—black magic, as it was called—just as everyone believed in the opposing power of miracles—white magic. But one was sinful, and the other was holy. One defied God and incurred his wrathful retribution. The other was pleasing to God and entailed his bountiful intervention.

The ethical war between black and white magic was carried over into actual attacks on generations of magicians who practiced the black arts of alchemy and astrology and employed a full assortment of spells, secret words, cabalistic designs, talisman charms, and amulets to gain power over the spirit who controlled all events. As the various departments of magic matured into the early sciences their practitioners and pioneers were anxious to purge science of its traditional reliance on supernatural forces and at the same time proclaim their own orthodoxy in matters of faith. This was the claim of martyrs such as Copernicus, Galileo, Brahe, and Vesalius. But the theologians still looked at the world in the old manner. As a result the war between black and white magic turned into a war between science and religion, and this war continued unabated throughout much of the modern era.

The leading apologist of the new view of science was Francis Bacon. He claimed that science had no theological significance at all. Science and theology were completely different worlds. One could be perfectly faithful to the requirements of each without causing difficulty for either one. The principles of religious faith and the canons of scientific evidence spoke to entirely different realms of truth. According to Bacon one could be both a proper scientist and a devout religious believer just as easily as one could be an impartial judge— abiding by strict canons of evidence no matter what the religion of the defendant —and at the same time live out the private life of a committed religious person.

Beyond this Bacon argued that there was something intrinsically humanistic about science. It automatically furthered human knowledge. The advancement of knowledge in turn automatically contributed to human progress. All that was necessary was to keep science completely free of dogma and authority. This became the professional ideology of modern science. It seemed a self-evident truth until the scientific revolution reopened some ethical issues that had remained closed since the 17th century.

Recall that the older Faustian ethic had portrayed science as resting upon the special intervention of supernatural forces. Medieval science dealt with the realm of ultimate power and knowledge, omnipotence and omniscience. But these are the attributes of God. Medieval scientists pursued the most fundamental quests. They tried to plumb directly to the ultimate secrets of the creation of life. They sought the secret elixir that would bring everlasting youth. They searched for the philosopher's stone that would convert the baser metals into silver and gold. They puzzled over the secret "signatures" of events that would unlock the mysteries of past and future, furnish control over the paths of the planets and the vagaries of the weather. They propitiated the spirits who would help them move mountains, change men into different shapes and bodies, and permit moving about through space and time at will. Medieval science was far more interesting and exciting than modern science. Its goals were more fundamental, its prospects more revolutionary, and the risks incurred by its practitioners were more dangerous by far than those of their pedestrian modern counterparts. This was why their ethic was a more profound one. It raised the ultimate questions of the man who would play God.

Modern science, in forsaking the realm of ultimate dreams and aspirations for the prosaic world of the possible and the immediate problems of the here and now, avoided the need to confront the ultimate issues posed in the Faustian ethic. It was as if a new contract had been written in place of that which Dr. Faustus negotiated with Satan. According to the new pact scientists would abandon all the quests that were disturbing to theologians and statesmen in

113

return for freedom to work undisturbed at their lesser tasks. This meant the scientist now needed an ideology rather than an ethic: a doctrine aimed at nonscientists rather than guidelines for themselves. It was necessary to convince nonscientists that the public interest would best be served if scientists were permitted to follow their own professional pursuits undisturbed.

The needed ideology was produced by Bacon. It guaranteed to mankind that nothing but benefit could result. Ultimately this came to be expressed as the need for maintaining the free market in ideas. As with the free market in commodities, everything would turn out well if no one interfered with the scientific process. Francis Bacon's memorable statement was that even though arguments about the ideal form of government couldn't be settled, the realm of knowledge was ever a democracy.

In science as in economics the laissez-faire approach was appropriate only so long as it did not produce results that were harmful to society as a whole. But the atom bomb was to science as an economic depression was to the free market. The implications were clear in both cases. Public controls and regulations were needed. In economics the solution had been relatively simple. But in science the scope of its potential ill effects promises to be so extensive that nothing less than control on a world scale can possibly be effective. This is an idea as repellent to scientists as economic controls are to industrialists.

Beyond this, however, science in its maturity now begins once more to concern itself with the deeper problems associated with medieval magic. The deliberate synthesis of miracle fabrics, exotic metals, and precious stones has become an everyday occurrence. Biology and mathematics are plumbing to the deepest secrets of life. The contemporary scientist is again face to face with the problems of Dr. Faustus. The ideology of unfettered freedom for science could persuade the world only so long as science remained prosaic and the scientist remained powerless. But the scientific revolution, in revolutionizing the capacity of science and the role of the scientist, has invalidated science's liberal ideology without supplanting it with an adequate ethic.

This was one of the poignant complaints of the conscience-stricken scientists who had participated in the creation of the atom bomb. The bomb proved that science was not automatically beneficial to mankind. It possessed deep and horrifying satanic potentials. Moreover, its capacity for evil seemed easier to exploit than its capacity for good. This was underscored for a shocked world by revelations about the inhuman medical experiments that had taken place in Nazi concentration camps. They were all the more disturbing because medicine was the one science that possessed a hallowed professional ethic. The lesson for science seemed to be that a new professional ethic was not alone sufficient. Individuals, even if they were well motivated and buttressed by a noble ethic, were no proof against the bureaucratized brutality of modern despotism.

A moral force, superior to the power of governments and yet reliably available to individual citizens, was a logical requirement of the times. Appropriately, scientists were the first to perceive the need. And because science itself was international they were also the first to appreciate the necessity for a world order with authority adequate to render scientists secure from governments and people secure from science. For the first time in its history, science became political. Inside nations scientists began to organize in order to confront the social and political implications of their work. And because, in addition to being a democracy, science is also international—the most truly international of human endeavours—it was in science that the earliest and most effective steps toward the creation of a true international community took place.

In 1955 Cyrus Eaton, an authentic old-fashioned American capitalist reminiscent of the individualistic tycoons of the 19th century, inaugurated the Pugwash Conferences for scientists of East and West. It was a tentative rupture in Cold War barriers. The need for expanding cultural intercourse had been formally agreed to by all governments and they believed that science would provide an ideologically innocuous starting place. And yet, the whole idea was political more than scientific. The results were impressive. Information was exchanged in an increasingly open environment. Technical details of thermonuclear test ban schemes were patiently explored by the very men who would likely be the chief actors in whatever policies their own countries decided to adopt. Now that they had come face to face each one knew that their future acts would be judged not only by their political superiors at home but also by the ongoing organization of their world scientific peers. For already, before a decade was out, the earmarks of a genuine community began to appear.

Loyalties of state and ideology by no means disappeared; but now scientists perceived with a new clarity the areas in which the canons of science might run counter to the *raison d'etat*. Like all revolutions, the scientific revolution had left a corps of casualties in its wake. The Russian physicist Kapitza had defied Stalin and lived; others, though fully as noble, were not so fortunate. In the United States the shifting currents of politics pushed scientists such as Teller, Oppenheimer, Urey, and Wiesner in and out of favour in cadence with the changing administrations. A few notorious espionage cases revealed the enigmatic treason complex of the scientific revolution, part fact and part myth. It involved conflicting loyalties of scientists to their governments and their ideological beliefs; the conflict between the governments' demands for secrecy and science's commitment to the free exchange of information.

Norbert Wiener publicly contracted out of governmental science a few years before he died. Leo Szilard devoted his last years to world order. The earliest martyrs to science had been punished for what they believed—such persecutions were by no means over—but the new pattern was different. It involved penalizing acts of fealty to something higher than state or ideology. They were acts of noncompliance and acts of treasonous divulgence performed by men conscious of their own power. Scientists were playing roles once reserved for generals and statesmen. But in doing so they were serving what they felt were the needs of the special world community they had joined in becoming scientists. The worldwide political implications of the scientific revolution came from many sources.

Recall again the way the atomic bomb came about. One of the salient features of that story was the change in the roles of experts and politicians. It was not a complete reversal. Scientists as a group never displaced political and governmental leaders. But science itself moved faster and went further than did its practitioners. Political issues and decision-making problems that once would have been resolved according to common prudence now required the application of the methods and procedures of science. In part this was due to the increasing complexity of the problems themselves, in part to the expansion of information relevant to their solution. It was just as easy as it always had been to make the ultimate decisions about war or peace or whether governments should foster cultural in preference to material enjoyments. But once one looked beyond the larger issues of justice and security, the arduous problems of implementation defied the processes of ordinary reason.

It was relatively easy for Soviet leaders to conclude that a larger effort should go into agricultural production. Americans could appreciate quickly the need for compensatory welfare measures on behalf of the Negro. It was apparent that the developing nations would have to make a strenuous effort to convert raw labour into capital. Under the simpler conditions that existed hundreds of years ago such decisions were hard to make but once made they were relatively easy to carry out. In our day the reverse is true. It is the decision that is the easiest to produce and the implementation that poses the gravest difficulties. Contemporary political decisions merely bring the beginning of troubles rather than their end. But this is also the nature of scientific decision-making. In science there is the same relationship between ends and means. To go to the moon, to decipher the genetic code, or to cure cancer are relatively easy decisions to make. To carry them out is what is hard. It is only after goals are determined that real problems begin.

This correspondence between decision-making in politics and science was made apparent during World War II. The major war goals all required the creation of items that had never before been conceived, much less invented. Operations research teams had to be assembled to focus all the related sciences upon the implementation of a basic strategic decision. In order to destroy enemy airplanes and ships it was necessary to have radar and sonar. Of course the principle of radar was known by the early '30s. But applying it and making it effective required inventions whose characteristics were far from being apparent in advance.

The mere conviction that something is necessary may contribute little to its achievement. By the 1960s this condition had permeated throughout politics. There was widespread agreement that the modern city had become dysfunctional. It was unable to maintain a healthful and peaceful environment for its citizens. Bluntly put, cities began to cost more than they were worth, and their exorbitant cost was reckoned in human and cultural, as well as financial scales. Novel modes of internal and interurban transport were needed, and this was only the beginning. The city confronted man with a long catalog of insistent requirements. Everyone could see what they were but none could perceive their answer. Nothing short of the concentrated application of sophisticated scientific and analytical approaches would yield answers to the problems that were apparent to all.

In the fall of 1965 America was stunned by two disasters, one social and the other technological. The Negroes of Los Angeles rioted and burned to the ground the core of their own community. The electric power serving New York and the New England states failed completely for twelve hours. The two disasters, different though they were, had one thing in common. Efforts to pin down their precise causes were like efforts to isolate the first germ to produce an epidemic. In other words, they were examples of a pervasive breakdown, the one in the functioning of a cultural system and the other in the functioning of a technological system. These were the kinds of troubles that promised to occur more and more frequently as the scientific revolution progresses. Being systemic rather than local their solutions could be sought only on the same level as their causes. But this required the application of highly complex procedures of investigation and analysis. One such mode of investigation was called the "systems" approach. It was pioneered at research and development institutes and involved the use of sophisticated information-processing and analysis with the aid of computers.

The political leader may have the authority to act. He may see clearly the goal to be achieved. Yet he stands helplessly immobilized until scientists, technicians, and systems analysts have been able to display for him the range of systemic solutions appropriate to his problem. There is also the opposite side of the same development. Any particular policy proposal may appear to have only a local or isolated impact, as, for example, the problem of mass urban transportation. However, there are intricate interconnections between all urban functions, and these are disrupted whenever any one function is altered. Moreover, the relationships between individual cities and the rest of the world are affected by any urban proposal anywhere, no matter how isolated and

117

localized the place may seem and no matter how restricted is the proposed action. This means that every policy must be analyzed carefully for its larger systemic implications. Only the new analytical devices can reveal these implications. These analytical aids must be employed because systemic effects are not immediately apparent to ordinary political prudence.

The political order is an ecological system. Under simple conditions politics needs only the application of practical wisdom to perceive society's ecological imperatives. Now, however, the most sophisticated tools of the scientific revolution are required to provide contemporary political leaders with the basis for making wise ecological judgments. Science and technology make inroads on decision-making even when issues are seemingly simple and local.

## Toward Political Ecology

This introduces a curiosity that cannot be left unremarked. Earlier the problem of revolution was discussed. There we gave it a simple definition: systemic change. Now it appears that one of the results of the scientific revolution may be to institutionalize revolution, for one of its results will be to focus attention on the systemic, or larger ecological, implications of every major social issue. Stating the matter in another way, the policy recommendations flowing from the sophisticated analytical devices of contemporary science will take in the entire ecological, or systemic, implications of every problem. They will produce systemic rather than piecemeal policies, and this is the definition we have given to revolution.

Alfred North Whitehead described the scientific revolution as a result of the perfection of the science of producing science. We have tried to present this revolution in its broadest aspects, that is, in a scope similar to that used by historians when they portray the industrial revolution. The parallel is justified. The scientific revolution portends a transformation so fundamental that all other social institutions will be required to adjust themselves accordingly. The essence of the scientific revolution can now be stated quite simply: it is the collection of fundamental social transformations that are implicit in the reversal of the relationships between theory and practice that were established by the industrial revolution. Consequent upon this is the reversal in the relationships between theoreticians and practitioners that have existed since the late 18th century. The world of the scientific revolution will be one in which the critical force in society will be the nature and the rate of the flow of scientific innovation. The critical struggles in such a society must take place over the efforts to direct and control that flow.

This way of characterizing the world of the scientific revolution is quite consistent with the way we have understood the social systems of the past. Our most perceptive historians explain the crucial institutions of the great ancient river valley cultures by the ways in which they were dominated by the overriding problem of controlling the flow and utilization of water. One perceptive analyst dubbed all such societies "hydraulic" cultures. In Western medieval feudalism the critical factor was the control of land with special emphasis upon its convertibility into military power. Industrial society, even in the developing nations and the collectivist democracies, has been dominated by the problems associated with the control and utilization of capital. So in speaking as we have of the scientific revolution it will be clear that we have merely appropriated this quite generally accepted approach to previous cultural systems and applied it to the transformations occurring in the most highly developed cultures of the present.

It is apparent that the scientific revolution will have a profound effect upon politics. In the first place, it seems to subvert the architectonic function of politics. Since the times of the Greeks politics has been regarded as the queen of the sciences, the "predirective" science. Its office was to adminster and control all the other sciences. Through politics men laid the groundwork for the developments of the future. But this function of laying the groundwork for the future has now become the province of the separate sciences. They are now providing the foundations from which the technologies, the institutions, and the material inventions of the future will be derived.

Science has become society's legislature. This is the most general political implication of the scientific revolution. All our ideas about legislation and the ways we conduct our legislative institutions are based upon two assumptions: that men of common prudence and wisdom are capable of understanding even the most perplexing issues that may arise in society, and that the deliberate determinations of representative institutions are adequate to control them. The scientific revolution discredits both of these assumptions. It faces us with the necessity of inventing new deliberative and legislative processes that will be as adequate to the issues of today as our traditional governmental institutions were to the kinds of issues characteristic of the times of their founding in the 18th and 19th centuries.

Nor is this all. It might seem sufficient merely to equip traditional governing institutions with auxiliary bodies of scientific advisers. But this cannot really deal with the problem. For the scientific expert has his own characteristic limitations that inhibit his ability to be useful in such a situation. The scientist, by his nature, must be such a narrow specialist that he cannot perceive the more general social implications of the very issues about which he is expert. In becoming a specialist he deprives himself of the possibility of functioning as a generalist.

The same thing applies in reverse for the person of general knowledge. He finds it impossible to comprehend complex technical issues of our times.

119

The ramifications of this difficulty become clearer if we consider the more specific political implications of some of the basic subdivisions of modern science. Molecular biology has deciphered the code through which the rudimentary substances of life are ordered into their distinctive shapes and functions. We are led to visualize not only the possibility of synthesizing foods and other kinds of organic substances but also living forms. The French physicist Pierre Auger once suggested that even previously extinct animal forms might be recalled from the burial grounds of history through the maturing skills of the scientist.

Once the decision is taken to synthesize foods, fantastic institutional changes are entailed. The entire agricultural industry is affected. Production and distribution methods must change. The labour force changes. The prospect of eliminating famine from the world opens out to us. But in that case, what functions are to be provided for the displaced peasantry of Africa and Asia? Will they be specially disadvantaged, as happened to the American Negro as a result of automation? What will happen to the population distribution of the world? The world contains something over three billion people. Roughly a third of them are Caucasian. Even without a solution to the problem of famine the world will more than double its population by the end of the century. The Caucasian proportion will steadily dwindle. When one adds to this the prospective elimination of famine, the result becomes impossible to forecast.

If traditional modes of agriculture disappear this will also bring a change in the earth's basic chemical cycle. This is the well-known cycle through which the proper levels of oxygen are maintained by plant life. Plants in turn remove from the air carbon compounds which otherwise would make animal life impossible. To introduce large-scale synthetic food processes all over the world would not only arrest mass-farming operations, and thereby decrease the natural generation of oxygen, but would also raise the level of noxious chemicals in the atmosphere harmful to the animal life. This harmful atmospheric effect would be magnified by the massive cities to be thrown up in the wake of the population expansion. For as people increase, new lands must be converted from foliage to use for streets, residences, shops, factories, and offices. Oxygen-producing vegetable matter is replaced by smog-producing vehicles and furnaces. In a short fifty years, some time following the turn of the 21st century, the problem of managing the chemical composition of the earth's atmosphere may assume crisis proportions. This will clearly pose a new problem for politics, but not for politics as it has been known in the past. For it is a problem that cannot be solved on a political scale smaller than that on which it occurs. It is a world problem and its proper solution cannot be achieved short of world order.

The aging process, like the growth process, can be traced to its foundation in the cybernetic systems that are built into the complex code-bearing and messenger-carrying protein molecules that design and regulate all forms of life. We are led to visualize the postponement, if not the abatement, of the aging process. The result would be a world in which human longevity had been measurably extended. (See further HUMAN NATURE in this series.) That this would add to the population problem is obvious. Already scientists have begun to speculate upon the drastic population control measures which may be required. The Israeli mathematician Bar-Hillel suggested that virtually every grave social problem can be traced to unchecked and unmanaged birth. He voiced a proposal that many find repellent. It is to devise a way of prohibiting all childbearing, except in specially approved and licensed instances. Human reproduction, as with that among valuable animals, would occur in accordance with careful calculations, both to maintain world population amounts at the proper level and also to insure that the quality of the genetic endowment of the world be maintained at the highest possible level.

The greatest philosophers and the most illustrious aristocracies have always believed that human breeding is at least as important as plant and animal breeding. Indeed, the problem was first broached in Plato's *Republic*. Soon, however, it may force itself upon the world republic. Population management cannot be effective on any smaller scale. If one government were to begin it others might feel forced to do likewise merely from fear of becoming genetically outclassed by a developing nation of thoroughbreds. But that all nations would follow suit is extremely unlikely. One holdout the size of India or China would be enough to nullify the salutary achievements of all the others.

If this problem seems politically insoluble another one related to the extension of human longevity is even more so. This is the complex issue that will arise if it becomes possible to increase human longevity measurably. Two dimensions of this challenge are apparent immediately. Much of what we now assume to be an indelible aspect of human nature may in truth result from the fact that during all his previous history man has been an animal who could look forward to little more than seventy years of life, if that. Suppose a relatively modest advance in medical science were to stretch this out to something like 150 years? For a long while, perhaps for a hundred years following this advance, those benefiting from this increased longevity would have a new conception of life itself. It would seem to reach out into an almost infinite future. During that time men would certainly think and behave differently from the way all men who have lived before them have done.

These new longer-lived men would become, in effect, a new human species. In one sense the prospect of death would cease to dominate their every calculation. Planning for the future, both on individual and collective levels, would assume less urgent characteristics. There would appear to be time for everything.

But at the same time, accidental death would become a much more colossal tragedy. Much of man's time and effort would be devoted to preventing accidental death. It is even conceivable that the struggle for longevity would take precedence over the struggle for wealth and power. Politics would accordingly move to a new level. We are already able to observe foreshadowings of what this might bring.

Those individuals who occupy the leading positions in the great bureaucracies—leaders of great nations, of great armies, huge industries, mammoth churches, and vast institutions—already command the services of elaborate life-support systems unavailable to lesser men. To be the head of the United States or the U.S.S.R., to be the Roman Pope or at the head of the British trade unions, entitles one to enjoy a massive, around-the-clock personal-care staff devoted to easing, guarding, and preserving the life of the leader. Elaborate security precautions occupy the attentions of professional corps of guards. All the normal causes of accidental injury, disease, and death are warded off with unflagging energy. Vehicles must be kept in perfect condition. Traffic is dispersed along the leaders' road of travel. Aircraft are specially maintained. Their operators are of the highest competence. Standby systems back up every conceivable item of use. Food, exercise, medication, and leisure are carefully administered and monitored by a watchful staff of experts on immediate call throughout the day and night. The slightest indisposition is occasion for mobilizing the most expert medical staffs and the most advanced hospital facilities.

In the winter of 1965 Dwight Eisenhower experienced a slight heart attack while on a golfing vacation. A large team of medical experts was dispatched instantly to the closest army hospital to furnish the former president with the best possible medical care. When he was well enough to be moved to Washington, where the world's most elaborate hospitals could provide even more careful attention, a special eight-car private train, converted into a mobile, one-patient hospital, was commissioned to make the transfer. There is no way to estimate the increased longevity great leaders enjoy as a result of these carefully organized life-support systems. Perhaps, on the average, they provide those who command them with an additional ten years of life. There is also no way to calculate the effect of political decision-making that results from the fact that medically pampered leaders exist on a special regimen of behavioural and preservative drugs. This was the case with the most spectacular of the world's recent leaders: Roosevelt, Churchill, Stalin, Khrushchev, Eden, Eisenhower, Kennedy, Johnson, De Gaulle, and Mao Tse-tung. How is it possible to determine the effect wrought on the Cold War by the fact that certain of its leaders at crucial moments were consuming steady doses of hormones, tranquilizers, and energizers? What must we guard against as this increases in the future? For the danger is enhanced, as we recall from the discussion of bureaucracy, that bureaucratic situations tend to magnify the numbers of crises presented to leaders.

But what about the future, after potential longevity has been stretched out considerably? Is it not readily conceivable that in such an event the dominant motive spurring men to greater heights of achievement will stem from the fact that with high office will come acquisition to the most perfect possible life-support system science can provide? The accidents which can cut down the lowly while they are still in their prime will be carefully eliminated from the environments of their great leaders. People cannot be expected to maintain their traditional evaluations of professions and occupations as if this change were of no moment. Time promises to replace money as the scarce value after which men struggle.

The second imponderable resulting from the expansion of longevity is somewhat more opaque. Throughout history man's entire conception of politics has developed in relationship to death. The earliest utopias were often patterned after religious doctrines of a heavenly city where the normal petty motivations of men were overcome because of knowledge that they possessed immortality. Mundane politics, of course, was of a different order. It was for men who died; for men who plotted the displacement, the retirement, or even the death of those who stood in their way. It was for those who had always to hurry. Even money was affected. Time was money, so it was said. Rates of interest based on its lease were influenced by the allotment of wealth-producing time given man at his birth. When life was short interest rates had to be high. For life *was* short. And it was shorter by the full measure of eternity for those of the late 20th century who absorbed the shock of the so-called death of God. This was what furnished the content of the late 20th-century philosophy of the absurd.

The Spanish philosopher Unamuno cried out in despair over the shock of death—saying, "if it be true that nothingness is our fate, let us not so act that it shall be a just fate." But if this nothingness is to recede further and further into the future, will not the absurd disappear from man's fate by the same measure? If so, what will be the result? Will the essential tragedy of life lose its biting edge? Will utopianism leave the heavens to take command of the politics of everyday life? Does the gulf between idealism and realism depend upon death? Does the stretching out of time eliminate that gulf? If it does it also springs philosophy from the academy and installs it as the most practical of the professions. Science, in building its revolution, by that same act prepares the ground for its own subordination to philosophy.

## The New Capital

One of the most tumultuous occurrences in the history of politics took place when capital replaced land as the major source of value. We have suggested that a similar replacement is brought about by the scientific revolution. What are the implications of this replacement? Let us assume that the significant role previously occupied by the flow of capital is taken over by the flow of scientific innovation. Can we then simply take the leading institutions of mature industrial orders and reread them as they stand, substituting science for capital and scientists for capitalists? It is tempting to do so. It is the first thought that comes to mind in visualizing the political content of the scientific revolution. But no sooner does the thought occur than we detect our error. For that is not what happened when the industrial order displaced feudalism.

Medieval institutions had simply ceased to be workable. And if they had become unworkable for feudal relationships they were even less appropriate for industrial conditions. You could not merely pump capital through channels previously occupied by land. Moreover, when feudalism itself was new, it had not taken over merely by taking the empty shell of Roman urban institutions and filling them up with manorial relationships.

It was not what happened when Rome's imperial *polis* supplanted the static modular *polis* of Greece, nor what happened when the *polis* supplanted the sprawling river valley cultures based on the control of waterpower. Each one of these distinct power systems possessed an equally distinct political system. We have no reason to doubt that the world of the scientific revolution will also produce its own distinctive constitutional structure. On the contrary, confirmation comes from two sources: the visible organizational effects of cybernation and the international scope of the scientific revolution. Cybernation transforms prior organizations by shifting their foundations from man-machine and man-routine relationships to computer-machine and computer-routine relationships. Just as the component functions and departments of traditional organizations were influenced by human capabilities and peculiarities, so also will cybernated organizations change in accordance with the peculiarities of computers. Not only will such organizations look and work differently, they seem destined to function differently and to operate on a different scope.

In the past the location, the size, the complexity, and the communications systems of organizations were determined by the natures, needs, and capacities of the human beings who composed them. What man could do and what he could control depended upon man himself. The form of the industrial corporation, its architecture, its location, and the administrative staff system by which it was managed, all were determined by the fact that men were the primary components of organizations. Double-entry bookkeeping had expanded the individual's power of control, making it possible for one man to manage more and larger firms. Scientific management and advanced precomputer business machines were further aids, but they merely expanded the number of people and the degree of complexity that could be controlled. However, cybernation breaks the dependency of organizational size and complexity on human nature and makes it possible to conceive of a vastly expanded scope of control. But this does not necessarily mean that the unit size of enterprises will expand. On the contrary, the computer makes it possible to decentralize functions at the same time that the scope of their integration is expanded. We can imagine control being exercised on a world level, but the objects of control being smaller than those known today. For physical contiguity between related functions is no longer required in the same way it is when human beings perform functions. Moreover, previously unrelated functions can be performed together. We can conceive of central materials-processing and information-processing centres serving a host of functionally unrelated operations.

With the break in the tie between functions and men the need for the concentration of functions in one location disappears. All considerations based upon the economy of collecting, training, and organizing human beings disappear. Questions of corporate morale and status anxiety disappear. All this adds to the potential for operating decentralized organizations.

Cybernation permits us to centralize and decentralize simultaneously: centralization and amalgamation of control functions, and reduction in the unit size of operational functions. If the unit size of autonomous functions decreases while the ability to control and integrate expands—as when several different industries employ the same computerized information-processing facilities—new vistas of community planning and organization appear. For the break in the ties between men and machines and men and routines eliminates another of the underlying causes of urban congestion. We are led to visualize the possibility of completely reorganizing the social order on the basis of the optimum unit of human culture rather than allowing life to be determined by the mindless forces of technology and industrialization. Each city can become a self-sufficient community. It can integrate and organize its own functions through common computer systems. It can relate itself to all other communities through a new form of computer-based central information-processing system. These are some of the forces that portend a considerable change in the organizational structure of society. They are also forces that reach out across national boundaries to demand resolution on a world scale.

It is often said that science is international. It is certainly true that it is more international than is any other human institution. Moreover, scientists make up an implicit international community. They rely upon the authoritative judgments of their own international peer group. The scientific approach has built into it a universalizing tendency. These features of science have gradually worked toward the sublimation of the national, ethnic, and ideological peculiarities that historians such as Spengler and Toynbee have pointed to in the history of science. There was once a prominent distinction between the Baconian empiricist tradition of English science and the Cartesian tradition of France. This has virtually disappeared.

A famous example of scientific nationalism occurred in the 18th century. English mathematicians dogmatically followed the Newtonian calculus while German mathematicians just as adamantly supported the notation system of Leibniz. Politics played a role when the controversy became heightened by the succession of the German house of Hanover to the English throne, and the result was a comparative stultification of English mathematics. The intrinsically universalist characteristics of science finally won out over the forces of nationalism.

The ideological tribulations of Soviet science are notorious. Einstein's theories were branded as decadent cosmopolitan heresies. Linus Pauling's tireless work in behalf of East-West coexistence did not save his Nobel prize-winning theory of the molecular bond from being banned from Soviet science by Stalin's physicists. The disaster visited upon Soviet genetics by Lysenkoism is well known. But gradually in the U.S.S.R., as it had earlier in English mathematics, the inner universalism of science won out over ideology. Perhaps the most dramatic example occurred in economics. This was the one realm that seemed destined to remain forever Marxist. And yet, throughout Russia and Eastern Europe there occurred a tentative and partial reception of neo-Keynesian doctrines and linear programming techniques. This was much like the "reception" of Roman law doctrines that began to seep through the legal systems of Northern Europe toward the end of the Middle Ages.

At the same time this was taking place in Communist economic systems something quite similar was occurring in the West. Stimulated by the organizational necessities of the Cold War, the growth of bureaucratization, the requirements for social justice, and in goodly measure by the forces unleashed by the scientific revolution, the nations of the West adopted quasi-socialist systems of central planning and control. Economics, the most scientific of the social sciences, was partaking of and contributing to the same universalizing tendencies observable throughout the sciences.

No national or cultural barriers are completely impermeable and science has an especially corrosive effect on the ideological walls which nations attempt to erect. It is even possible that the long-hoped-for cultural meeting of East and West may make its way first through scientific thought. A possible illustration may be found in the contributions to theoretical physics made by the Chinese physicists Yang and Lee. In 1957 they received the Nobel prize for work in parity theory that had direct implications concerning the symmetry of matter and antimatter in the universe. The conception was philosophically profound in its own right. But what was almost equally remarkable was its resonance with the traditional Oriental doctrine of Yin and Yang. Scientists who knew Yang and Lee as young men at the University of Chicago had prophetically dubbed the inseparable pair as "Yin and Yang." When we recall the influence national styles of thought had on early science in England and France it would not be surprising to find a similar occurrence taking place as scientific traditions become more firmly established throughout the Orient. If the work of Yang and Lee is a reliable guide the result will be a marvelous enrichment of scientific thought. Beyond that, however, lies the prospect of science serving as a democratic melting pot for sublimating and amalgamating the philosophic residues of the world's separate cultural traditions.

## The Management of Science

Against this prospect of peace and order in the universe of speculative thought it must be recalled that the actual scientists and intellectuals who inhabit the real world behave much like other men. We have been talking about science, not about scientists. And as C. P. [Lord] Snow pointed out, scientists are often the very ones who are least qualified to perceive the deeper philosophic and cultural implications of their special world. In this aspect science is like business and politics. It is not necessary to understand their deeper principles in order to become adept practitioners. Much of what scientists tell us about science must be taken on the same level as what industrialists tell us about economics.

Scientists, like others, tend to produce an ideology expressing their professional interests through a series of general maxims such as: what is good for science is good for humanity; science is intrinsically progressive and beneficent; its well-being requires an environment of freedom not unlike that extolled by Western businessmen, and so on. Scientists understandably see little virtue in the new "science of science" which proposes to treat the work of scientists as economics treats the world of material production and exchange. But the testimony of scientists to the contrary, some device for controlling and managing science is necessary.

Science, in the idiom of the well-worn cliché, is too important to be left to the scientists—too important for the world as a whole, intrinsically too important, too fraught with potentials of evil, and too full of potential promise to be allowed to proceed according to chance and individual whim. As soon as this is said, however, it is immediately apparent that the very universality of science requires that whatever is done to submit it to overall political direction must be done on a plane commensurate with its essentially universal nature. The control and direction of science requires world order.

Suppose, for example, that the welfare of the world requires the prohibition of something that is scientifically possible to achieve. Let us say that what we wish to prohibit is the scientific reduction of human beings to docile, mindless slaves who will be effective and content in the performance of disagreeable and menial tasks. History teaches us that leaders may arise who will not blanch at posing such ends, and that scientists can be found who would work toward them. But, as in all other aspects of science, this is something that cannot be regulated only in part, or only in some parts of the world and not others. It can be achieved only on a world level. No matter where we touch the problems of science we find that its politics is world politics and that the politics of the scientific revolution is world politics.

This was made apparent at the beginning of the scientific revolution. The first encounter of science with politics came through an issue similar to the above example, the threat to human germ plasm arising from the detonation of thermonuclear devices. This was a question that could be answered only by scientists—physicists and geneticists—and all over the world they debated the issue vigorously. Related to this was the question whether it would be possible for nations to test thermonuclear devices secretly and the question of how agreements to cease testing could be policed. Here science was thrown directly into the highest political problems facing the world.

The Pugwash conferences brought leading scientists together in the first breach of Cold War antagonisms. Awareness of a responsibility transcending national boundaries emerged. In the United States the issue was joined by two world-famous scientists, Linus Pauling and Edward Teller. Their debates about radiation levels and detection possibilities made them into the contending representatives of millions of people whose sympathies and preferences could not otherwise find expression. Science had produced a new type of representation and a new form of deliberation through the famous Teller-Pauling debates.

Radiation was only the most spectacular example of a series of ecological problems that shared in common two features: they could not be solved on any scale less than the world and they could not be solved without the help of the world scientific community. Perhaps the most immediate problem is that of maintaining an adequate balance between world levels of food and population. It is a problem that will soon come to a head as the world's colonial areas acquire full autonomy and press forward their claims to share in the enjoyment of the world's resources.

We learn from the article on NATURE that the deep-lying beds of the world's oceans hold our last great treasure trove of natural resources. Soon the seas will become our farms and our factories. But how will we portion them out? And how will we regulate their exploitation? The seas belong to the world and only world order can administer them. Already the fisheries of the world are being rapidly depleted but in the absence of world order this fact merely speeds the competitive efforts of individual nations to harvest the dwindling resources before others beat them to it. It is a species of mob behaviour not unlike that observed when passengers panic on a burning ship. It will become an even graver problem as the world turns its attention to harvesting the vegetable and mineral resources of the oceans. Nothing less than a scientifically sound, world-administered system of regulation will suffice.

A final control problem may seem more remote but it is like the others in that it is a problem with a worldwide incidence and one that can be solved only with the aid of science. It is the problem of preserving those characteristics of the ionosphere which make electronic communications possible. The danger arises not only from exotic weapons designed to disrupt electronic communications but also through national experiments that may have deleterious effects on the Van Allen belt. If anything were to make electronic communications impossible, civilization would collapse like a house of cards.

Man's genetic endowment, his food supply, his air, and his communications systems are about as basic to his pursuit of life, liberty, and happiness as can be imagined. The time is not far distant when their maintenance will depend upon political controls scientifically developed and administered on a world scale. It is from such needs that the scientific revolution may realize its fullest potentials for human betterment and it is also from such needs that the drive toward world order may acquire its most insistent force.

## Science and Administration

One of the most exotic aspects of the scientific revolution is the prospect of conducting political affairs scientifically. This is different from the substantive employment of science to achieve a political aim. Calling upon physics to produce atomic bombs, and chemistry to produce defoliants are examples of the latter. No matter how extensively science is employed by government the result is not scientific government. We would only be justified in speaking of scientific government if the procedures of science (not the substantive sciences) were to become applicable to or replacements for the procedures of government.

Since ancient times there have been two opposing traditions about the establishment of political goals. The conservative tradition has favoured restricting decision-making to specially distinguished elites: generals, priests, landlords, capitalists, bureaucrats, philosophers, etc. The democratic tradition places its trust in the wisdom of the people as a whole. The political institutions of democracies are designed to facilitate the expression of popular will, to elicit as much wisdom as possible from the people, and to prevent elite groups from expropriating popular authority. These are the two traditional ways of discussing the establishment of political goals. If only people can make decisions, decision-making must be either elitist or popular. However, in the chapter on bureaucracy we discussed bureaucratized decision-making. When this is combined with recent advances in science we perceive a third way of looking at decision-making.

In politics one doesn't start out from the state of nature each morning. Fundamental goals do not have to be established anew for each new decision-making situation. Moreover, at any one moment only a limited number of goals are feasible, for the practicability of goals is largely determined by the means at hand. If a country does not possess atomic bombs it is automatically foreclosed from adopting a number of political goals which depend upon the possession of bombs. Countries that do possess the bombs have forced upon them special decision-making problems whether or not they like it. Every established social order exhibits a fundamental system of goals which permeate all its institutions.

One of the chief functions of social institutions is to reduce the need for individuals to make decisions. Institutions are to some extent depersonalized or nonanthropomorphic reason. A culture's family system limits the range of courtship possibilities open to each individual in the culture and thereby effectively "decides" the nature of the families to be created. Taken all together the institutions of a society express similar basic goals and exhibit built-in forces for the accomplishment of those goals. Left to themselves the institutions of a society will tend to preserve the status quo, and they do so powerfully, often in spite of occasional efforts by individuals to substitute new or modified goals.

American political scientists are fond of pointing out that regardless of the campaign speeches made by candidates for the presidency, once in office each new president is surrounded by a continuity of institutional forces which permits him but a narrow range within which innovation and personal discretion may be exercised. The office molds the man. Each new incumbent, whether of the American presidency or the Soviet presidium, is forced to administer the same programs as his predecessors and to administer them in just about the same way. Harold Laski described how the same forces operated in British government. There were certain things no socialist majority could do even though it might have received an impressive mandate from the people at the polls. Laski believed that there was an unwritten agreement on fundamentals permeating all British institutions. Any measure which conflicted with these fundamentals would be like trying to put square pegs in round holes. The alien measures would be "vetoed" almost automatically.

This aspect of social institutions is what has led sociologists to describe organizations as congealed reason. One of the most important motives leading individuals to join organizations is to "purchase" the rationality they maintain. The large body of the members of an organization are relieved from the necessity of attending personally to the range of decision-making allotted to organization.

Electronic data-processers have been explained as analogues of the human mind. The same analogy can be applied to social organizations. In addition to functioning like one man writ large, they also operate like vast data-processing machines. Because of this it is possible to conceive of computerized decision-making in quite large organizations. A third form of organization, neither elitist nor democratic, but scientific, now becomes conceivable.

The phrase "automated decision-making" rings in the ears with a sound as modern as that of the latest supersonic aircraft. However, it is one of man's oldest ideas, one of his perennial quests. Plato wrote of scientists governing scientifically in the *Republic*. Later, in the *Laws* he conceived of their place being taken by a rigidly programmed system of laws. Indeed, one of the most hallowed of constitutional principles is the rule-of-law tradition: government by laws rather than men. Francis Bacon's *New Atlantis* carried forward both of these components of Platonic political theory. He provided for the overall direction of society by a scientific elite in the institution he named Salomon's House. In his system of jurisprudence he conceived of a rigorously nondiscretionary system of laws.

The great founders of the behavioural sciences, Locke, Hobbes, Smith, and Rousseau (together with American practitioners such as Madison, Jefferson, and Adams), dreamed of a kind of precomputer automated decision making. Both the economic and the political orders were to function on mechanistic principles. Political scientists were needed only one time—at the constitutional convention. After their intricate constitutional machinery had been set in motion ordinary people following only their own self-interest would produce the general welfare automatically, as if guided by an unseen hand.

This is really the ideal of every corporate body. The ideal is brought to its highest development in modern bureaucratic organizations. In the 19th century the scholars who first studied the large-scale bureaucracy of modern times detected this factor and devised the theory of the real personality of the group to account for it. This was the idea that organizations have lives and personalities of their own apart from the personalities of their members individually or collectively. Earlier we described how it happens that large organizations create conditions in which every member may be in fundamental disagreement with the policies he devotes his life to carrying out. When the principle of staff organization is carried out effectively the highest decision-making functions become very nearly automated. Recall the earlier example of Admiral Radford who defined a decision as what one does when the solution to a problem is not implicit in the evidence available. This is especially true of large military organizations and it applies even to their highest officers.

World War II was a preeminently bureaucratic war and General Eisenhower was its most peremptory bureaucrat. We have related how, on becoming President of the United States, he carried the same mode of operation into the White House. He insisted that no problem be presented to him until elaborate staff work had been completed. The standing order was that all conflicts were to be resolved in the lower echelons of the departmental and White House staffs. The end result of this process of conflict resolution was to be a one-page statement of the proposed policy. The President had but to approve or reject with the flourish of a signature.

All this near-automation of the decision-making process predated the computer. It received a great deal of adverse criticism. This is but a foretaste of what can be expected when computers are utilized for decision-making. Yet even the primitive, precomputer efforts at automated decision-making had very beneficial consequences. They were indispensable for the conduct of the mass of run-of-the-mine presidential business. Without it the presidency would have been a shambles. Indeed, the world was fortunate that just at the time the American presidency was becoming the most complex executive control centre in history it was occupied by the man who better than anyone before him knew how to bureaucratize the decision-making process.

When John Kennedy succeeded to the presidency his first act was to dismantle Eisenhower's bureaucratized decision-making system. Later on, political scientists contrasted the orderly and tranquil general-staff atmosphere of the White House under Eisenhower with the hectic, crisis-laden, combat command post atmosphere of the Kennedy White House. It has been noted previously that memoirs from the Kennedy days indicate that the worst errors of the Cuban invasion and the missile confrontation with Khrushchev might have been avoided had President Kennedy maintained the bureaucratized decision-making apparatus of his predecessor. Recall also that President Eisenhower became personally incapacitated by a series of crippling illnesses. Yet all during the time he was absent from office the presidency continued to function effectively.

There are limits to what can be done through automated decision-making procedures. They cannot inaugurate drastic new policies. They cannot resolve grave crises. However, when large and complex bureaucracies are involved it is far from certain that even the most energetic and indomitable executive can work such effects in any case. Surely few executives in history ever sought more avidly for the reputation of a daring innovator and a courageous crisis commander than did Eisenhower's immediate successor, John Kennedy. And surely few were so consistently thwarted. Much the same fate befell Premier Khrushchev. The consistent frustration of Khrushchev's grand schemes for economic reorganization, for agricultural reform, and for international comity betrayed a fundamental misunderstanding of decision-making in bureaucratic institutions.

## The Governing Principles

The Eisenhower administration has been chosen to illustrate automated decision-making because of its general familiarity and because it concerned decision-making at the most exalted levels and of the highest gravity. Moreover, a study of its procedures reveals the chief operating rules that may come to govern automated decision-making. Four principles emerge: (1) the subsidiarity principle; (2) the minimax principle; (3) the cost-effectiveness principle; (4) the balance-of-power equilibrium principle. All are designed to deal with the exceptional situation, namely, what to do when the solution to a problem is not implicit in the evidence available. When the decision-making situation is fraught with ambiguity conflicting modes of action appear to be equally feasible. The problem then is that of devising programs to follow, or to put into information-processing systems, so as to resolve conflicts and reduce ambiguities.

*Subsidiarity* is a principle with a long-standing tradition in Roman Catholic political theory. It amounts to approaching a decision-making situation with the initial assumption that there is no real need for any central executive action at all. Every effort is made to force the subsidiary components of the political sys-·tem to resolve their problems and conflicts independently, without referring them to higher authorities. The soundness of the principle rests upon its efficacy. Problems are best solved where they arise. Moreover, the subsidiary components of an organization are the instruments of political action. Whatever solution is ultimately adopted the subsidiary components will be the ones to carry it out. Inasmuch as their consent is essential, the optimum condition is for them to resolve their conflicts independently. If the subsidiarity assumption works out the need for decision making by higher authority disappears.

*Minimax* is a term applied in games theory. It refers to the general proposition that where conflicting alternatives are present the most rational strategy will always be the one that promises to minimize the maximum possible losses.

The *cost-effectiveness,* or cost-benefit, approach is related to and in part derived from the minimax principle. It was made world famous by the U.S. Secretary of Defense, Robert McNamara. It meant programming information relevant to a decision-making situation so as to reveal the ratios of values sacrificed to values realized for each competing alternative. The process of elimination is determined by the rank order of the resulting ratios. The cost-effectiveness method of eliminating all but the project with the most favourable ratio is closely related to a long-standing principle of industrial decision-making whereby alternative capital investment proposals are ranked on the basis of their prospective rates of return.

The *balance of power* principle is familiar enough. When applied to conflicts over alternative policy proposals it requires evaluating them on the basis of the extent to which they imply an alteration in the existing balance-of-power positions of the various subordinate departments affected. That decision is favoured which least disrupts the existing equilibrium of the bureaucratic forces.

All of these practices developed before the advent of the computer. Two of them, minimax and cost-effectiveness procedures, lent themselves to immediate computerization. However, all four procedures can be employed to program sophisticated information-processing and evaluating systems. We have seen already that bureaucratized functions, like those of a factory assembly line, will become relatively easy to computerize. If we can computerize the routine operating functions at the bottom and then employ programs to automate the decision-making process at the top, an entirely new prospect opens to mankind. The possibility presents itself of destroying the autocracy and controlling the willfulness of large organizations. The centralizing bias of their present decision-making processes can be reversed. We can even visualize a post-bureaucratic form of organization. It would make possible a renaissance of democracy. For the processes discussed above are devices for referring decision-making crises back to popular processes rather than referring them up to executive resolution.

This has been discussed in terms of bureaucratized and automated decision-making and in these terms it sounds somewhat futuristic. Actually, however, it is merely a modernization of what constitutionalism tried to do for the nation-state. The intricate machinery of the American Constitution was aimed primarily at preventing the exercise of unchecked executive authority. Its specific devices were federalism, checks and balances, and separation of powers. They were very similar in principle to the devices just described for automated decision-making.

Federalism incorporated a principle of subsidiarity. It was designed to preserve the autonomy of the component parts of the American political decisions. Checks and balances were designed to prevent the development of an autocratic decision-making capacity in any of the chief branches of government. Separation of powers was designed to maintain an equilibrium of authority between the three governmental branches. Computer techniques make it possible to achieve similar results in the operation of bureaucratic structures. We are on the verge of being able to constitutionalize the composite parts of the state the way we did previously for the state as a whole. One of the most promising of the many facets of the scientific revolution is its prospect of making automated decision-making possible. The result would be bureaucracies programmed so that crucial decisions were referred back to popular deliberative institutions for definitive action.

## The Ethical Issue

The scientific revolution has been described as involving the reversal in the relationship that industrialism had established between theory and practice. The philosopher Cassirer explained this process. He called it symbolic transformation: the transformation of technique into symbol. A familiar example of the process is provided by the way in which architecture was produced from the building crafts. But architecture is not, strictly speaking, a science. The sciences seek the truth about nature. The scientist can be compared to the architect only when he sets about designing a symbolic model of nature to correspond with what science has uncovered. But even here there is a fundamental difference. Architecture, and all similar professions, aim at the advancement of human purposes. Science aims at the revelation of natural processes. The design created by the architect must be scientifically sound, but more important than this is the demand that it also be good and beautiful. The only demand we impose on science is that it not be untrue. The difference is that between a situation to be described and a function performed.

The classic professions such as medicine, law, and architecture, including even the traditional guild trades such as masonry and knighthood, grew from functions to be performed. Their processes were controlled by the functions from which they were derived. A function that creates things for men must face the deepest questions of ethics. It must submit to domination by the human issues of goodness, beauty, and justice. The mature mark of that submission is seen in the emergence of the true professions from their initial trades and services. The professions employ the arts and sciences, but also furnish them with philosophic expression and ethical control.

As far as the specific sciences are concerned, this kind of professionalization is impossible. The sciences produce an ethic of means of what it is proper to do when engaging in scientific activity. There is no ethic of ends with canons of goodness and justice as found in the true professions. As a result, the growth of the sciences, and their invasion of fields traditionally allotted to the professions, has had the effect of corroding the codes of ethics which once surrounded the major fields of human endeavour. Medical science provides a most gruesome illustration.

The glories of modern medical science are related in the article on HUMAN NATURE. But the science of medicine is different from the profession of medicine. The difference is more than that between researcher and practitioner. It is the difference arising from the substitution of an ethic of means for an ethic of ends. This is the substitution that accompanies science everywhere it reaches. One of the most distressing episodes in all the annals of history was that associated with the inhuman medical experiments conducted by Nazi physicians on concentration camp prisoners during World War II. And

135

yet, once medical science had triumphed over the profession of medicine it is difficult to see how medicine could ever again be subordinated to ethical ends.

The physicist Max Born, reflecting in his old age on the scientific revolution in which he himself had played such a remarkable role, pointed to a further source of ethical corrosion in modern science. In order for an ethic to be observed it must be possible for men to perceive the different ethical consequences of the alternative choices of action open to them. For ordinary conditions this is obvious. If a military superior orders the commission of an odious crime against humanity, his subordinates may decide they have no alternative but to obey. However, they cannot claim ignorance of the ethical issue. But when the scientist sets to work unraveling the secrets that stand in the way of detonating atomic bombs or perfecting death rays, the preliminary research is carried out on such a profound scientific level that the connection between the action of the scientist and the effect of his work disappears. But this is the connection that must exist for an ethic of ends to be operative. Moreover, a time element may be involved. The full ethical implications of a scientific endeavour may not become completely apparent until many years after the work's consummation.

Of course, it has been true always that an action in the present may have unforeseeable harmful effects in the future. The invention of the automobile is an all too familiar illustration of this separation of actions from their effects. In the earlier chapter on bureaucratic cultures, it was pointed out that this separation is one of the effects of bureaucratization. However, science expands the separation between actions and effects to a new level. For the more profound a scientific innovation the more universal will be its potential application and the more difficult it becomes to forecast what its future effects will be. Max Born's mournful conclusion was quite simply that science has destroyed ethics; the scientific revolution threatens to usher us into a new world that is not only postindustrial and postbureaucratic, but also postethical.

This is aggravated because of a further difficulty existing between science and ethics. Scientific knowledge is logical and mathematical in form. Ethical knowledge is philosophical and functional in nature. As a result, scientific knowledge accumulates from generation to generation like compound interest. Each new scientist stands on the shoulders of all those who have gone before and he leaves behind him in his teaching laboratories a hundred more who do the same. The fledgling scientist begins his career by acquiring only the distilled essences that remain of the work of his predecessors. His lifetime is devoted to adding further elements to the accumulating edifice of science. He need not, and indeed he cannot, start out by retracing the laborious steps that brought science to its present state. If that were necessary, the progress of science would be limited to how much of it could be assimilated anew by each successive scientist. Science could not progress beyond the limits of the scientific powers that one man could bring to bear in the course of his life.

This was roughly the case prior to the development of modern science. Then the quest for both scientific and ethical knowledge proceeded in much the same way. Both were subject to the same limitations and neither possessed the power to develop and accumulate findings. When modern science acquired this power in the 17th century the growth of scientific knowledge shot up at an exponential rate. Ethical knowledge remained as before, its social effects limited to the wisdom individual men can acquire during a lifetime. One does not assimilate the truth of an ethical precept the way one perceives the truth of a mathematical solution. And the fact that someone in the past may have succeeded in learning and applying ethical principles during his own lifetime cannot provide the foundations upon which successors may achieve even nobler ethical heights. Each person must learn and apply ethical truths for himself, for ethical knowledge is noncumulative. This means that there is an objective foundation for the way science separates ethics from action in the fact that the ethical problems posed by modern science have become progressively more numerous and complex whereas the ethical capacities of men have remained static.

Some relief might occur were science able to extend longevity measurably. Short of this, the only solution would appear to lie with a concerted effort to constitutionalize science, subjecting its progress and development to planning and control at the same time that more concerted attention is given to the fostering of man's ethical nature in a thoroughgoing reformation of the purposes of education.

# *Chapter 6*   Ideology

THE INDUSTRIAL REVOLUTION embarked the West upon a wild cultural adventure whose like, measured in turmoil, rapidity of change, population growth, war, revolution, and the exploitation of resources, the world had never before seen. Among the developments of particular significance in politics were two innovations of the modern world: political parties and ideologies. Closely related, at least in Europe, were problems attributed to the interrelations of the social classes. It became customary to explain the political developments that accompanied the industrial revolution as the story of the ascendancy of the middle class over the other social classes. On the one hand were the declining aristocratic and peasant remnants of feudalism; on the other hand was the range of conflicts that arose between the middle class and the new species of factory worker produced by the industrial system.

Several different theories were offered to explain why things happened as they did. Marxism emphasized the primacy of material factors. Another theory argued that the change from the other-worldly ethic of feudalism to the prosaic, work-oriented capitalist ethic of Protestantism was the crucial development. Still another reduced matters to the special psychological repressions that were characteristic of the middle classes. And there were many more proffered causes.

None, however, ever quite matched the explanatory power or the widespread popularity of Marxism. Indeed, no other philosopher has so succeeded in stamping the qualities of his own mind on the thought and action of an era—something of a paradox, considering what Marx taught about the subordinate role of ideas in history. This would be reason enough for us to give some consideration to Marxism. It is made even more necessary by the imponderables of the scientific revolution. For if the scientific revolution carries an import as large and as disruptive as that of the industrial revolution, then some very direct questions pose themselves: Is there a basis for a development in social classes comparable to that which accompanied the industrial revolution? Is there a basis for ideological developments similar to those that accompanied the industrial revolution? Both questions are speculative in the extreme. The most that can be done is to canvass the possibilities of the future in the light of the happenings of the past. This requires taking a retrospective look at the problem of ideologies and social classes as they first developed.

According to Marx, ideologies develop dialectically out of the conflict between objectively distinct social classes. Objectively distinct classes were said to develop out of relationships to property and production. This idea seems to work fairly well in explaining European politics. It suggests that the medieval aristocracy became threatened by the rising middle classes. The aristocracy responded by developing defensive doctrines proclaiming its own intrinsic governing superiority as the proper guardian of the providential virtue embodied in long-established social institutions. The ebullient middle class replied with its own doctrines of individualism, freedom of economic opportunity, the career open to talents, representative democracy, and criticisms of the evil of restrictive social and political barriers. Spokesmen for the newly created working class railed at their oppressions by the middle class, proclaiming that the workers should do the same thing to their bosses that the bosses had done to the aristocrats. They criticized the industrial system and demanded that society recognize their right to a fairer share of the goods they produced.

These were the historical European ideologies of conservatism, liberalism, and socialism. As Marx said, they were indeed the products of social classes. But more than that they were products of the way the social systems of 19th-century Europe led these three classes to compete against each other for political power and popular following. For the mere presence of an industrial order was not by itself sufficient to produce social classes and ideologies like those native to 19th-century Europe. This is seen from the American example. There a rampant industrial society developed without producing the class system or the ideologies typical of Europe.

Similarly, even in Europe, a change is taking place. The aristocracy has all but disappeared. The peasants are changing into middle-class farmers. The middle class is becoming bureaucratized and professionalized. The working class is improving its conditions of life and enhancing its political power. Class distinctions are becoming blurred. Class conflict is moderating. Consequently, the older ideologies are losing their clear-cut demarcations. Conservatism has become largely an admonition to proceed slowly in making political changes. Liberalism has become primarily a skeptical and wary attitude toward government. Socialism has become essentially an effort to employ government to achieve egalitarian and humanitarian ideals.

But not even these somewhat seedy, middle-aged versions of Europe's once virile ideologies are really applicable anywhere else. For example, what Europe calls liberalism has a rough counterpart in the United States, but there it is found on the right and goes under the name of conservatism. What is called liberalism is most akin to Europe's socialism. But the kinship with socialism is at best remote. Moreover, the United States, the one country virtually devoid of a socialist movement, has been the one most anxiously fearful of its imminent outbreak. The fear may prove justified, but the advent of a future American socialism would appear to be attendant upon the fuller development of the scientific revolution, which promises to extend affluence throughout society, to eliminate distasteful labour, and to provide the control technologies required for the proper working of planned society.

Nowhere else in the world has there appeared a system of classes similar to those of Europe, with the possible exception of Japan. And with this exception, no other nation produced the peculiar European array of class-based parties and ideologies. This is a proposition that cannot go unchallenged. The world is simply too deeply habituated to viewing political problems in the context of the European pattern. As a consequence, the general relevance of the American political tradition is often questioned. This requires a brief discussion of the setting of American politics.

## The American Model

America never possessed a European-type class structure, but it did have a sharply stratified social system. The so-called WASP (white, Anglo-Saxon, Protestant) always constituted an ethnic elite. Its psychological impact on others was often quite cruel. Circulation into it was very hard for Negroes, Jews, Catholics, Orientals, Latins, Asians, and other non-English peoples. The cruelty of ethnic discrimination in America was intensified by the very equality and individualism and classlessness that were proclaimed to be the American Way.

Inside America's overall system of ethnic discrimination resided others. The Eastern Seaboard—the original colonies—developed a quite rigid Brahmin elite. The Seaboard South produced its ersatz Cavaliers. Under them lay the sharply distinguished stratum of poor whites, and of course on the bottom were the Negroes. This led to the perplexing subculture of the Southern gentleman and his highly ritualized ways of life. These distinct social strata have furnished sharp social and ethnic divisions but they seldom acquired self-conscious expression in political movements and parties. There were the Know-Nothing Party, the Ku Klux Klan, and a few others, but these were like the Cagoulard eruption in France. They were violent, intense, sometimes threatening, but more a manifestation of group paranoia than of an ideology in the European sense. Has anything been left out? How about the persisting division between the rich and the poor? These two social classes have always existed in America. Their opposition has stamped its mark on American politics. This forces us a little more deeply into the nature of social classes.

In the ordinary view of things the upper classes are the rich; the lower classes are the poor. It is a clear and simple idea and it is as old as civilization itself. Aristotle comments that all polities tend to become divided into two cities, the city of the rich and the city of the poor. He believed that this polarization was the cause of political instability and revolution. The solution seemed obvious: see that the polity contains a large and vital middle class capable of mediating between the two extremes. We remember also that Aristotle was the philosopher of the golden mean and it is not difficult to see how a philosophy and an economics of moderation would entail a middle-class politics moderating between oligarchy and mobocracy. It is a commonsense notion and many others have thought of it independently. It is an idea that comes naturally to Americans, Canadians, and Australians. When they speak of a middle class they usually have in mind the group that occupies the middling income ranges of society.

But this raises the problem of knowing how to identify these three classes and how to draw the lines between them. It turns out to be a problem without a solution. For we are not dealing with descriptive categories like the class of all those with red hair. Rather, we are dealing with a statistical distribution such as the average, the below average, and the above average. The three classes occupy arbitrary divisions plotted along a numerical scale. It is relatively easy to tell the difference between those at the extremes but not those who occupy the border regions. The thing that is missing is the objective determinant of class status that was so clearly established in the Marxist theory. Without this there is no way to use the categories of rich and poor to explain ideologies and parties, for the members of a class must be able to know for certain what class they belong to. Only then is it possible to recognize clearly the ideology and party corresponding to one's own status.

But a statistical scale is like a ladder and people who feel they occupy positions on society's ladder look for betterment to come through individual efforts to ascend the ladder. Personal misfortunes seem to be just that, the result of personal failings rather than insurmountable blockages that are built into the social system itself. When people believe that they may circulate to the pinnacles of society by their own efforts they do not become revolutionary. Revolution is only indicated when a social system contains structural barriers capable of frustrating the efforts of even the most gifted. Otherwise, reform alone will suffice to correct the maladjustments that may occur from time to time. A system of class analysis that distributes all people along the one income scale implies that the society to which it is applied contains no built-in barriers denoting distinct social classes. Otherwise a separate scale would be required for each distinct class.

Modern social scientists have improved on Aristotle's statistical conception of social classes by adding several refinements. In addition to income they correlate level of education, occupation, residential location, life style, social clubs, professional associations, and the like. On this basis they produce more sophisticated descriptions of social strata and more objective demarcations between them. But the resulting strata still all fall on the same scale. Circulation between strata is seen to be more difficult than it was formerly thought to be. Sudden wealth or professional success is not alone sufficient to provide its possessor with immediate entry into the highest strata, though this may permit the children to acquire essential upper-class attributes lacking in the parents. But even though circulation becomes somewhat more painstaking, it is not completely forestalled. If it were, one would not speak of strata along one ascending scale but rather of separate scales in a system of distinct social classes.

There is another way of dividing societies into separate classes. Like Marxism, it rests upon an objective foundation. But the determining factor is politics rather than economics. It is possible to distinguish those who hold political power from those who do not. This produces the idea of a political class, a ruling elite, and it may lead to what has been called the iron law of oligarchy. This states that all societies, regardless of how different their constitutions look from the outside, always have the same internal constitutional structure. But this alone does not get us very far. For if there is free circulation from the bottom of the social structure into positions of political leadership one is not dealing with a rigid social class so much as with a fact of social action. In order to accomplish any collective action there must be some who exercise executive direction of the others. By itself the idea of a political class means only that there must be leadership functions in any social system.

However, when this is combined with the previous idea of social strata, the result is the conception of a stable "power elite" and a ruling "establishment." This is a condition that appears to develop in all bureaucratic cultures. It helps explain the rigidities in the educational systems of contemporary mass societies.

The article on EDUCATION explains the so-called streaming process that separates children into different ability levels at a very early age. In the liberal democracies and the collectivist democracies alike, a class system reminiscent of that in Plato's *Republic* is produced by the school system. The difference is that in Plato the educational class was to be determined on the basis of innate ability, whereas sociological studies show that in modern societies actual selection is determined by the prior cultural environment of the child. Those born into elevated cultural levels tend to be the ones to qualify for advanced university training and ultimate membership in the Establishment. Those who belong to the more numerous group are destined to be shunted off into clerical, service, vocational, and technical training programs. These divisions are often determined by the age of 10. The result is the production and maintenance of social systems containing sharp cultural demarcations that individuals are almost powerless to surmount.

In the collectivist democracies this was criticized in books on bureaucracy and the "new class." In America it was dramatized by the Negro Revolution. This latter was a protest against the fact that a series of forces had developed among the lower income groups, among special ethnic groups, and in certain residential and cultural environments that had the effect of permanently locking them into an inferior, second-class status. It does not take much reflection to see that the difficulty is structural. It is not a problem of local incidence, as when one isolated community is relatively disfavoured. Rather, it is as if the social system as a whole had been specially designed to prevent some of its members from ever being able to participate in its highest bounties. The solution could only be to redesign the system. The implication is revolutionary in the traditional meaning of the term.

In the liberal and the collectivist democracies, in Japan and in Latin America, similar deterministic social forces have produced similar expressions of class antagonism. A regrouping of political and ideological movements is taking place as a result. Moreover, the problems of the lower classes inside their own societies are directly comparable to those resulting from the division between the Afro-Asian countries and the elitist Western nations within the larger world community. In both cases a form of imperialism is at work, holding down nations in a self-perpetuating pattern of cultural stagnation just as it holds down the lower classes inside nations. The class revolution of our times is genuinely universal. It is anti-imperialist and it carries the same imperatives within nations as it does between them.

In Europe, England especially, it came as something of a shock to discover that it was not enough to eliminate the older class distinctions. For when these had gone it was merely revealed that the source of the problem ran deeper than had been thought. A literature of protest appeared after World War II in which Britain's Angry Young Men complained about the new imperialism of the Establishment that had taken over from the exclusiveness of the former class system. In America, however, the new European protest had an all too familiar ring. This was the sort of class problem that had been present there from the start, even though it was given new content by the mass, urban, bureaucratic culture that had grown up since World War I. There is a class system in the contemporary world but it is not the same as the 19th-century European class system described by Marx. The new class system has produced ideologies, but not those familiar from European history.

## Ideology and Class

The ideological tradition that grew up in America was as different as was its class system. In Europe the traditional social classes seemed to be real objects, like ethnic societies or religious communities. In America the divisions between the rich and the poor, between the power elite and the people, the highly educated and the dropouts, were less readily discernible and more readily permeable. The type of social stratification found in America is perpetuated more by psychological, political, and social forces than by heredity or property status.

These differences help explain the different types of corruption that exist in the two different social systems. American politics is notoriously corrupt. Sociologists have even been prompted to write learned treatises on "Corruption as an American Way of Life." The implication is that European politics are somehow less corrupt, and this seems to be true. Yet, the difference is largely one of appearances, attributable to the differences in the way the two class systems operate.

In England the larger class structure is reflected in the bureaucracy in the rigid distinction that is still made between the ruling "Executive Class" (note that it is *called* a "class") and the clerical functionaries below. The distinction is similar to that made in armies between commissioned officers and the lower ranks. This is a division that is also much more rigid and impermeable in England than in America. It is true that exceptional individuals from the English lower classes can now gain entry into the executive aristocracy by fighting through the educational system into the top universities, but for reasons previously noted the cultural barriers remain quite formidable.

Corruption is also much less apparent in France than in America. There, as in England, an elitist executive tradition has grown up and has been perpetuated through the great national *hautes écoles*. A kind of Jeffersonian, not to say Platonic, aristocracy of the highly educated has replaced the aristocracy of birth of the *ancien régime*. Something quite similar obtains in Germany and throughout Scandinavia. These countries are all examples of proud and incorruptible bureaucracies. Politics and administration seem more corrupt in America than anyplace else in the world except in the collectivist democracies and the developing nations.

Of course, Europe was not always so exemplary. England during the first half of the 19th century practically invented all the modern forms of political corruption. There was even a specially established paymaster in Parliament through whom members sold their votes. The parliamentary "whip"—imagery borrowed from the master of the hunting hounds—in large part based the sting of his lash upon the bounties at his disposal. This system of corruption was in full swing at the time of the founding of the American Constitution. It became an explicit point of contention between Hamilton and Jefferson. Hamilton, a self-avowed Anglophile, saw himself as the new world's First Lord of the Treasury. He assumed that in America as in England organized legislative corruption was the only effective engine of politics. However, England was not the only model of corruption he might have chosen. Nineteenth-century France must loudly protest any attempt to award England first prize. French deputies were bought and sold like shares on the bourse.

The fact of corruption was universal, but the forms it assumed in Europe and America were different. Where politics is dominated by a system of classes, as in Europe, or by a caste system like that traditional to India, corruption may seem to disappear into the paternalistic ideology of the ruling class or into the sanctified social and ritual prerogatives of the religion. A Brahman caste or a middle class securely in power may administer the society it controls in its own interest without seeming to be at all corrupt. But once it is deprived of its opponents—once there is a relatively classless society—government in one's own interest loses its aura of ideological nobility and becomes merely bald-faced corruption. Ideology—European class-based ideology—provides its adherents with a blank check made out to self-interested government. For the essential message of the typical European ideology is that all people will be better off if a given class is awarded exclusive trusteeship over society.

But this gives us a moment's pause. Self-interested government was precisely what the philosophers of classical antiquity defined as corruption. Plato and Aristotle used this definition as the basis for their famous classification of the various forms of government. The virtuous forms of monarchy, aristocracy, and democracy were those that governed in the general interest. Their corrupt counterparts were tyranny, oligarchy, and mobocracy; those that governed according to private interests. In both Greek and American democracy, corruption lay more open to the eye than in the case of Europe. If we are to find a historical model for the American political system we must skip over the class-ridden conceptions of the European tradition and refer back to the political forms and preoccupations of classical antiquity.

Classical politics and classical political speculation were designed for a society whose citizens were all thought of as members of the same civic family. Corruption arose out of struggles over the distribution of the family patrimony. When there was injustice it was the type of injustice that occurs when some members of the family are given unfair treatment. Complaints were made about how the decisions were arrived at and executed. The solution to this type of injustice was found not by destroying the family system but by eliminating its corruption. This was the issue in the struggle between the ancient aristocratic and popular factions. It was like that between Hamiltonians and Jeffersonians in Greek-revival America.

In the case of traditional Europe, corruption was built into the mutually antagonistic class system. If there was injustice it was not primarily self-interested corruption that was responsible. It was the built-in corruption of the overall system of class relationships that gave one class dominance over the others. In such a case the solution was not reform—the purging of corruption—but revolution: the elimination of the social system whereby one class was permitted to exploit and subordinate all other classes and claim that this amounted to the essence of justice.

This line of speculation leads to a curious conclusion. Americans are accustomed to acquiesce in the judgment that the ideological pattern of European politics is somehow more sophisticated than their own. In the light of European models they often feel their own tradition has been quite superficial. And yet, without going to the other extreme and becoming as ideologically chauvinistic as Europeans, Americans can point out that the two political traditions rest upon entirely different social foundations. This difference has stamped the classical rather than the European pattern upon the American political tradition. That this was not an ignoble pattern needs no special pleading from Americans. What may not be quite so obvious is that once Europe has transcended her own historically conditioned, class-confined pattern of politics she will be confronted inevitably with the same kinds of issues that have dominated the American political tradition since the "political revolution of 1801" when the Jeffersonians routed the Hamiltonians. What is of even more interest is that once the collectivist democracies had eliminated their own traditional class systems they also began to develop a classical pattern of politics similar to that found in America.

## Ideology and Change

An interesting confirmation of this proposition comes to us from the Soviet Union via Yugoslavia. It is illustrated in Milovan Djilas' strange little book on Russia, entitled *The New Class*. This is essentially a book about corruption in the classical, and the American, sense. Djilas uncovered in Russia the existence of a power elite. He failed to make the link with classical politics because of the fact that he wrote and thought in the terms of Marxism: terms derived from the 19th-century European class system. And so, in order to talk about the appearance in Russia of a ruling establishment with its accompanying forms of corruption, Djilas had to convert his discussion, by main force, into the somewhat archaic Marxist class categories. This was, indeed, a curious irony: the disciples of Marx in power had rendered his doctrines inapplicable to their own behaviour.

On this basis one can readily appreciate the possibility of an end to the European ideological tradition. It would follow, after a considerable time lag, the dissolution of the traditional European class system. However, we cannot very easily imagine a complex industrial society that is completely nonideological. In addition to the persisting conflict between the power elite and the people there is the fact that one of the leading characteristics of modern mass industrial societies is change. American society has turned itself inside out every generation or so for the past 200 years. Russian society has compressed the same process into an even shorter span. Both societies have exchanged in their turn a series of energy sources—coal, oil, and hydroelectric and atomic power—and now they prepare for new exotic ones yet to come. They have revamped their industries and their cities in adjustment to each change. They have transported their people and things by horse, train, motorcar, and air, and have remodeled their peoples' lives and environments to suit each one. They have organized their affairs through shops, clubs, trusts, bureaucracies, and mass parties. They have arranged for intercommunications through a changing series of mass media from public postal services and book printing, on through newspapers, radio, and television. They have progressed from hand tools through power machines to automation. When America and Russia began the industrial revolution their cities were as occasional demographic islands pushed up out of a sea of agrarianism. As we look about America now, we see the countryside all but devoured by urbanization, and Russia is but a short step behind. The generation now on the wane could still assume that the nation-state was here to stay; that which is now arising feels in its bones that world order cannot be long postponed. The industrial revolution with its opulent American magnates and its powerful Russian bosses yields now to the scientific revolution with its new breed of scientists and intellectuals.

Throughout all this in America one of the functions of political movements and parties was to facilitate both the preservation of continuity and the adjustment to change. The overall political system accommodated what we have called a dual myth system that combined together both conservative and utopian features. The dual myth system and the classical pattern of politics functioned in unison with the special class system. At each critical development stage one of the prerequisites to change was the displacement of the particular power elite that had accompanied the preceding stage of development. So when we turn to Europe and speak of the ultimate demise of her traditional class-based ideologies we do not mean that the function of combining continuity with change will disappear. It must continue to be served, but the American experience indicates that it may find expression through a system of opposing ideological forces based upon the circulation of elites. The fact and the function of ideologies seem destined to remain, but their content seems just as surely destined to change. For it is the old content—the old class-connected issues—that are no longer applicable to contemporary conditions. It is not only that issues have changed, though they have. Even deeper is the fact that the old goals and the old procedures have become outmoded.

The traditional goal of ideological politics in Europe was revolution—or counterrevolution. Liberalism acquired power through revolution. Socialism aspired to power through revolution, though whether this aim could be achieved only through violence remained a persisting topic of controversy among socialists. Conservatives were counterrevolutionary by definition. But these are goals special to the modern European tradition. They don't fit either the rest of the world or the rest of history.

Not only revolutions but also political parties are different in the non-European world. In Europe, especially in England, parties grew out of court factions, those that assumed opposing sides in the high courts of Parliament. Such court disputes led ultimately to the creation of ministerial factions. The chief ministers rose to their positions through apprenticeship and mastery in the arts of parliamentary politics. When they fell into irreconcilable conflicts their disputes could only be resolved by carrying them back to Parliament for a vote of confidence. The head of government (the prime minister) and all his chief assistants (the cabinet ministers) always remained sitting members of the nation's law-making body. Their parties grew from parliamentary factions and never lost the distinctive characteristics produced by this fact. Inasmuch as they acquired ascendancy through their ability to command a majority of votes in Parliament, it made sense for a ministry to resolve any internal crisis among its members by going back to the full membership of Parliament and putting the issue to a vote. In Europe this came about as naturally as did the habits of civility and the handling of a fork at table. But something quite different was established in American politics.

The new American president was independent of the legislature by constitutional design. Everyone was aware of this fact. But the different factions gave it different interpretations. Washington thought it meant the president was to be like an elective king of England. He was to review the troops, hold levees, make progresses with great pomp and to the pace of a carriage and six. But the actual conduct of government was to be in the hands of his would-be First Lord of the Treasury, Alexander Hamilton. His job was to manage the new American Congress the way Peel had done with the British Parliament. The American Constitution, like the American common law, was at first thought to be little more than a written version of what had become hallowed by custom in Britain. But the British constitution suffered somewhat in translation. The president could not be a ceremonial alter-king even if he tried. For one thing, it was he, not his ministers, who possessed true authority. And it came from the states and the people directly, not as filtered through Congress. Under this situation it was of no avail to try and follow the parliamentary model. For legislative votes alone could not resolve a cabinet or a policy conflict. The latent functional logic of the new American Constitution required that policy disputes be carried directly to the electorate for resolution.

It was Jefferson who perceived what the Founding Fathers of the Constitution had not forseen: they had constructed a constitution that required the invention of an entirely new mode of politics. It even required its own new form of corruption, as was seen later in the Jacksonian spoils system. The English, we recall, mobilized parliamentary votes through the distribution of spoils among M.P.'s. The new American system was to require a method of distributing spoils to those who could mobilize the electorates of the various states. The difference reached also to matters of ideology. This was to mark the distinction between the American and the European political traditions, just as it was to reveal the kinship between the American and the classical political traditions.

Recall Jefferson's conviction that Hamilton had organized a powerful monarchical plot. Had this issue arisen in a European setting it would have taken the shape of a struggle between the aristocrats and the middle classes. Each side would have tried to explain and rationalize its class aims through opposing ideologies. The famous debate over monarchy between Filmer and Locke and that over mercantilism between Steuart and Smith were ideological illustrations of the way this issue assumed the form of a class struggle in England.

In America the absence of a European class structure made it difficult for these ideologies to find ready translation. The Hamiltonian Federalists were true monarchical mercantilists, but they were merely the right wing of the Federalist Party, not the spokesmen of a class with sharply defined interests. The ideas of John Adams came closer than those of Hamilton to the beliefs of the typical Federalist, yet Adams was also closer to the tradition of the English middle-class theorists Locke and Smith than he was to the English monarchical mercantilists. American Federalists simply could not be read in terms of English aristocrats. Moreover, another factor stood in the way. The mere existence of the 13 states—resulting in a federal form of organization instead of a centralized state as in England—mitigated against the easy translation to America of the English ideological polarities. The states had opposing interests. Factors that might otherwise have put Hamilton and Jefferson into the same camp were overshadowed by the opposed interests of commercial New York and agrarian Virginia.

The differences between the governmental and class structures of England and America made for two different systems of parties and ideologies. The American class structure induced the formation of parties based upon the opposition between the people and the power elite. Federalism provided a dual structure of political authority to be fought over by the competing political forces. Both factors together combined to convert the substantive differences between political factions into different interpretations of the Constitution. Constitutionalism and democracy are legal and organizational matters. They provided the ideological content of American politics. Jefferson, in his constitutional arguments with Hamilton and the electoral invention with which he hoped to oust the Federalists, was setting the pattern for the future.

149

From this point the American political tradition set off on a tack entirely different from that of Europe. Instead of producing a dialogue of competing class ideologies it produced a dialogue of controversy over constitutional structure. Again, however, it must be remembered that this was the classical mode of politics. It identified the quest of Plato, Aristotle, Polybius, and Cicero. In the long reach of political ideas it is the European ideological tradition that is atypical, standing as a curious, sometimes brilliant, intellectual island pushed apart from the main body of human political speculation by the special constellation of contending social classes that appeared in Europe when industrialization was engrafted on the remnants of feudal society.

## Beliefs and Goals

We were led into this consideration of social classes in the course of contrasting the politics of America to the politics of Europe. And while the ideologies of Europe do not help us understand American politics, there is another meaning of ideology, different from that of Marx, that is more typical of the non-European world. This is the notion that every social system tends to produce its own belief system, or ideology—that is, a body of defensive and conservative beliefs supporting the established goals of the society and explaining away any deviations from those goals as temporary and transient lapses. It is the Chamber of Commerce, *Pravda,* Rotary Club, Komsomol, Commencement Day view of the society. In the United States it is the tradition of the American Way. In Russia it describes the New Soviet Man.

In progressive societies, especially in modern ones, there is a second body of ideals. It expresses the more utopian goals at which the society aims. Christians, especially, are familiar with this dualism on the level of personal morality. Indeed, this ethical dualism was one of Christianity's distinctive features. It enabled the Christian to make his peace with the practical requirements of everyday life and at the same time maintain his loyalty to a higher ethic of love, equality, and brotherhood. At the worst this appeared in the form of a pietistic hypocrisy in which six working days were given over to the practical necessities of improving one's immediate lot. The seventh was reserved for utopian idealism, with the attention of the believer diverted from the city of man to the city of God.

This was the mechanism by which the Protestant ethic furnished the special combination of practical industry with visionary utopianism that distinguished capitalist economic endeavour from its predecessors. Jansenism was the Catholic version of the Protestant Ethic. American Pragmatism provided the doctrine with its highest philosophic expression. When Marx turned the Hegelian dialectic upside down, placing primary emphasis on the material factors of history, he provided the foundation whereby socialism could acquire the same ethical dualism. The result was the doctrine of "socialist morality." The true believer in socialism could obey the practical necessities of the day without endangering the purity of the utopian goals of the future.

The "doctrine of progress" was the name given to this dualistic ethic when it was applied to society. The established order was portrayed as the best of all presently practical worlds. This gave day-to-day laws and regulations a provisional validity. However, the utopian ideals of social progress looked further into the future. They portrayed a secularized heavenly city toward which society was believed to be heading. This two-way idealism first assured everyone that the present was as good as it possibly could be. Secondly, however, it confidently promised that the future would be miraculously better. Societies with such dual-myth systems turned out to be like Christians with their dualistic personal ethical systems. They were startlingly progressive. Changes and innovations which might otherwise appear seriously disruptive in the light of the society's conservative myth could be given validity through association with its utopian myth.

Societies with dual-myth systems regard themselves as cultures in transition. They are like transients, stopping for a while in their present institutional quarters. During that stay they attempt to arrange things as well as possible. But they live at an address that is only temporary. They are a people who have a rendezvous with their special utopian destiny.

Take the American example more concretely. America has a conservative myth that proclaims America to be God's country. Its citizens are the chosen people. Nothing could be better than the American status quo. On the other hand, the utopian myth, often referred to as the American Dream, holds out to all the promise of affluence, full civil liberties, and perfected democratic institutions made completely applicable and effective. This was the utopian myth announced by men like Paine and Jefferson. It was the subject of Tocqueville's great study of American democracy. It has been appealed to ever since by a long line of reformers starting with Jackson and including not only the liberal and progressive politicians in American history but also most of the leaders and writers in the American radical tradition.

The collectivist democracies are similarly dynamic and progressive. The dual myths of socialism (the here and now) and communism (the utopian future) represent the conservative and utopian components of their dynamism. In their early stages, as represented in Russia by the regimes of Lenin and Stalin, an important prerequisite to dynamic transition was to sanctify the authority of the cultural elite, the monolithic party. This gave the party elite free reign to employ manipulative devices to mobilize the consent and the energies of the masses for the arduous tasks of industrialization. In doing so the party elite made numerous twists and turns of policy. From the outside these policy shifts

151

were exceedingly perplexing. This was primarily because outsiders fixed their attention permanently on the ultimate ideals of communism and failed to see how the day-to-day tactical shifts could square with the ultimate goal. Socialists, for their part, applied the same criticism in reverse when they looked at the day-to-day failings of Western cultures.

This mutual tendency characterized the polemics of the cold war. Each side explained away its own day-to-day contemporary failings in light of the nobility of its ultimate goals. But at the same time each side did the opposite when considering the other. Each disparaged the validity of the other's utopian goals in the light of its day-to-day failures.

Dynamism and flexibility took different forms in the two cases. In the collectivist democracies it was expressed in the twists and turns of party policy that acquired such notoriety before World War II. In the constitutional democracies it operated through the alternation of political parties in and out of power. The one reflected the fluctuating and progressive interpretations of a culture's utopian myth by its dictatorial elite. The other appeared merely as the changing interpretations of their myth by a sovereign people. With the death of Stalin the monolithic nature of the Soviet Communist Party began to dissolve ever so slightly and the progressive changes in Soviet society began to take on some of the colour of decisions made in response to popular pressure rather than solely by elite dictation.

Following World War II some Western observers began to write about what they called the end of ideology. They argued that the utopian ideals of the West had become eclipsed by actual achievements and discredited by recent philosophic trends. America provided the best example. The conservative status-quo component of her beliefs caught up with and devoured the future-oriented utopian component. The good life that had been a utopian dream seemed a practical achievement. Automation promised to eliminate poverty once and for all. The doctrine of progress itself was subjected to derision. Presidents Eisenhower and Johnson, one a conservative and the other a liberal, both disavowed the dialectic of partisanship and aspired to a politics of consensus. The dissidents of left and right were split off from the massive mandate of the centre, leaving America a one-ideology society and consequently a static society with a conservative goal system.

This did not mean that change would not take place nor that the conservative goals were fully realized in practice. The political, economic, and constitutional events that transpired from day to day still left much to be desired, but their failings were believed to be nominal and temporary. They were like the failings of automobile drivers to conform perfectly to traffic regulations: minor failings of insufficiency and deviation. For the main point was that despite these failings Americans came to believe that all of their traditional utopian goals had ceased to be truly utopian and were practically realizable within the confines of established institutions and practices. No large transitions or transformations—no great institutional or behavioural modifications—seemed any longer required. Americans revealed this in two ways. They announced on the one hand that their goals of affluence, constitutionalism, and popular democracy were at the point of accomplishment. Automatically this meant that the major political struggle would have to become a preservative rather than a progressive one. In the second place, they engaged in a great public struggle to revitalize their old utopian myths, an effort that confessed its own futility by what it admitted.

In the past, utopian myths often have been generated out of religions: from heaven-after-death myths and heaven-on-earth myths. The Western utopian tradition was just such a development. The historian Carl Becker explained how the birth of 18th-century political theory, with its romantic state of nature and its heavenly city on earth, was related to the prior theological heavenly cities of the medieval philosophers. Heavenly cities have always been pictured in material terms. This was the only way masses could visualize them. Their facilitating revolutions have been directed toward material ends.

The American experiment in democracy, and the industrial revolution, are examples of this. Traditionally, the United States was a culture striving toward a material utopian future. The U.S.S.R., China, and the entire underdeveloped world today strive for the same utopian materialist future that spurred the United States relentlessly through the 19th century. The People's Democracies now tell their citizens that they too are on the verge of realizing the same goals. Premier Khrushchev never tired of announcing to his own people, and to the world, that Russia would soon catch up with and then surpass America.

Nineteenth-century capitalism in America and 20th-century socialism in Russia and China do not really represent different types of utopianism. Both revolutions aimed at affluent, materialist utopias. In the process both suffered considerable violence and injustice. More violence in the case of Russia, less, perhaps, in the case of China. The primary difference is that one revolution has been achieved and the achievement of the other is just in the offing.

Because her revolutionary goals—her utopian ideals—have been realized, America has lost the dynamic component of her myth system. This means that she is now in the position of a static culture—one unable to visualize how fundamental changes or drastic improvements could make things better. The collectivist democracies have still a few historical moments of dynamism to spare. But their days are numbered; numbered by the time remaining to the industrial epoch now drawing to a close; numbered by the dawn of the scientific revolution now on the horizon. This amounts to saying that the advanced industrial nations of East and West are all going through a transitional era in which the goals of the past have lost their relevance and new goals must be put in their place. Transitional periods of this sort take a special form.

## Cultural Transformation

Turmoil reigns in the world at large, revolution rules throughout its parts. In the large world community the Western hegemony is being dismantled at the insistence of national liberation movements, and inside the nations of the West the scientific revolution is dismantling the institutions that flourished during the heyday of the industrial revolution. The scientific revolution brings new problems—it strews the paths of the future with grave impediments. Yet the essential predicament it poses is not entirely new. History has already seen three or four previous transformations that were equally profound. This fact may be of little solace in retrospect, however, for mankind's success in coping with them was sorry indeed. Each brought war, violence, and rebellion. They were times in which the institutions on which culture rested were themselves at war with one another. And when the facts underlying men's lives are at war, men in arms may not be far behind.

What are these warring facts which threaten to become unstable fuse caps to a world whose cultures are mined with thermonuclear bombs? The one big fact within which all other facts must receive their evaluation is the great cultural transformation to whose brink the scientific revolution has brought the world. It is comparable in profundity and significance to the greatest transitional periods of the past. For the late 20th-century world, regardless of its other shortcomings, at least can lay claim to membership in the select club of those epochs which have given history its headiest moments. The historical siblings of our times are only to be found in the Greece of the 4th century B.C. when the transition from Hellenic to Hellenistic cultures was made; in 5th century A.D. Mediterrania when the transition from ancient Roman culture to medieval Christendom was begun; in 18th-century Europe when the transition from feudal Christendom to modern industrial culture was forged. For Western culture is now transcending all of the fundamental institutions that have been associated with the great cultural epoch introduced by the 17th century.

As with the others that have gone before, this transformation will affect the forms of economic endeavour, the forms of international and domestic politics, the educational and religious institutions, the forms of urban and community organization, the forms of family organization, and most certainly our conception of human nature. This much history teaches about the great cultural transformations of the past, and we cannot expect our own future to be any less gravely affected than has been true of similar transformational periods in the past. These great transformations did not occur easily. Each one was associated with an extended period of warfare and violence.

In each case a similar cause seems to have been at work. It can be summed up quite briefly. During each of the previous transformations it was not possible to look at their social orders—the Athenian *polis,* the Roman empire-city, or mercantilist England—and discover therein one integrated cultural system. Great cultural transformations seem to proceed in a quite special way. They have their own form, but that form is dualistic rather than unitary. The great transitional cultures of the past have been dualistic cultures. The same thing is true of our own times. We are witnessing the evolutionary dynamism associated with dual-myth systems giving way to the revolutionary dynamism of dual-cultural systems. Consideration of the way this happened in the past will make contemporary problems of transition clearer.

Medieval England did not die promptly with the last battle of the Wars of the Roses or the accession of Henry VII. Nor did modern England spring full-grown to life with the 17th-century installation of William and Mary. In the more than 200 years separating these two events England was not a unitary, homogeneous culture. It was more like two separate cultures, each existing within the other. But herein lies the difficulty, and herein resides the foundation for the institutional detonators that seem capable of triggering war and revolution almost of their own accord. For what occurs in a period characterized by two fundamentally different cultural systems that reside inside each other is a series of profound and well-nigh irreconcilable conflicts that course through every element of the social order.

The old form of economic endeavour is at war with the new form. The old form of religion is at war with the new form. The old form of politics is at war with the new form. The old form of education is at war with the new form. The old form of family organization is at war with the new form, and so on throughout the social order. With all of these built-in situations of diametric conflict, the result is a culture in which every one of the fundamental institutions is capable of being detonated at any moment and of sending explosions throughout society like a pack of firecrackers ignited by a spark.

One contributory reason for this is that men are only dimly aware of the fundamental transition taking place in their midst. They are even less aware that they actually live in two cultures at once. Finally, there is an underlying conflict produced by the discord between the stability required of any ongoing social order and the instability that always accompanies profound cultural transformations. No social order can work unless men can go about their daily affairs with some assurance that the arrangements, contracts, and institutions on whose basis they plan for the future will remain predictably stable so that day-to-day plans can be expected to bear fruit in the future.

This is one of the primary functions provided by law. Men think and plan their way into the future on the basis of the laws, traditions, and institutional forms they have always known. The maintenance of law and order supports men in the assumption that the future will look pretty much like the present. If this were not believed to be true no form of social organization could exist. Cultures depend upon the ability of men to control their future in this fashion. But what control is possible in a time of widespread transformation? In such a time if men follow their hallowed traditions the result is not the stability they expect but rather the aggravation of instability. The very behaviour which in normal times produces peace and tranquillity turns back upon itself and in times of fundamental transition aggravates the causes of discord and stimulates the outbreak of violence.

For example, today the traditional economic system of the West is being supplanted. The marvel of the industrial revolution was the mass-production factory. Cybernation promises to invade the production lines of the factory and the clerical corridors of its offices, displacing blue- and white-collar workers right and left. Work itself promises to disappear and the most advanced countries are entering an era in which income is no longer dependent upon work.

The economically elite nations of the world see the elimination of work as a direct possibility. The world's have-not nations fear their population explosion may prevent them from ever getting as far as the 19th-century stage of industrialization, much less to the postindustrial workless world of the contemporary West. If incomes are guaranteed to all as their birthright, the struggle for subsistence, which has been with man since his expulsion from paradise, ceases to occupy his energies.

This does not mean that the traditional industrial system passes away at one swoop. Nor does it imply that all of its vestiges are destined to disappear in the near future. But it does mean that the world in general is hung up in confusion. It is unable to plan economic affairs except in terms of its familiar industrial system and that is what is being transformed before its eyes. The very policies which in earlier times might have stabilized an industrial economy cause only aggravation when applied to the new economic conditions.

This is seen when Americans attempt to counterbalance the growth of monopoly in agriculture with guaranteed prices to farmers, paying them not to produce. It is seen when communities, politicians, and labour leaders, fearful of unemployment, devote their efforts to the artificial creation of jobs—when jobs are the very things the scientific revolution is bent on destroying. Such programs, rather than being ameliorative, serve rather to intensify the underlying forces which caused the disturbances in the first place. Quixotic behaviour such as this, by increasing discord, acts as a kind of fuse cap threatening to magnify the existing stresses.

In the collectivist democracies the displacement of the industrial system is not so far along, but similar problems are already appearing. In the early stages of industrialization the problems of planning are not very complex. Everything is scarce and everything is needed. Lack of coordination and unevenness of quantity and quality are problems, but so long as there is not enough of anything such problems are not serious. No matter how bad production is it is better than no production. Factories may make more left shoes than they do right, but where most people are shoeless, ways will be found to utilize what would be wastage under more affluent conditions. However, once relative affluence approaches, planning acquires a new scale of complexity. Consumer demands become more and more insistent. Substandard goods go unconsumed. Lack of coordination becomes more serious under advanced economic conditions, for it affects a so much larger network of functions.

The possibility of increased leisure appears under socialist as well as under capitalist industrialization. But if leisure is a disturbance in the nonsocialist world it is virtually subversive in the socialist world. The political and economic philosophy on which all socialist plans rest are based upon assumptions about labour and about the industrial system. The socialist ideal was for the state, not industry, to wither away. Yet contemporary automation promises that just the opposite will occur.

The educational systems of the industrial nations have remained basically the same since the opening of the industrial era. In some nations this began nearly 300 years ago. The article on EDUCATION explains how industrial needs came to dominate the schools, converting them into vocational adjuncts of the economy. As automation renders one job after another obsolete, displacing as it does so their practitioners, society turns to its schools for the answer. The schools are supposed to retrain those who are technologically displaced, preparing them on an instant's notice for the new jobs that are confidently expected to appear. But the schools can do little more than struggle to keep one job ahead of the displacement process. As the article on EDUCATION explains, this is not only a degradation of the educational function—it is also a losing battle. The conclusion is that the schools of the future must serve the needs of a learning society rather than those of a labouring society. It is not easy to see how this transformation can be brought about anywhere, and especially not within regimes that govern in the name of the labouring man. One expression of this problem is found in C. P. [Lord] Snow's doctrine of the growing gulf between the sciences and the humanities. He predicted that the gulf would be further deepened by the scientific revolution. The world of the scientific revolution will be in desperate need of education devoted to deeper philosophic pursuits. But the more education follows the dictates of science the less well suited it becomes to serve the deeper philosophic and ethical needs created by the scientific revolution.

The article on the law helps us perceive further aspects of the cultural transformation through which the world is moving. On first thought the jurisprudential differences between the East and West appear to be those of two alien cultures. The supporting case is quickly made. On one side there is constitutionalism and the subordination of law to the requirements of a property system. On the other is the subordination of law to the tasks of building the collectivist institutions of a socialist order. There is no disputing the fact that these are two entirely different legal systems. Yet this alone need not imply incompatibility.

Quite different legal systems have often in the past operated within the same society. During the Middle Ages an almost unbridgeable gulf existed between the church law of professional and occupational relationships and the customary land law of feudal institutions. Their conflicting principles continued in conflict during the long centuries of the church-state struggle. However, this internal discord was dwarfed by comparison with the larger conflict between feudal institutions in general and the industrial order that appeared later. Church law and feudal law were more like each other than either was like the jurisprudential system of an industrial society. This was true even though on the Continent both the Code Napoléon and the medieval canon law of the church developed out of Roman law sources and in England, on the other hand, both the medieval commentaries of the English jurist Bracton and the modern commentaries of Blackstone were treatises on what purported to be basically the same English common law.

A similar point can be made of the legal systems of the two most advanced industrial nations, the United States and the U.S.S.R. Even after all their many differences are acknowledged the fact remains that the social systems they serve are remarkably similar. Both operate at the same level of technological development. Both are mass, bureaucratic cultures. They share the same educational and scientific traditions, they partake of essentially the same cultural heritage. The Byzantine heritage of Russia is no more alien to Western culture than are Nordic and Latin traditions alien to each other. Today East and West are both preoccupied with achieving the conditions of an urbanized mass-consumption society. This means that both will meet the challenges of the scientific revolution at about the same time. Their different legal systems will both be forced to accommodate its novel jurisprudential requirements, just as both the Roman law and the feudal law systems of medieval times had to accommodate the industrial revolution.

In law, as in all other fundamental institutions, a profound cultural transformation is taking place. For all our institutions seem threatened by forces that appear to discredit the ways of the past. The result is a cultural crisis that pervades the institutions of the most advanced societies and promises to spread from there throughout the entire world.

## The Challenge of Crisis

Our normal presupposition about crisis is that it permits obsolete institutions to be supplanted. History tells of many occasions in which this has happened. Courageous leaders have arisen to meet the challenge of crisis with institutional reforms and revitalized laws. This seemed to be the effort of President Roosevelt in America's New Deal and of Premier Khrushchev in the post-Stalin period. However, the opposite may also occur. When the causes of the crisis run too deep, reformist efforts are often ineffective. Leaders who attempt reforms see their efforts fail and find themselves discredited along with their inadequate programs. Examples are Marcus Aurelius during Rome's Christian revolution, James I in 17th-century England, and Kerenski in prerevolutionary Russia. For this reason the actions of would-be reformers may actually worsen the situation they try to remedy. For when their reforms fail and when they fall in disrepute the result may be to discredit all reform and all reformers. This plays right into the hands of conservatives, depositing authority in their care even though they are the very ones who are least aware of the causes and the cures of the crisis. The result is to further intensify the underlying crisis and magnify the scope of the ultimate disaster. For when every conservative effort designed to restore the ways of the past fails, the only alternative is some form of violence, terror, war, or counterrevolution.

This is the pattern of a paralytic "conservative crisis": one that produces *reaction* rather than *reform*. It has occurred in all of history's great transitional periods. In no previous case was it possible to avoid violence. Usually there occurred an apocalyptic combination of war and revolution that swept away the malfunctioning elements of traditional institutions. This was always a terrifying prospect. In our own day it is a cataclysmic prospect. For the world now stands dependent upon the self-restraint of threatened regimes who have ready at hand an ever expanding arsenal of culture-killing weapons.

The alternative is for the world to become fully aware of the profound cultural transformation it is undergoing; to become politically mature enough to confront this revolutionary prospect with a new politics capable of providing the basis for a new political order that will be tranquil and yet dynamic. One mark of that maturity would be the appearance of a new, dynamic dual-myth system capable of superseding the present dual transitional cultures found throughout the world.

The world needs a new ideological system. But this condition cannot be fulfilled in a world based upon the nation-state alone. Indeed, the world system of sovereign states, familiar since the 17th century, is being superseded just as steadfastly as are the domestic institutions it comprises. The ideologies of the nation-state are at an end. The class systems that nurtured them are disappearing from their European birthplaces. The renaissance of ideologies here fore-

159

casted will be for a different type of class system in a different, postindustrial type of economy. It will develop a different creed of democracy appropriate to the challenge of the scientific revolution. Finally, it will be committed to world order. This latter ingredient is seen by considering what has happened to the balance-of-power system of international politics that was traditionally associated with the world of the industrial revolution.

# *Chapter 7*  Balance-of-Power Politics, Old and New

MOST OF US think about international relations as if they were conducted by sovereign nations, or even sovereign rulers themselves. This is the way things seem at first glance. It is the way world affairs were always conducted in the past. Even our closest approximation to a world organization, the United Nations, proclaims itself to be, and technically is, made up of nation-states. Moreover, nationalism, that is, the struggle to become a nation-state, is one of the most potent factors in contemporary international politics.

All of this seems to confirm what the facts at first appear to be, namely that autonomous nation-states are the leading actors in the drama of contemporary international politics. But merely because we would like to be able to operate on the basis of certain assumptions about the world does not mean that the world will automatically see that its facts will fit our fancies. Today the world is trying to teach us that our traditional assumptions about the nation-state no longer conform to the facts. Our dogged pretension that they do continues to be one of the chief stumbling blocks in the way of efforts to create a more rational world.

The world of politics today is in a condition comparable to that of the world of the 4th-century Greeks. They, too, lived in an international world that had made their separate states—their city-states—obsolete. Like ourselves, the ancient Greeks continued to actually practice international—interurban—politics with a complete disregard for the revered sovereignty of the individual *polis*. They behaved as imperialists while still retaining the autonomous *polis* as their basic concept. The same behaviour occurs today.

Pause for a moment to consider: what is the Soviet nation? Is it that territory which formerly was Russia? The United Nations does not think so, for two of the larger soviets have the legal status of nation-states in the General Assembly. Are Russia's Eastern European satellites true nations? Or are they part of a larger Communist commonwealth? Again, at international law they are nations. But in fact, what is East Germany? What is Finland? Suppose Afghanistan were to become sovietized. Would it be a nation? Would Russia become that much bigger a nation? Or would it be the Communist commonwealth that had expanded?

161

What is West Germany? Six powerful European nations, including West Germany, have operated the European Common Market. They look forward to following this preliminary economic union with some degree of political union. What would the new political entity be? Would it be a nation? If so, would its components lose their former status as nations?

What of the United States? Where does its nationhood stop? Alaska and Hawaii are "organic" parts of the United States. That has been made clear by their becoming states. But what of Panama? What of the Philippines? What of Puerto Rico? What of Santo Domingo? Such are the political communities which should be kept in mind as one asks the question: What is the nation-state? The answer given must apply to the European Economic Community as well as to the Congo; to Byelorussia as well as to New Zealand; to the Philippines as well as to Finland; and to the United Nations as well as to the United States.

Historically, the nation-state arrives with "Made in Europe" stamped on its base. It was never quite the same anywhere else—neither in the Western Hemisphere, nor east of the Danube, nor south of the Mediterranean. The nation-state was born in Europe following the 16th century. European political philosophers and lawyers were the first to detect its birth. They described it and furnished it with a complete body of political and legal theory. European states in their maturity proceeded to stamp their image and their aspirations on the rest of the world. Accordingly, images of the communities which flourished in Europe between the 17th and 20th centuries still today control our conception of the nation-state.

Several points need to be recalled about these early European nations. In the first place, they represented a process that never in history occurred the same way anywhere else. It was a double process of generation and disintegration. Inside areas like France and England feudal institutions were disintegrating. Along with their decay came the erosion of baronial sources of autonomy and independent military power. A somewhat modern way of summarizing this process is to say that the absolute monarchs of the 16th century did to military power what the socialists of the 20th century did to economic power: they nationalized it. Moreover, kings nationalized and monopolized military power in much the same way as did their modern economic counterparts. They expropriated it, took legal title to it, and prohibited any further private ownership or exploitation.

If one had looked inside England in 1500, when the Wars of the Roses were beginning to peter out, one would have been more impressed by the pluralism and the confederate nature of the English political community than by its integrated corporate nature. But a hundred years later—time moved more slowly then—by 1603 and the close of the Tudor dynasty, a political consolidation, integration, and nationalization had irrevocably taken place. The other European nations, following somewhat different time schedules, went through similar nationalizing experiences. That was one side of the simultaneous generation and disintegration process. But there was another side as well.

Medieval Europe in one regard had been an organic community. True, that community existed only in a very loose sense, but it did exist. For the notion incorporated in the word Christendom was applicable throughout the European continent. The overall Christian world was even less tightly organized than were the separate ethnic communities which composed it, but it did exist. However, the political effect of the Reformation, proceeding in rough unison with the developing autonomy of the nation-states, was to accomplish the disintegration of Christendom as an overall European community.

Christendom had been a world community. Communications and conceptions in the world of Christendom were such that as far as its inhabitants were concerned, it was in effect the whole world. So, one of the things that accompanied the growth of the nation-state was the disintegration of a world order based on religion. In its place was substituted an oligarchy composed of the chief European states. Ultimately they would produce an imperialist world order. Our own ineffectual contemporary efforts to move beyond this inherited world oligarchy to a more effective form of world order should give us caution in disparaging the kind and degree of world order once represented by Christendom.

True, the world order known to medieval man existed primarily on the level of faith and spiritual allegiance, rather than on the level of politics and full authority. But this fact also should provide 20th-century man with instruction. If today's world can achieve even a partial type of union in some way analogous to that of medieval Christendom a great deal will have been accomplished.

By the 18th century, then, the forces of generation and disintegration had taken place on two levels; on the level of world order there was disintegration with Christendom being supplanted by autonomous nations struggling for empire. And on the level of the nation-state there was disintegration with autonomous federal baronial forces being supplanted by centralizing monarchs. These were to become later the targets of businessmen's demands for economic autonomy.

## The Theory of National Power

Ideas for describing and dealing with these developments were close at hand. Since the first stirrings of the nation-state, whose ontology was foreshadowed in Renaissance Italy, our notions about international relations have been dominated by ideas first developed by Machiavelli. In the Italian city-states Machiavelli confronted conditions which led him to develop ideas that would later be applicable to the nation-states of modern Europe. Machiavelli lived during the disintegration of papal authority and the decline of the ancient Roman secular authority, yet before the rise of modern national Italian authority. Accordingly, he was observing a conflict situation among the Renaissance Italian city-states comparable to that which later was to appear among the early-modern European nation-states.

Machiavelli derived the logical answer to the question: What form of order could take the place of the spiritual and secular authority that had disintegrated beyond the possibility of regeneration? The answer he gave was both prescient and ingenious. He concluded that in the absence of a rational, overall, coordinating source of authority everything would be determined by a struggle for power. He applied this principle of power struggle both to the relations between the competing city-states of his day and to the intraparty and factional struggles inside Italian city-states. This was not merely the birth of power politics and its rationale—it was also the birth of balance-of-power analysis. And this was the principle that was destined to permeate every institution of the industrial world.

Machiavelli saw balance-of-power principles most clearly on the international (inter city-state) level. But similar conceptions were implicit in the way he described competition between political factions within city-states. Only one thing was missing from Machiavelli's analysis. This was the proposition that somehow, out of all this struggle and clash of interests, there would be operating an equilibrium mechanism not known about or purposely sought for by any of the parties to the struggle. Nonetheless, it would assert itself automatically as a result of their mutual competitive efforts. We have noted already that this equilibrium feature was not formally added to power analysis until much later—in fact, not until the 17th and 18th centuries when there flourished the founders of liberal social theory: Thomas Hobbes, John Locke, Hugo Grotius, and Adam Smith.

Balance-of-power relationships are of a very special kind. They are summed up with such words as autonomy and individualism. These are the terms that have been used to express the ideal and sometimes the reality underlying the fundamental institutions of the industrial West.

In *religion*, the Protestant Reformation stood for the ecclesiastical autonomy of the individual God-seeking believer. Neither a single system of belief nor a monopolistic religious order was deemed appropriate or possible. Only an environment which guaranteed free, private individualistic faith-seeking and God-seeking could hope to provide some unpredictable and undetectable individuals with grace and salvation.

The ideal of autonomy and individualism is most familiar in the *economic* institutions that grew up in association with free-market practices and theories. The analogy between balance-of-power politics and free-market economics is immediate and apparent. Individual traders in a market are like sovereign nations in conflicting power relationships. Money, prices, and contracts take the place of power, diplomacy, and treaties. An equilibrium price is the commercial counterpart of the state of peace which hangs delicately from day to day on the balance of power.

The *political* institutions of the West are similar. Western constitutional democracy has rested upon a notion of the primacy of the individual over the state. Electoral processes and legislative institutions were founded upon a notion similar to balance-of-power politics on the international level. In democratic theory the free electoral competition for individual votes and the open clash of political forces will, if unhampered, permit the principle of majority rule to establish the wisest policies and elect the wisest statesmen. No one confused any particular majority vote with wisdom, just as no one confused any individual market price with economic equilibrium. But an ongoing pluralistic process of freely competing political forces relying upon the majoritarian principle must, so Western democratic theory claimed, produce greater wisdom in the long run than is possible through any other device.

The most direct parallel in domestic political institutions to international balance-of-power principles occurs in the pulling and hauling of legislative pressure groups. The defenders of pressure-group politics admit that individual pressure groups will seek their own interests rather than those of the public, just as individual traders in the market or sovereign nations in international politics are motivated by their own self-interest. Yet it is argued, following the classic exposition of James Madison in *The Federalist*, "Number 10," that so long as there are numerous pressure groups vying against each other in a legislative chamber the compromises and adjustments which each will have to make in order to produce majoritarian legislation will result in the closest possible approximation to the public interest even though no single pressure group may even have had the public interest in mind. This obvious parallel to international balance-of-power doctrines and economic free-market doctrines was seized upon a few years ago by J. K. Galbraith when he applied the notion of "countervailing power" to the combined political and economic forces that he saw taking the place of the classical free-market economy.

Religion, economics, politics, and international relations are unquestionably four of the most fundamental functions of any social order. To find that a culture has operated upon the same underlying principle in each of these important areas suggests strongly that the principle, in this case the balance-of-power principle, is the fundamental, and at the same time the identifying, process of that culture. This, indeed, is the claim of all those who profess to find the highest ideals of the West embodied in its free enterprise market economy. Political philosophers who extol pluralism as the West's distinguishing virtue are really making the same point in slightly different language. If we study the institutions of the modern industrial West during the 19th and early 20th centuries the way anthropologists study the institutions of primitive cultures we must conclude that the balance-of-power mechanism has been the distinguishing pattern that has furnished the foundation for all leading Western institutions. On the level of international relations this pattern began to break down following World War I. How it operated and why it broke down requires special consideration.

## The International Mechanism

Machiavelli, we have seen, applied balance-of-power ideas to interstate relations, without a clear notion of an automatic harmonizing principle. This ingredient was added in the 17th century by Hugo Grotius. Grotius, figuratively speaking, placed himself in the middle of the 17th century North Sea and observed about him the existence of a number of corporate persons—nation-states —in a violent struggle for power among themselves. Considering each nation as if it were an autonomous person, that is, a legal sovereign, he concluded that, appearances to the contrary, their violent struggles need not necessarily produce cataclysm. On the contrary, such was their calculation of interests and their mode of contractual diplomatic alliances that the interest of each nation in preserving its own autonomy and in preventing others from developing too threatening amounts of power would lead all to combine against any other who seemed bent on upsetting the status quo.

The result of these constantly shifting and countervailing power struggles would automatically produce a kind of balance or equilibrium in which each nation would be relatively secure. No nation need be guided by any vision of ultimate overall equilibrium. No nation need seek explicitly for the balance which would protect them all. Rather a true equilibrium would result, as if guided by an unseen master diplomat, out of the effort of each to follow its own national self-interest. For those who believed this it followed that rationally imposed world order was neither necessary nor desirable. The self-interested balance-of-power struggle would achieve world order if left to assert itself, and it would do so better than could any actual master statesmen sitting down in advance, trying to calculate the appropriate conditions for balance and order.

The most succinct application of balance-of-power ideas to war was provided by the late 19th-century German military theorist, Clausewitz. Clausewitz's famous proposition was that, superficial appearances to the contrary, war is not the opposite of diplomacy or politics. It is merely their continuation by other means. We are led to think of nations as if they were warriors in the gladiatorial arena. Each may try to achieve his goal of self-preservation and ultimate victory through combination, negotiation, trickery, or diplomacy. But when such methods no longer suffice, war and violence must and should be resorted to. In this view, politics and diplomacy are but embryonic forms of war. Their natural issue is in warfare and this destiny of violence dominates their characteristics even during times of seeming peace. Indeed, peace disappears as an intrinsically valid diplomatic goal. Like politics and diplomacy, peace is merely the interim between wars. It is useful primarily as a breathing space, a time of jockeying, a period during which the gestation of the next war takes place.

Not all balance-of-power apologists have carried their views to this extreme. A few were like Woodrow Wilson. He truly believed that there should be a large number of autonomous sovereign states in free trade and open communications with each other. They would create a host of interrelated power struggles. But the result would not be war. On the contrary, they would produce the same process of checking and balancing on the world level that Madison described for the factions of domestic politics; the same wholesome result that Justice Brandeis had attributed to an antitrust economic policy. Self-regulating world peace would automatically result.

But either way, whether we favour Woodrow Wilson's idealism or the *Machtpolitik* of Clausewitz, we cannot avoid the conclusion that the history of balance-of-power politics has been one of intermittent warfare rather than stabilized peace. The unseen hand theory has been an even worse failure in international politics than it has been in economics.

The explanation of why this has been so concerns the quality of international relations which must obtain before the balance-of-power mechanism can escape issuing in war. It is not enough that there be numerous nations in open competition—"open covenants . . . openly arrived at"—as Wilson had proclaimed. More important is the requirement that the power of all competing nations must be truly and effectively counterbalanced at all times. This means that each nation must conduct its affairs steadfastly and solely on the basis of power politics. Each nation must subordinate all its interests, when occasion demands, to insuring that no one of its competitors becomes strong enough to overwhelm any other at war. According to classic balance-of-power theory, the way in which all of this was to be accomplished was through a completely flexible and virtually automatic process of rearranging national alliances and treaties in immediate response to any imbalance of the international status quo that might be detected. By these new alliances the scales of international power would be quickly adjusted in such a way as to counterbalance any disequilibrating augmentation in the disruptive power of a given nation-state.

Again the analogy to economics was believed valid. International alliances were to be in a constant state of flux and realignment. "England," said a famous power balancer, "has no permanent allies, only permanent interests." But the two sister systems of self-regulating equilibrium shared the same congenital defects. War, the violence of states in a balance-of-power relationship, is like depression, the violence of entrepreneurs in a market relationship. The causes of instability are similar in both cases. Monopolistic (imperial) tendencies develop among states as well as among entrepreneurs. Moreover, states frequently place other values ahead of national self-interest just as entrepreneurs frequently place other values ahead of economic self-interest. Either tendency, the oversuccessful courtship of power (imperialism) or its underevaluation in comparison with other international goals, will prevent balance-of-power mechanisms from producing international equilibrium or peace. In any case, balance-of-power politics could never really be said either to produce or to aim at peace. Counterpoised equilibrium, or the temporary absence of war, was the most that could be said to result, even when the mechanism was working perfectly.

In fact, the theory never claimed to eliminate war completely. From time to time there would be certain errors and miscalculations. This was where war entered. But war merely proved out the system. For when the diplomatic struggles failed to produce a transparently obvious equilibrium adjustment, war would quickly test out the true power situation and reveal to all the exact state of the forces available to each of the nation-states. After a short struggle a peace treaty would express the new conditions of equilibrium and provide the ground rules for the next stage of balance-of-power diplomacy. War was an essential, but an unusual and atypical part of the system.

In theory the process could proceed perfectly without war if all the partners to the system undeviatingly followed their national self-interest and played the balance-of-power game without regard to any other consideration. Indeed, it might be said that war, far from being a result of the aggressive pursuit of national self-interest, occurred only when national self-interest was abandoned in favour of some more chimerical goal such as justice, revenge, or the propagation of a religious or ideological tenet. But the chief requirement was always that the world continue to consist of autonomous nation-states. In a different kind of world, balance-of-power theory would be inapplicable.

Some have argued that the mechanism did work fairly well during parts of the 18th and 19th centuries and prior to the time when the Western imperial powers had completely parceled out the non-Western world among themselves. However, once this latter condition had arrived the Western empires could expand only by acquiring colonies from one another through warfare or incitement to rebellion. This was the stage that had been reached by the time of World War I. Imperial systems were beginning to feed off each other's preserves just as business monopolies and cartels warred against each other in the economic orders. Woodrow Wilson spent his political life combating monopolistic tendencies in the economic order. When he turned to the problems of world order he applied the same approach. This was the underlying principle of the League of Nations. It was to function the way the New York Stock Exchange did. It was not to control, but rather to facilitate the balance-of-power process.

But Wilson's international trust-busting failed. A between-the-wars period of monopolistic competition began in earnest. The end result was a bipolar world divided on the basis of ideology rather than power. The conditions of such a world are completely inapplicable to the conditions required for traditional balance-of-power politics to produce equilibrium and peace. The problem is something like that of balancing a two-legged stool. The balance-of-power mechanism will not work any better in politics than it does in economics if its special requirements are not met in practice. Indeed, in domestic politics it was Madison's fear of the development of a bipolar political standoff, with North and South pitted against each other, that had led him to propose breaking up these two blocs in a federal legislature composed of numerous power factions. Only then, he argued, could the balance-of-power equilibrium emerge.

One can imagine the world setting out politically and constitutionally to produce—on the international level—conditions similar to those James Madison prescribed for the domestic level. But one can imagine this only *after* the establishment of a world constitutional authority comparable to that Madison could rely upon for the institution of his scheme of legislative balance-of-power politics.

Politics in a world of ideologically motivated thermonuclear powers is qualitatively different from the balance-of-power pulling and hauling of numerous small nations. In the latter case, one can visualize (even though history has shown how improbable it is) a perpetual condition of equilibrium resulting. In the former, however, both sides proclaim that their ideological conflict is irresolvable. Each side vows to remain forever committed to the destruction of its ideological opponent.

How is it possible for balance-of-power mechanisms to work when this condition obtains? It is not possible. This truth is megamagnified in a world that calculates warfare in terms of megadeaths per megaton. The very idea of a military victory disappears as a meaningful notion. With the death of victory goes the death of war and with the demise of these there disappears forever any possibility of relying upon balance-of-power politics for international relations.

## Failure of the League

It must be reemphasized that this fact underlies the essential tragedy of the Wilsonian League of Nations. The avowed aim was a world rule of law. Yet it was a rule of law that was to be given its expression and find its enforcement without a world legal order. The League of Nations was to function as a free market in world power. This involved the League in the initial effort to break up international power blocs and empires. Empires were the same sort of disruptive, monopolistic forces in the international balance-of-power equilibrium mechanism that economic monopolies were in free-market theory.

Next the League tried to rationally reconstitute the entire world as a series of ideal nation-states competing together according to the classical definitions of national sovereignty and balance-of-power politics. Most of the non-Western world did not fit this ideal. These areas were regarded as being in various stages of development toward nationhood. One of the functions of the League of Nations was to help nurture them through their prenational childhood and adolescence into full maturity as nation-states. All was to proceed under the tutelage of various of the senior powers of the League of Nations.

If everything went according to schedule the classical balance-of-power mechanism could again produce international harmony. However, it was also necessary for the great powers to follow the American lead and renounce imperialism as a goal. Like bidders in an open market, nations were supposed to function only through "open covenants, openly arrived at." This meant that the League could be given no authority of its own and no enforcement agency. It was not to superimpose world order on the sovereign nations. Rather, it was to operate like a neutral power arena: the political counterpart of the ideal free market.

One of the results would be freedom of the seas. This Wilsonian conception was perfectly consistent with the balance-of-power mechanism he was trying to revive. First the nations must agree to maintain their naval forces in proportion to the power status revealed by the war. Then the interests of all would be to see that no one power altered the balance. This would insure freedom of the seas for all. Freedom of the seas meant the neutrality of the seas. It was essential to the working out of a balance-of-power mechanism able to generate an equilibrium reign of law out of the free competition of the various high contending parties.

Leading European statesmen can be forgiven if they did not immediately perceive the rationale or the practicality of the Wilsonian program. They had not participated in the peculiar American political tradition to which Wilson belonged: the trust-busting progressive revolt. For, as we have seen, the Wilson scheme essentially applied to the international scene the same ill-fated corrective policies American progressivism had designed to cope with the growth of economic monopolies in a free market system. League of Nations empire-busting and nation-building was the international counterpart of domestic trust-busting and regulations to insure that the marketplace would consist only of numerous small firms in free competition with each other.

170

The Wilsonian League of Nations was to be the antitrust division of the international market in political power. Like its American counterpart it was to have no coercive authority. But progressivism was even *less* applicable to the international scene than it was to national economic affairs. For the new nations constructed at Versailles did not represent political realities. And the expectation that the European imperial powers would somehow abandon their foreign interests and investments was as romantic as the notion that domestic economies, made up of such giants as Standard Oil, I. G. Farben, Philips, Krupp, and General Motors could somehow be made to operate as if they were composed of numerous small economic units on the classical free market model.

The fact of imperialism and the nature of imperialist relationships were in fundamental discord with the conception of the nation-state assumed in the traditional balance-of-power model. For the ideal nation-state of the classical model was a self-contained political and legal entity. It was conceived of as an integral legal person negotiating contractual rather than organic relationships with other similar persons throughout the world. This was the condition implied in being legally sovereign in a world composed of legal sovereigns.

Imperialism, politically, was a maneuver in which one country—one mature European nation-state—attempted to acquire jurisdictional controls over a large number of political communities, thereby rendering them subordinate. It is not important whether the motivation was economic, military, or a struggle for prestige. The important thing is that the relationship purported to be one of permanent submission. It implicitly denied to the inferior political community the possibility of ever becoming politically coequal with its imperialist master. This was true even of the mature, sophisticated arrangements ultimately produced in the British Commonwealth of Nations. No matter how much local authority nations like Canada and Ireland might acquire they could never become the equal of the Mother of Parliaments herself. As the colonial system matured it made the imperial powers into something more than nation-states and something different from the autonomous legal persons implied by balance-of-power diplomacy.

## A New Kind of State

Meanwhile, an entirely different principle of monopoly growth was under way in the New World. Already in the 19th century the United States had created an arrangement which was in fundamental discord with the classical conception of the nation-state. Its original 13 colonies grew into 50 states in a steady process of national, rather than imperial, expansion. This was a departure from the nation-state idea. It represented a new principle of political and territorial aggrandizement.

The traditional European mode of national growth consisted of acquiring colonial possessions. In that classical imperialist relationship the nation-state always maintained a sharp distinction between itself and its colony. This was obvious when a native culture was acquired in fact, as in Asia and Africa. It was not so obvious in the Western Hemisphere where European countries sent their own nationals out to capture and colonize underdeveloped areas. Even so, it was colonial opposition to this rigid insistence on the primacy of the motherland that gave rise to the American Revolution.

The sharpest distinctions between European imperial powers and their colonies became apparent in the second phase of colonial expansion, as the European nations acquired control over already well-established cultures in underdeveloped areas of the world. For in the latter case, the European nations formally and explicitly insulated their own cultures, their own political systems, and their own economic systems from those of their colonial communities. There were local variations. France permitted colonials as individuals to become "French." The British held out the promise of eventual commonwealth status. But the overall result was for the non-European colonial dependencies to become second-class communities. Following the conception of the nation-state as a corporate person, their colonies were analogous to slaves rather than true citizens.

The form of expansion represented by the growth of the United States was based upon a non-European principle. It produced the first example of what were later to be called satellites when Russia began to expand in the same fashion. The explicit principle of federal expansion was that the various communities who were candidates for inclusion into the political system of the United States had first to develop within themselves political and cultural institutions which were mirror images of those already present in the United States. Once they had done this, they were eligible for inclusion in the larger community. Only in this way could the organic expansion of the larger community take place.

America soon was wielding great power throughout the world. She virtually declared the entire Western Hemisphere to be her own exclusive sphere of influence. As her power expanded in the 20th century, the same approach that had worked in Latin America was attempted for the rest of the world. America never acquired colonies in the European pattern. Dependencies not suited to becoming "territories" and ultimately states were controlled more indirectly through financial and economic policies.

After their revolution the Russians built their soviets into a federal union similar to the American federal system. As in the American case, this led to the territorial expansion of Russia. However, Russia is different from America. Its national creed expresses the goal of international socialist unity. This issued in an ostensible desire to add soviets from all over the world rather than limiting the extent of expansion to immediately adjoining territory. In fact, however, the U.S.S.R. actually followed the American pattern rather than her own creed. The result of the expanding power of these two federal giants was to supersede completely the traditional European pattern built on an unchanging sovereign state at the core and a flexible collection of subordinate colonies on the outside.

The world was confronted by a collection of political anomalies which made traditional balance-of-power politics impossible. Leading off were two great continental powers. Each was expansionist. Classical balance-of-power considerations obviously could not apply to the two federal giants. Recall the two-legged stool. Balance-of-power required at least three members before the game could be played. Ideally many more than three would be required for the system to work smoothly according to its classical model. Moreover, there were no theoretically "natural" boundaries or limiting ethnic characteristics for the two new supranations. If their examples were to be followed in the future the world's new nations would all be "melting pots"—nonnations.

Behind and below the two bipolar giants there lay a series of archaic European nation-states. Their empires were breaking up. Their ex-colonies were assuming independence, as in the case of India, or falling into the orbits of the great federal giants, as in the cases of Santo Domingo and Finland. The traditional European type of nation-state was unable to play the game of world power politics in its new form. Yet it was held in its old inapplicable forms by seemingly immobile international traditions and by the seemingly insuperable animosities with which each European state regarded its political siblings. Gaullist France seemed to offer the most creative model for the future. For, having dissolved its empire and transformed its constitution, it was prepared to become a part of a more effective world order. Meanwhile, not even the two federal giants were secure. Their own satellite systems were becoming unglued. The underdeveloped areas of the world were themselves politically on the move, striving not only for national independence but also for the formation of their own regional federal blocs of influence. Hopefully they would then be able to counter or to compete with the great bipolar giants contending over them. The appearance of pan-Muslim, pan-African, and pan-Asiatic movements threatened to visit the world with a whole series of post-European federal giants. When the growing powers of India and China are added it is more than ever apparent that the once dominant "made-in-Europe" nation-state system has seen its last days.

The European nations themselves have been forced to abandon the nation-state form. European economic union was already in its first stages by 1960. Political union in some form would follow, and when this occurred the classical nation-state system would be completely dismantled. Along with it would disappear the classical balance-of-power mechanism which had grown up in association with the nation-state. The Machiavellian episode in world politics would be at an end. What would take its place? Would it be some form of world order built on regional federal blocs? Or would the world of international competition follow that of the economic order and devise a new form of monopolistic competition?

The U.S.S.R. had every reason to view with alarm the potential formation of a federal union composed of the former nation-states of the continent of Europe. For if such a project were to become an accomplished fact, extremely strong forces would be set in motion counter to her own. Ultimately these new forces might be capable of drawing away from Russia's orbit some of the Eastern European members of the socialist camp who had no alternative but to side with Russia so long as the European nations remained disorganized. All of these developments brought with them a dramatic shift in the methods by which the game of international power politics was played. Recognition that this shift has occurred has been slow in coming. Realization of its implications has occurred even more slowly.

## Fuse Cap Politics

The legal theory of the old balance-of-power politics was that each national "person" was as inviolable as were real human persons. That is, each was assumed to be encased in a suit of legal armour created by its own sovereign law. The world was viewed as being composed of a series of such armoured legal vehicles. Each total national armoured vehicle moved through the world as an integral unit and it dealt with every other national capsule as if it were the same kind of unitary legal entity. Each nation was like a complete person. It had a collection of interests which were the interests of its total personality. Speaking with one voice it approached its competitors assuming them to be similarly constituted and similarly motivated.

We have seen how the real world of international relations has outmoded this conception. It has been eroded from another side by the advent of thermonuclear weapons. The thermonuclear weapon is a total means of destruction. It cannot be used as an instrument of war in a traditional sense, and especially not in the kind of warfare Clausewitz and the chief apologists of balance-of-power politics had in mind. To resort to thermonuclear war would be an act of suicide.

Suicide on the individual level is called an irrational act because it is not a rational way to solve problems. The force of this argument applies even more strongly on the cultural level than for individuals. For although we may imagine a person whose condition is so horrible that we sympathize with and under-

174

stand the choice for self-destruction, this kind of an argument does not apply on the cultural level. A slogan such as "better dead than red" is no more rational than is its converse.

No culture can be so sick or so completely full of corruption that reforms, changed leadership, or revolution may not revivify it. No leader or oligarchy—not even an electoral majority—can be accorded the right to choose to destroy its culture out of despair over the gravity of the problems facing the culture or incompetence in dealing with its international opponents. Failure, defeat, demise, and even destruction may be a culture's fate; it can never be a culture's goal. A decision to wage a thermonuclear war is tantamount to deciding to commit cultural suicide.

If this much is granted then it follows that the same can be said for a decision to remain in a system of relationships which threaten to break out into thermonuclear war. But we have seen that this is precisely the effect which can be predicted should the world "decide" (either positively through a conscious act or negatively by doing nothing to supersede it) to remain in traditional balance-of-power political relationships. For the balance-of-power mechanism, when there is added to it the presence of thermonuclear weapons, amounts to an extremely delicate and sensitive fuse cap connected to each of the world's thermonuclear weapons. The whole system becomes not only war-oriented but suicide-oriented as well. Any hope for the preservation of peace, and of human culture, is doomed to frustration unless this form of fuse cap politics can be superseded by a new form of international politics which is not intrinsically directed toward war.

## The Bipolar World

One thing that inhibits us from perceiving the need for a successor to traditional balance-of-power politics is what can be called the paradox of post-European nationalism. We live in times which seem to be the most aggressively nationalistic in history. More separate nations are now in existence than at any other time in history. The spirit of nationalism and the demand for national autonomy are coursing irresistibly throughout the non-Western world. At the same time, however, our world situation is such that for the first time in history the sovereign, autonomous nation-state is no longer a workable form of political organization.

There are many reasons for this. One of them is technological. The size and scope of organizations always tend to expand in unison with the capabilities contained in man's techniques of control. Double-entry bookkeeping was a control technique that expanded enormously the size and complexity of economic organizations men could control. The joint-stock corporation expanded the amount of capital one firm could assimilate and deploy. The general staff command system expanded the executive function and released it from dependency upon the capacities of one man. Bureaucratization did for office work what mass production assembly lines had done for manufacturing. Cybernation promised to synthesize and then go far beyond each one of these technological advances.

For several centuries the European type of nation-state was the largest and most complex political community man knew how to operate effectively. Federalism made this obsolete. And recently new techniques of communications, coordination, administrative management, and information processing and analysis have become so highly developed that man can manage vastly larger and more complex political communities than either the nation-state or the federal union. Inasmuch as political communities are in a form of competition with each other they daily measure themselves in comparison with their peers throughout the world. Accordingly, each political community must find its relative position among its fellows on the basis of its size and power and the degree of sophistication with which it is able to organize and utilize the human and physical resources at its command. This means that today's political communities are forced to utilize the new technologies of control and power. They must grow to the limits of size and complexity made possible by the new tools of organization, information processing, and administration.

Inevitably, therefore, even if none of the preceding factors were of any force the European type of nation-state would still be driven to supersede itself. It would do so simply in realizing its maximum organizational, territorial, and demographic potentialities under contemporary conditions. It must expand beyond the limits which traditionally circumscribed what was meant by a nation-state. Failing that it will find itself relegated to a position of inferiority, as did Spain when she refused to develop a modern industrial economy.

This is the compelling logic of the economic and political union now being attempted on the continent of Europe. If this effort succeeds it will reveal the final demise of the European type of nation-state, for it will be the European nation-state self-consciously superseding itself in response to the political, technological, and military imperatives of the contemporary world. As was previously the case with the Greek *polis,* self-supersession is the price of survival in today's community of nations.

But European union may not even be enough. It may be little more than a primitive, foredoomed effort. Not even a national organization of the size and scope of the continental United States nor of the U.S.S.R. is any longer adequate to cope with the competitive conditions of national existence presented by today's world. Yet the most Europe can achieve is a federal organization comparable in size and scope to what has been known in the past as the United States. This is simply not sufficient in a world consisting of the type of extraterritorial international power blocs that the United States and the U.S.S.R. have become. Neither may be adequate when confronted with the industrial and demographic potentials of such Oriental powers as India and China.

However, for a while yet ours will remain a bipolar world. This is for ideological as well as for organizational reasons. The entire world is like the city of Berlin, like the city of Jerusalem, like Korea, like Vietnam; and so on through the catalog of world communities in which demarcation lines have been drawn by the two great power constellations that dominate world politics. In such a situation, the very idea of the traditional European nation-state ceases to have vitality and is rendered as archaic as was the feudal morality Don Quixote wished to preserve after the time it had ceased to be relevant to the social conditions of his day.

Similarly today it is both quixotic and foredoomed to attempt to preserve the nation-state form of organization in a world in which it can no longer cope with the political problems presented to it. If it were only windmills at which today's archaic nation-states were tilting, our quixotic nationalistic behaviour might be little more than a matter for idle amusement, or at the most, pathos. But unfortunately these outmoded warriors of ours are possessed of some very nonquixotic armaments. It is as if Don Quixote had gone jousting through the late medieval world mounted on an armour-plated cannon-firing tank rather than on a jousting horse.

Few warriors able to destroy their opponents have instead peaceably put down their arms and prepared unresistingly to die. Yet this is what the survival of the world today demands of the traditional nation-state. Despite the forces previously cataloged it seems likely that among the nation-states of our day there will be found at least one "Spain." And if it happens to be a thermonuclear power, it may be able to involve all mankind in its own irrational, suicidal compulsions.

Humanity's problem is set. It must find a method for superseding the nation-state and with it traditional balance-of-power relationships. It must become politically self-conscious about the fundamental cultural transformation taking place in its midst. It must develop a new politics within which a new family of ideologies may find expression. If the new ideologies transcend the limitations imposed by traditional European political and class systems, how can we visualize them?

## The Epic Function

To do so we must start with the foundations of ideas. Ideologies served functions similar to those served by the myths, epics, and tragedies of classical antiquity. A society's epic function does not refer merely to a literary, poetic, or dramatic work of art. It refers to something much more central to the functioning of a social system. The epic function of a society consists of the devices whereby the society gives symbolic expression to its fundamental unity and the goals at which it aims. In the most primitive cultures this symbolic epic function is accomplished through rituals. Elaborate and intricate primitive *rites de passage* reveal to all members of a culture what their larger purposes are and the roles members must perform in order to accomplish those purposes. In complex societies many institutions, religion most prominently, serve to express overall goals and to define the roles appropriate to individuals. But in a primitive society religion is not a separate and subdivided institution. There is a general amalgamation of the institutions that become separated in more complex societies. Education, politics, and religion are examples, as is war.

As societies become more complex, a transition occurs. Religious rituals subdivide and develop into separate institutions. One is a formally and explicitly organized religion. The other is a myth system with epic characteristics. This is the stage which in Greek culture is represented by the appearance of the Homeric myths, the religious maxims of Hesiod, and the mystery religions. It is at this point, and especially in the case of Homer, that the more restricted and familiar use of the term epic becomes applicable.

The important point is not that the Homeric Greeks had a literary form which typically has been known by the term epic. The point is rather that the specific literary form—the symbolic idiom—known as the Homeric myths had the function of revealing to the ancient Achaeans the larger goals and purposes of their cultures. This was accomplished through novelistic tales about symbolic culture heroes who were larger than life and yet who confronted the typical problems of life and coped with them in ideal ways. The epics, in this form, were animated, anthropomorphic representations of the goals and purposes of the culture as a whole. They were presented in a fashion that revealed the ideals of behaviour, that is, the rules and roles necessary for human beings to follow if those goals and purposes were to be realized.

The Homeric myths, like the similar epic myths of other cultures, employed a great culture war as the setting for the portrayal of their ideals. A mythic war does what real wars do. It unifies a people. It distinguishes the virtues of the chosen people from the evils represented by the "enemy." In this way epic myths serve as great cultural textbooks. They provide education. They are the basic acculturation and assimilation manuals of societies. In short, epic myths are instruments through which the civilization and the acculturation of the members of a society take place. This is one reason for the elevated position of the poet in all societies that fulfill their acculturation functions through epic myths. His function is like that of the religious leader, the teacher, and the elder statesman combined together. The Achaean poets of classical times and the druidic poets of ancient Europe were the teacher-philosopher-priests of their societies. Plato clearly understood the acculturation function of the Homeric poets. He attacked them with such vigour because he felt the education being purveyed through the Homeric myths was no longer appropriate to the needs of 5th-century Athens.

The world's great epics have always served a teaching, an acculturating, and a unifying role. Nor have men ever consummated their most serious revolutions without an accompanying galvanic myth or epic celebrating the conflicts which arose at the outset of the revolutionary threat and immortalizing the achievements through which ultimate unification and consensus was produced. Great unifying commemorational epics and myths have taken many different forms, but whatever the form, they have been necessary for the preservation of the settlements of mankind's great revolutions. As the essay on THE FINE ARTS shows, this is why the work of the greatest dramatists comprises what is called an "epic theatre." They portray a war, actually or symbolically, and reveal the heroism appropriate to its special demands. This is also the function served by ideologies.

In all these instances, it was not the case that war as an institution had disappeared. This was not the aim of myths, epics, tragedies, or ideologies. On the contrary, all prior societies have been, in the idiom of Walter Millis, war systems. War was one of their most crucial and centrally necessary institutions. And actual wars served a purpose for the society analogous to that provided by its great myths. Indeed, one of the eternal problems of a war leader is to associate an existing or impending war with the great struggle-oriented myths and ideologies revered by his society. If he succeeds, the actual war may achieve the same result as is portrayed in the cultural myths. For actual war, like mythical war, also mobilizes the energies of the people and at the same time expresses a communal struggle for the achievement of the goals of the culture.

The Cold War presents the world with an ironic paradox.[1] It is the time in man's history in which the military resolution of conflicts is most intolerable and most hazardous. Yet it is the time in which militarism and trial by battle seem to hold their greatest sway. A look across the governments of the world discloses little but "warfare" garrison states, usually headed by military dictators. It is characteristic in such states for domestic, political, and economic issues to yield precedence to paramount considerations of armaments and defense. Warfare states internationalize domestic issues in the act of militarizing them. This reverses the traditional meaning of diplomacy. Originally diplomacy served the dictates of domestic power. Contemporary warfare makes it serve the dictates of the exotic, new, logistical sciences instead.

The European nation-state, archaic, illogical, and dysfunctional though it is, still dominates the theatre of world politics uncertainly and unpredictably like

1 See Walter Millis, COLD WAR, in *Encyclopædia Britannica* (1968).

179

a crazed and willful king in the closing scenes of a Greek tragedy. Balance-of-power politics, having failed during its 19th-century zenith, finds its most extensive utilization during its 20th-century nadir. Paradoxical it is. Rare it is not. It conforms to what was earlier described as a "conservative crisis" that sets events on a headlong collision course with disaster. At the very time when the informal forces for world integration and peace are at their apex they are blocked at every turn by the loggerheads disposition of the formally organized forces of the world's nations.

## The Military Mode

Traditional balance-of-power politics can no longer truly resolve *any* question; yet for the first time in history it is being relied upon for the resolution of *all* international disputes. This fact takes on special significance in the light of the recent work of revisionist historians who are reinterpreting 19th-century diplomatic history to show how ineffective was the balance-of-power principle for that world. Though conditions then existing made its principles applicable in theory, nonetheless it was constantly ignored in practice. In our day the change is that while actual conditions make its theory totally discreditable, the world's political practitioners are making the most sedulous effort in history to apply it. Never before in human culture have people tried so hard to resolve every type of political conflict through the threat of a resort to actual violence rather than by deliberations and negotiation. This is what is meant by the policy of deterrence in international relations. The riots, the uprisings, and the demonstrations in the world's domestic affairs merely show that the world's people have learned well from the lessons in power politics taught them by their bomb-brandishing superiors. The novel element in world politics is that violence and force have come to be used for nontraditional purposes: they are used to acquire the right to control the direction of the internal cultural development of political communities, rather than to reduce them to the type of colonial subservience formerly typical of European imperialism. The states of the world have become pawnlike, valuable as indicators of the changing tides of ideological fortunes in the larger world bipolar struggle rather than as the intrinsically valuable objects of acquisition they were in olden times. Imperialism, like most other institutions, has become politicized and ideologized even though its methods have remained militaristic.

This pattern was foreshadowed by the post-World War II elections in Greece. There the American aim of preventing a Communist victory was accomplished through relatively delicate, though forceful, means. The Greeks themselves rounded up and jailed local Communist leaders. The presence of American gunboats outside Greek harbours could not be considered more than an implied threat. A more indicative model was provided by the Russian invasion and satellization of the states of Eastern Europe. Of course, these were contiguous territories and by one mode of reckoning Russia was merely behaving as did America when she took over Spanish Texas, New Mexico, and California. Both abandoned politics in favour of overt violence. America was unchallenged. But she was the one who challenged Russia's 20th-century acquisitions. Her unwavering opposition throughout the globe resulted in the complete militarization of American foreign policy. Communism was to be contained throughout the world—by local military action in the first instance; by more generalized thermonuclear attack against Russia if necessary.

The United States had always regarded Latin America as her special imperialist preserve. When a Communist-oriented regime appeared in Guatemala it called forth the application of modern counter-insurgency techniques. The Truman and Eisenhower Doctrines expanded the area within which such tactics might be employed. The new policy was sometimes called a "roving" Monroe Doctrine. It extended the Latin-American principle to the entire world. America committed herself to the political guidance of the uncommitted nations of the entire world. She preferred to use economic incentives. This failing, her vast network of undercover operations could be relied upon, as in Guatemala. Finally, there was the resort to overt violence, as in Santo Domingo. Russia replied in kind. Examples were the Congo, Cuba, Afghanistan, and Egypt. On both sides the readiness to resort to violence increased the closer one came to the homeland's boundaries. However, Russia was able to avoid overt military involvement in cases like Korea and Vietnam.

The entire world came to be involved in a vast power struggle. Though each side preferred to avoid warfare and achieve its aims nonviolently, each was prepared to, and frequently did, fight to gain its way. Overt military power had never in history played so prominent and so constant a role in international affairs as it did in the post-World War II period. Even where negotiation would have sufficed, as in Santo Domingo and Hungary, the great powers appeared to prefer force to diplomacy. As the two federal giants reduced world politics to violence, the small powers followed suit with seeming relish. The Arabs and the Israelis were always in some form of war or near-war. The members of the Arab world seemed increasingly disposed to settling their internal affairs by military violence. Throughout Latin America military dictatorships—always a familiar political landmark there anyway—increased until hardly any regime existed on that continent which was not held in power by armed might. Military power is the most primitive of the ways of influencing politics. In the new African states affairs devolved quickly upon those who monopolized the armies and the police forces. In all such cases the result was obvious. The army would be used to resolve serious internal as well as border difficulties. Everywhere the aggrandizement of the military grew apace. In Asia, each of the smaller countries followed suit as the big powers vied with each other in the quest for satellites. China had never been much more than a vast, subcontinental collection of garrisons. India, the land of Gandhian pacifism, quickly grew into a modern Cold War nation and showed no hesitation in applying military force to the solution of her troubles with Pakistan, Goa, and China.

It is incredible, in the light of all this, how optimists can survey the history of the Cold War and conclude placidly that it has revealed the end of power politics. On the contrary, the argument above is that this has been the period of the most unmitigated militarism, in domestic as well as in foreign affairs, throughout man's entire history. The postwar world can be regarded as little less than a world in counterrevolution. It has been engaging in the steadfast, if partly unconscious, effort to preserve the nation-state. It has been forced into adopting ever increasing applications of violence in the attempt. This has helped to bring power politics into its own. However, these are conditions making continued utilization of power politics extremely hazardous, for the conditions of its invocation are completely discordant with the facts of the world to which it tries to address itself.

## The Satellite System

Under the colonial system the internal shape of the culture of the colonial territory was almost a matter of unconcern to the imperial power. We have seen that in the contemporary quest for satellites the crucial factor is the ability of the imperial power to induce other political communities to develop in harmony with its own ideological and political forms. Former economic relationships have been reversed. Contemporary imperial powers may even give their satellites more in goods and services than the economic value of what they receive in return. And if the reply is that "security" is what the great powers buy through their Cold War struggles, then the situation is ironic indeed. Security seems to be what is in least supply. Theoretically the goal of each of the new-model imperial powers is to create a world made up only of its own satellites, all exhibiting allegiance to its own official ideology. Ideally each satellite would be aiming ultimately to acquire governmental and organizational forms patterned after those of the imperial power.

Along with this change from empires made up of colonies to empires that are made up of satellites, a comparable change took place in the relationships between the new-model, major imperial powers themselves. Now each of the federal giants began to design its foreign policy on the basis of calculations about how to discredit the official ideology of its opponent and how to foster the ultimate victory of its own ideology inside the opponent's country. As a result, these new imperial giants ceased to view their political opponents as unitary legal persons. Instead, they sought to X-ray the other side's internal political structure. They looked directly inside each other's borders and made the manipulation of internal political and ideological forces an explicit aim of foreign policy.

International victories were previously consummated by formal concessions of land, reparations, and agreements granted by one national power to another. Such was the way of the old balance-of-power politics. Now, however, international victories have come to be registered in a new way. They are revealed by changes in the electoral strength of the various political factions and parties and by changes in the composition of the ruling elite. Each of the contending nations regards all other polities in the world as if they were battlegrounds of warring internal factions rather than as integrated wholes.

In the chapter on bureaucracy we observed how the internal factions of each country wage an incessant struggle for power. They combine and recombine into constantly shifting coalitions of ruling oligarchs. At any given moment the coalition that happens to be in charge expresses the domestic balance-of-power situation at that time. Changing policies come and go in cadence with the shifting tides of the internal balance-of-power struggle.

This leads nations to design their own foreign policies with the dynamics of other countries' internal balance-of-power struggles well in mind. The success or failure of a nation's foreign policies is truly revealed by their effects on policy formation and factional changes within other nations. This is why the great powers have made it an explicit aim of foreign policy to manipulate the internal politics of other nations. International victories are no longer measured by the amount of economic or territorial concessions the loser can be forced to yield. It is the quest for ideological allies that really counts. The means may include subversion, corruption, a guerrilla uprising, a coup d'etat, or even overt invasion.

This internationalization of domestic politics has affected the ideological characteristics of the political parties and movements inside every major country. During the 19th century internal politics of the great European nations were characterized by a fairly complete spectrum of politically organized ideologies. Their partisans waged a constant struggle in and out of elections striving for the victory of their special ideological versions of the national common good. In an earlier chapter we saw how this traditional European form of internal ideological struggle almost disappeared as the 20th century matured.

This process was abetted by the change in the terms of world politics. For as *international* ideological competition became paramount, domestic ideological competition moderated. The reason was simple. If national survival was proclaimed to depend on winning the world struggle against capitalism (or communism), domestic politics had to be purged of all traces of the enemy's beliefs. Each of the major powers—especially the great bipolar powers

—established an official spectrum, or range of ideological disputation. Within the confines of the permitted range, internal political differences could be expressed legitimately. Anything outside the officially sanctioned spectrum might verge too close to enemy ideas to be tolerated.

In the United States the spectrum of politics was much wider and the policing of ideological expression much more informal than in the U.S.S.R. However, following World War II the direction of change in the two countries was for the United States to become more restrictive and the U.S.S.R. to become more tolerant.

## Internationalized Ideology

This internationalization of internal politics added to the reasons that led many 20th-century sociologists and political philosophers to conclude that "the end of ideology" had arrived. In truth, however, what had happened was not so much the end of ideology. Rather there was a restriction or suppression of ideological struggle inside various countries. But there was also an intensification of ideology when it was displaced and sublimated into the realm of international politics. The old ideologies had been confined within the borders of the European-type nation-state. Now ideological struggle followed the general trend of the times and became internationalized. Only in the larger theatre of world politics was there the full-scale ideological struggle that had been so familiar inside nations during the 19th century. Nations themselves ceased behaving like states of old and instead began to act more like the 18th-century political factions described by James Madison in his famous essay in *The Federalist*, "Number 10." This novel development in contemporary world politics had been foreshadowed in the New World during the 19th century. America was then a revolutionary form of government beleaguered by monarchical enemies. As noted above, America's response was to proclaim the Monroe Doctrine. This anticipated by a century the contemporary struggle to control a foreign country's internal power structure rather than to possess it outright.

The Monroe Doctrine was basically at odds with the established principles of 19th-century European balance-of-power politics. Its concern was with internal ideology rather than territorial power, even though much later "dollar diplomacy" came to stand for a special American brand of economic imperialism. Originally, however, the Monroe Doctrine was both political and revolutionary. America proclaimed fraternal sympathy with revolutionary republican movements in the New World. Any counterrevolutionary interference would be interpreted as a hostile act against America. For her own part, however, she would not hesitate to extend brotherly aid and intervention throughout Latin America. Of course, the Monroe Doctrine had been developed to aid the 19th-century revolutionary struggle of republicanism against monarchy. But it stood ready to

184

be adapted to the mid-20th-century ideological struggle between the liberal and the collectivist democracies. This happened after World War II.

First came the Marshall Plan. Initially it had been concerned with aiding friendly European nations to reconstruct their war-ravaged cultures. Almost immediately, however, it was adapted to Cold War ideological needs. This meant in effect the extension of the idea of the Monroe Doctrine to include Europe. Gradually, the same principle was expanded to include the entire world. This occurred in two stages known as the Truman Doctrine and the Eisenhower Doctrine. The central theme was that of the containment policy. Communism would be prevented from spreading to new areas. Ultimately it would die out because of its own internal weaknesses and contradictions. This was precisely what Karl Marx had said about capitalism.

The Cold War, then, was a new departure in the history of world politics. It converted the struggles of world politics from conflicts between legally autonomous corporate persons, whose political integrity was tacitly recognized by all the rest, into a worldwide feud between two large families of opposed ideologies. Neither clan respected the national boundaries or the legal integrity of any country in the world. Each sought to penetrate the internal processes of all other political communities and influence them to develop in harmony with its own practical ideals. The internationalization of ideological struggles abetted the decline of the European type of nation-state. It also furthered the development of a new type of balance-of-power politics.

As we saw earlier, internal factional struggles of a Communist government are not very different from the factional struggles in a Western government. In both America and Russia the official actions and policies of the ruling faction are influenced by the results of their day-to-day analysis of the other government's policies and actions. The situation appears to be one of chessboard moves and countermoves, and so it is up to a point. But the pieces on the board are not whole countries, as formerly. Rather, they are internal factional forces. Just as careers of American officials and the ascendancy of Washington factions are influenced by the effectiveness of and the need for the policy proposals with which they have become individually identified, similar vicissitudes affect the ascendancy of the ministers and factions in the Kremlin. The new targets of international politics are not states as wholes but rather their internal political processes. Some novel policy conclusions follow from this.

## Dialectical Conflict

Traditional balance-of-power theory projected the antagonistic competition of monolithic nation-states indefinitely into the future. A situation that maintains the antagonism of state against state is one that is like the process Socrates long ago named "eristical." This was his term for the combative process which

185

could be resolved only in the victory of one side over the other. But Socrates also described a second type of conflict, which he called "dialectical."

An eristical conflict is one in which each party tries to prove that he is right and that the other party is wrong. A dialectical conflict is one in which one contending party tries to show that his position is really agreed to by his opponent even though the opponent has begun in disagreement. Or conversely, it might turn out that the opponent holds the more valid position even though this was not apparent at the beginning. The essence of dialectical conflict is that both parties proceed in the conviction that a solution exists which expresses the true interests of each. This dialectical solution puts both parties in the right and brings a resolution of their conflict. (See further EPILOGUE.)

This view of dialectical conflict is not the same as that described by Hegel and Marx. Rather, it is close to what has always been the ideal of statesmanship. However, traditional European balance-of-power politics frustrated statesmanship because the situation was eristical rather than dialectical. The contending nations were related in such a way that for one side to "win" another had to lose. It was hardly ever possible for such a situation to issue in conflict resolutions that guaranteed the integrity and the future of the opponent. War, not statesmanlike resolutions, was what it produced. This was true in fact as well as in theory.

However, we have seen that the present world situation is no longer the one described by Clausewitz. The nations are different and they relate to each other in different ways. They are massive, bureaucratized states composed of entrenched and institutionalized power blocs. Elites from industry, politics, the military, and science and technology furnish the internal factions of a shifting, amorphous, permeable confederation. Coalitions are formed and re-formed as different factions move in and out of ascendancy. We have seen how this has become characteristic of bureaucratic leadership everywhere, industrial as well as governmental. The only possible development capable of changing this would appear to be in computerizing bureaucratic functions. However, for the immediate future there is little prospect of such a change. Bureaucracies with their pluralistic power structures are going to be around for some time. Their guiding policies will continue to be forged by the oligarchical cluster of factional leaders who struggle against each other at the apex. Each power faction strives to exert as much authority as it can in the multiform struggle of all to influence the policy formation process.

We have already seen how this results in policies that are themselves as pluralistic as the confederate structure that produces them. This is not immediately apparent from the outside and, as a result, it is easy to misinterpret official bureaucratic statements. Moreover, a policy statement is carefully drafted with a view to making it appear unitary and unambiguous. But the hands of the pow-

186

erful are not so easily hidden from sight. Careful observers can always search down through the official phraseology and find enigmatic references and hints of contradiction that deny the major thesis of the announced policy.

Recall our earlier discussion: The ostensible purpose of a Soviet pronouncement may appear to be to propose a major settlement of the East-West conflict. But simultaneously, somewhere in that proposal will be a contrary sounding reaffirmation of the ultimate Soviet determination to "bury capitalism." A month later and the tides of factional power may have shifted. A new statement may affirm Russia's undying commitment to achieve victory in world socialist struggle. Inevitably, however, the same announcement will somewhere, in a minor key, endorse the belief that capitalism and socialism can live together indefinitely at peace. The minority policy of yesterday has been converted into the majority policy of today; the minority faction of yesterday has become the majority faction of today. The dynamics of factional politics is reflected in the reciprocating ambiguity of succeeding policy statements.

Each new policy statement must guard against the possibility that today's dominant faction may be out of ascendancy tomorrow. This results from the power of the minority to include somewhere their contrapuntal theme. Though stated in a minor key and ever so faintly, inclusion of the minority position saves tomorrow's newly dominant policy from seeming to appear from nowhere as a complete policy reversal. This is why the fundamental policy statements of contemporary bureaucratic cultures are double-faced. They attempt to embrace opposite goals simultaneously. This simultaneous inclusion of opposites appears confusing only if one persists in thinking in terms of the politics of the past.

Previously—19th-century England and France furnished the typical examples—a fundamental policy statement was issued by each new administration that came to power following a parliamentary or an electoral victory. The voice was that of the "government of the day," as the politically wary English phrase had it. But parliament also contained vigorous opposition parties. They looked forward to being able to defeat the government of the day in a parliamentary vote of "no confidence" and, ultimately, in an election. No sooner had the victorious party made its declaration of official governmental policy than the opposition countered with opposing statements, forewarning the world of the changes that would be instituted should they come to power. Domestic voters and foreign ministries alike were put on notice. Every foreign government was privately obliged to qualify its formal recognition of the official policy with its own informal estimate of the electoral durability of the administration announcing it. In reality, then, the policy posture of the nation was as variable and pluralistic as was the political system of the country as a whole.

187

There is in fact but little difference between these two types of policy formation. The system of 19th-century European politics produced a seriatim succession of the policies of the various groups in a pluralistic party system. The contemporary process expresses much the same variability, but it does so simultaneously. In the older system there was at any moment a deceptive appearance of unanimity.

As we have seen in an earlier chapter, the American party system was never exactly like the one produced in Europe. Its parties were called "parties of compromise" rather than "programmatic" parties, like those in Europe. Accordingly, there was never a sharp distinction in the policies of the two major American parties. Moreover, until after World War II foreign policy played only a small part in American politics. This was changed after 1946. But with the inclusion of foreign policy issues into the political process another development also occurred. This was the "bipartisan" approach to foreign policy. The major parties entered into an informal agreement not to make foreign policy a matter of partisan disputation. In effect this meant that the Cold War was not to be debated publicly. The point was driven home forcefully in the disastrous episode of the Wallace Progressive Party in 1948. After that, bipartisanship was unchallenged in foreign policy until the protest movements of the 1960s. Bipartisanship, together with the growing bureaucratization of American politics, effected in the United States a studied ambiguity of policy statement similar to that characteristic of the U.S.S.R. Similar causes were at work in both cases. They lead to the calculation of international balance-of-power politics in novel terms.

## The New Diplomacy

Since World War II, each American administration, regardless of party, has fluctuated between two policies toward Russia. This reflected the fact that there have been two rather stable factions within each administration. Some personnel even remained the same through the changing administrations. One group, the so-called Hawks, advocated firmness to the point of belligerency. The second, known as Doves, advocated comity to the point of peaceful coexistence. We also know that there were similar factions inside Russia. Moreover, the ups and downs of internal Russian power struggles influenced the ascendancy of the comparable factions in their competitive struggles inside America. When relatively more pacific counsels appeared to have won out in Russia and became reflected in peace-regarding actions and policies, the counsels of those who favoured comity carried greater weight in the United States.

Illustrations of this became especially vivid after the death of President Roosevelt. It is immaterial who may have started the Cold War, but the major stages in its development proceeded in accordance with the kind of fluctuations of policies and factions just described. Militarism in one country stimulated countermilitarism in the other. Following Stalin's death, peace overtures from Russia met tentative reinforcement from the United States—until the American U-2 surveillance airplane was downed over Russia just when Premier Khrushchev appeared ready to make serious peace proposals in Paris.

In 1962 this new mode of diplomacy was officially explained. The U.S. Senate was threatening to reduce aid to Poland and Yugoslavia. Speaking through McGeorge Bundy the White House made a carefully reasoned effort to forestall the aid cut. The argument rested entirely on the proposition that the aid programs were designed to have a beneficent effect on the factional struggles taking place within the Kremlin.

In the spring of 1963 word came of a new power struggle inside the Kremlin, threatening the supplantation of Khrushchev with a more Stalinist and militarist successor. The main concern of American foreign policy then became how to manage its own posture so as to forestall that Soviet shift. Further aggravation of Kremlin politics was produced by the worsening of her relations with China. Throughout the closing days of his administration President Kennedy's primary effort became how to marshal his Western allies so as to strengthen Khrushchev's hand at home. In 1967 ex-Premier Khrushchev explained over American television that the Kremlin operated in the same way. Vice-President Nixon's efforts in behalf of the American flier held captive in Russia were rebuffed because Khrushchev feared this might ensure Nixon's victory over Kennedy. Khrushchev did not hesitate to take credit for electing Kennedy to the presidency.

This was a new kind of international politics. It still relied upon balance-of-power calculations, but of an entirely new kind. The powers to be balanced were not nations entire, but their internal power factions. For it had become apparent that *within the limits of their ability to maneuver, the Russians could, by the nature of their own actions, influence the direction of American foreign policy. Their actions could also influence the composition of Washington's dominant power coalition. And America possessed precisely the same power to select her own policies and actions so as to influence the policies and the factions to become dominant inside Russia.*

Each of the great nations is involved in the domestic politics of the other and each "participates" in the selection of the other side's leaders and programs. Balance-of-power politics now works on an entirely new foundation. It is not states as wholes that are bargained for and against. In each of the major countries domestic power factions work to influence and control the political profile of the coalitions that rule the world. It was in this context that "personal diplomacy" by the world's great leaders seemed to reappear in world politics during the Cold War. This was a seemingly paradoxical turn of events because it ran counter to the bureaucratization of authority that was so prominent a feature in the two great antagonists of the Cold War. The numerous foreign excursions of heads of state in the period following World War II were not what they appeared to be on the surface. That is, they were not pure exercises of executive autonomy. Their purpose was to mobilize mass opinion and to influence the power elites, not only in their own counrties, but also abroad.

When Khrushchev toured the United States in 1959 it was not solely to bargain with Eisenhower. Indeed, only a "spirit" came out of their celebrated meeting at Camp David, in Maryland. Khrushchev's trip was really aimed at American opinion leaders. His actions were those of a man running for election. Not only that, his political style was thoroughly American. No English, French, or German leader ever could fit so well with the grass-roots tradition of American politics. And this was recognized in Washington. Khrushchev's every statement was blanketed with official corrections and his steps were dogged by official correctors. However, a change occurred somewhere between Los Angeles and San Francisco. Henry Cabot Lodge was specially dispatched by the President to change the signals and permit Khrushchev a respectful public hearing. After all, President Eisenhower could be obliged to follow suit.

Khrushchev's U.S. tour was in the pattern of the new personal diplomacy. It was adhered to by Kennedy on his tour of Latin America in 1961 and in his tour of Europe in 1963. It was the purpose of Johnson's Far Eastern tour and his Manila summit meeting in 1966. It had been the purpose of De Gaulle's trip to the Soviet Union shortly before. In 1967 De Gaulle went so far as to incite the French Canadians toward rebellion. The entire world has become the constituency of all the great leaders. No matter how well they might fare in domestic politics, if they failed in the arena of world politics they were slated for displacement. Khrushchev's deposition was primarily attributed to mistakes in foreign affairs. Kennedy won sainthood despite an unimpressive domestic performance, in large part because of his foreign successes. With Johnson, just the opposite occurred. His spectacular domestic successes could not redeem the disasters that beset him when he ventured into foreign policy. This ascendancy of foreign over domestic politics provided an added dimension of the new balance-of-power politics.

## The New Game of Diplomacy

Following the end of World War II it was said that balance-of-power politics was dead. It could not work in a bipolar world. So long as international politics is viewed as an arena in which great monolithic Western and Eastern behemoths parade before the world in counterpoised tension, that observation remains sound. However, as soon as attention is directed to the internal relationships between the various ingredients in an overall policy, the internal power cluster, which had to be amalgamated in order to put the policy position together, becomes more significant than the country's external appearance of unity.

Policy formation began to require a new level of calculation. The difference was that there had ceased to be a sharp distinction between the inside and the outside in international politics. Domestic and foreign relations became part of the same political universe. All policies must be constructed with this in mind. They must accord with the facts of domestic factional power. But they also adjust themselves in accordance with the range of policies that it is possible to elicit from the other side. Both situations furnish constraints and also possibilities. Policy formation must find the way to harmonize the internal processes of the world's many power centres. This is a qualification of traditional eristical balance-of-power politics, which is capable of conversion into a process of policy formation that is dialectical on each side. For under the new conditions policy formation may proceed on the assumption of ultimate harmony and synthesis rather than conflict.

One looks at the opposing sides of the world power struggle as if they were all federal organizations. Each side's policies are in fact as confederate as are the factions composing its dominant group, as described previously in the discussion of bureaucracy. This changes the process of making "moves" in world political competition. It is no longer the chessboard model that applied in the 19th century. The new problem is not merely how to counteract another country's disagreeable confederation but how, at the same time, to foster the reorganization of a new configuration of power and policies which will be more in accord with the dialectic of statesmanship.

Stated like this the demand may seem too idealistic. How could the separate policy decisions of the world's power centres yield uniform and harmonious policies? Perhaps they will not. However, there is a persuasive example from the world's largest industry, automobile manufacturing. Designing an automobile for the world market is like designing a foreign policy for world politics. It occurs at several places in isolation, but calculations must include estimates of the actions of all world auto producers. This complex decision-making process operates so as to produce automobiles throughout the world that are "harmonious." For the result is automobiles that are virtually indistinguishable from each other regardless of whether they are made in the United States, Britain, Italy, the Soviet Union, or Japan. The same kind of dialectical process may be the outcome of the new balance-of-power diplomacy.

## Inside and Outside

Following World War II it was no longer possible to pretend that the world was composed only of autonomous nation-states, all of whom were ideologically colour-blind to each other. The new aims of foreign policy were addressed to the internal processes of states. This was perceived by America's first secretary of war in the Cold War, Henry Stimson, whose chief aide was the young McGeorge Bundy. It was the end of World War II and Stimson meditated the diplomatic shape of the post-World War II world. The result was a recommendation designed to govern America's future relations with the Russians. Secretary Stimson began by stating he had lost faith in his earlier belief that the way to make the Russians trustworthy was to show them they were trusted. Whether or not the effort truly had been made is beside the point. For Stimson recognized the need for a new diplomacy. He was wrong about the cause. He said a new approach was needed because of two factors: the Russians' long and hardened suspicion of the West, and the fact that Russian negotiators (Stalin most particularly) were of recent peasant origins. He believed this was what prevented them from abandoning their ingrained suspiciousness.

Stimson concluded that the system of diplomacy that had grown out of European balance-of-power politics was no longer applicable. He prescribed a new dialectical diplomacy in which the United States would devise those policies truly in the interests of both the Russians and Americans. The wisdom and fairness of a given American policy might not be immediately apparent to the Russians. If so, mere argument and diplomacy alone would not persuade them. The untrustworthiness of Western words was a central tenet of their ideology. But where the language of politics failed, the logic of the situation might prevail. The procedure would be to envelop Russia with a series of realistic acts and situations that when calculated and analyzed by Soviet leaders would appear to them as a configuration out of which only one policy response could be extrapolated: a resolution which was truly in the interest of both sides.

As events actually turned out these conceptions were converted into their opposite. They issued in the containment policy and the chill of ideological warfare instead of the warmth of dialectical comity. The problem was that the world's leaders had contracted hardening of the categories. For if one takes the final propositions of Secretary Stimson and reads them in terms of a traditional nation-against-nation power struggle, the result is not the new balance-of-power diplomacy here described, but rather containment. Containment was the effort to play the new dialectical game of world politics under the old rules of eristical nationalism. The containment policy was counterrevolutionary in two respects. It was avowedly counterrevolutionary in being anti-Communist. But it was also counterrevolutionary in being an attempt to conduct international affairs as if nation-states were still the vital forces in world politics.

The Cold War was a period of marking time during which the world struggled to supersede the European nation-state and to supersede its form of diplomacy with a new design for the conduct of world politics.

# *Chapter* 8   World Order

IT IS RARE IN HISTORY that one can point to a definite event and say that one of its results was to pose an entirely novel problem for mankind. The advent of the atomic bomb is just such a historical occurrence. The reason for this is very simple. A tool, in order to be of use to mankind, must be finite. That is, it must be something that can be used in the accomplishment of a goal looking toward the preservation of life and the enhancement of the conditions of living. A tool with infinite capabilities has the perverse potential of refusing to remain a means for the accomplishment of another end. Rather, it becomes an infinite end in itself. But an infinite end is the end of ends; the end of everything. That is the gruesome potential of the atomic bomb, and that is the novel problem it has posed to mankind.

Even before the atom bomb was invented men had doubts about the efficiency of war as an instrument for achieving goals. For one thing, war has always been an inefficient, crude, blunt, and violent tool, much too imprecise to be really useful. Now, however, the problem of inefficiency has been superseded. After all, inefficiency is simply a comparative matter. One tool is inefficient only in comparison with another which is not. The thermonuclear bomb, being absolute in itself, supersedes the whole problem of efficiency. In making war absolute it thereby eliminates it from the stock of tools available to men.

This leads to a further novelty: the possibility of accidental war. It has always been realized that wars could start by accident. That is, unintended, or fortuitous, incidents have often in the past triggered the inauguration of large-scale conflicts. The most famous example is the assassination of Archduke Ferdinand of Austria at the inauguration of World War I. However, such accidents have never previously been the cause of serious concern. For in the history of every great war it is possible to prove that profound underlying causes had been festering for a long time. It was these that really made the war inevitable. Had this not been the case no mere accident could have brought about a war. Moreover, the fact that such potent underlying causes existed made it irrelevant which specific event or incident served to trigger the actual outbreak of war. Historians have concluded unanimously that none of the great wars has been accidental. Because there was really no such thing as an accidental war at any time in previous history there has been no reason to treat accidental war as a fundamental problem. .

Ominous facts now give new cause for worry. So far as the major powers are concerned the tables may have been turned completely. It would be bad enough for man to obliterate himself on purpose. Now, however, world obliteration can indeed occur through accident. This derives from the combination of two novel factors: thermonuclear weapons on the one hand and on the other the elaborate computerized thermonuclear delivery systems that are counterpoised against each other East and West, ready for massive utilization on an instant's notice.

These vast culture-killing "man-machine" systems *must* be capable of instantaneous activation; they *must* be always aimed at each other's jugular vein. Otherwise they could be wiped out in a surprise attack and they would have no deterrent effect on a potential aggressor. But this is where the novel factor enters. In possessing such irradicable deterrent capability, they also possess the possibility of accidental and irrevocable activation. This is the cost the thermonuclear powers pay to insure "credibility" for their deterrence systems. This possibility is what gives urgency to the problem of accidental war and its prevention.

Because of the infinite destructive capability of these counterpoised systems a mere reduction of the statistical probability of accidental war is insufficient. No matter how infinitesimal the statistical probability of accident might become, an accident would still be possible and threatening. For the mere fact that the statistical probability of an occurrence is small is no guarantee that the event will occur only in the distant future. One might think that if there is a one-in-a-million chance that an accident will occur that one instance will take place only at the end of a million chances. But, of course, the one-in-a-million chance can occur immediately. Several one-in-a-million chances can occur in immediate succession and still not disprove the mathematical calculation which assigned the one-in-a-million ratio.

J. C. Kendrew, the British Nobel laureate, voiced the fears of many who were knowledgeable about thermonuclear weapons and their "fail-safe" procedures. "However many switches you have," he stated, "it is inconceivable . . . that with one thing or another there will not simply be an accident, one will go off and will be misinterpreted and unleash much more than has been bargained for."

"Hot wire" telephone and teletype communications systems were established between the world's great chanceries. Their chief executives took great pains to reassure each other each time a military engagement against a smaller power was begun. But this did nothing to reduce the possibility of technical or human failures that might cause an accidental thermonuclear outbreak. On the contrary, such executive precautions underscored the danger without facing the problem for what it is: mankind held hostage by a statistical probability—a probability which, no matter how small it may be in theory, is vastly magnified in practice whenever instability occurs in the minds of men or in their social institutions. Unfortunately, as we have just seen, institutional instability is the order of the day. No matter what perspectives one chooses to look at in the world situation today the conclusion is the same. The maintenance of world peace and the institution of world order are the sovereign imperatives facing men everywhere.

## The Meaning of Peace

Peace, though it is invoked by politicians as frequently and as fervently as is motherhood, has a unique position among the magical incantations of politics. It has never had a positive meaning. Peace has been like a vacuum. If we try to picture it in our minds we must do so by imagining the absence of its opposite, war. War, on the other hand, is an all too positive idea. When a Cassius rises to plead the case for war, his listeners have a vivid, concrete idea of what he means. They have an even more graphic idea of what actions will be required of them if war comes. The advocate of peace can convey nothing so concrete. He cannot picture for his listeners the tasks of peace.

To plead for the prevention of war appears to propose doing nothing rather than something. It seems to ask only that war be avoided. Perhaps that is why history reserves a high place only for those peacemakers who have brought wars to an end, not for those who have prevented wars. For who can tell for certain when a war has been prevented?

Even if a threatened war fails to break out it is impossible to prove it would have occurred had it not been for the efforts of a peacemaker. And a peacemaker like Neville Chamberlain, who succeeds for a short time only, reaps only calumny. For if a war does ultimately break out, it always seems afterward to have been inevitable. Once war has started, those who worked to prevent it appear to have been weak and cowardly appeasers, even if they were completely in the right.

However, the peacemaker who presides at the ending of a war has something positive to do. There are definite arrangements that must be made to bring about the truce. There are peace terms to be negotiated. There are prisoners to exchange. The victors must be awarded their spoils and the victors' penalties must be meted out to the losers. This is the kind of positive peacemaking whose results can be seen and appreciated by all.

What is the task of the peacemaker who works to prevent a war? Usually he seeks for a compromise. Compromise itself has a bad name. It implies that principles have been compromised. The compromiser gets something for what he gives. But later the concessions he made can always be interpreted as dishonourable concessions to an implacable enemy. This makes the peacemaker appear to have paid blood money to a bully irrevocably bent on starting a fight. Opponents have little trouble in portraying the peacemaker's concessions as payments from cowardice: a price paid to keep from fighting.

One of the chief difficulties is that the peacemaker's struggle is a negative one. His back is to the wall. He is *for* peace, but he can only realize that aim by working *against* war. Seekers for peace are as rowers in a boat. They must work turned away from their goal, seemingly guided only by what they wish to leave behind. This negative nature of the struggle for peace is its most serious weakness. War has the opposite position. The positive nature of preparing to fight a war is its greatest strength. The result is that conflict creates an almost irresistible propulsion toward violence. From one side statesmen are inhibited from pursuing peace, from the other they are propelled toward war.

Negative goals are not always weak ones. Liberty, for example, is often regarded as a negative goal: the absence of restraint. But it is a goal whose realization often requires positive action such as in a war of independence or a revolution. However, there is also a positive meaning for liberty. We are free if we are able to do what we want to do. This requires not only the absence of restraint but also positive ability.

Freedom is seen to be a positive goal when it is identified with mastering the prerequisites to achievement. The untrained apprentice carpenter is not "free" to build a house, even if no law restrains him from attempting to do so. The fledgling mathematician is not free to work in the field of nuclear physics. Similarly in politics, a people may be free of restraints and still lack positive political freedom. An African nation may have thrown off colonial bonds and yet lack the political skills and abilities to institute and maintain free institutions. This is broadly true in politics.

A people, like an individual, is free to enjoy what it has mastered the prerequisites for and no more. Two nations may have governmental institutions that seem almost identical, but only one of them may be a free people—take Uruguay and Guatemala as illustrations. The same may be true of two states within the American federal system: Massachusetts and Mississippi, for example. Freedom cannot be enjoyed unless the people have mastered its prerequisites. Similar propositions apply to peace.

The mere ending of hostilities does not mean that the enjoyment of peace will follow automatically: witness the Cold War that followed the end of World War II. Peace *is* like freedom. It cannot be meaningful so long as it is thought of negatively, as the absence of war—as a battlefield on which nothing is happening for the moment. Peace is not an environmental condition, like a pleasant summer day; it is positive activity. It is like a child's game of statues, a still-

196

ness that cannot be maintained without strenuous effort. It can exist only so long as people actively keep it in being through appropriate actions and roles.

Keeping the peace has a different aspect inside nations. It sometimes appears cowardly in world affairs, when leadership attempts negotiation in the face of international violence. Yet the same behaviour is usually regarded as the noblest of activities when maintained in the face of domestic violence. In both cases the effort is to prevent the outbreak of violence. In both cases established political (diplomatic) relationships threaten to break down. Neither international nor domestic peace means merely the absence of conflict. On the contrary, conflict and the resolution of conflict are never absent. Conflict is at the heart of politics on all levels. But it doesn't exhaust the nature of politics, for politics arises out of man's harmonious and cooperative impulses as well as from those that cause conflict. However, at a minimum, politics—that is, the relationships found in a political order—must cope with conflict in such a way that war, revolution, and murder are eliminated.

Every conflict contains the potential of breaking into violence. Where social organization is simple and political skills are low, it may suffice merely to provide aggrieved parties with an acceptable way of making a comparable retaliation. This was like the retaliatory justice described in the Old Testament; like the law of the Colt .44 that maintained order "West of the Pecos." This was the justice of Moses: an eye for an eye and a tooth for a tooth. Where interrelationships are more intricate and require more stability, the social and political fabric cannot be left at the mercy of private feuds.

Politics must become the opposite of war rather than merely its regulation or even its absence. Remember Clausewitz' statement that war is the continuation of politics by other means. Exactly the reverse is true of politics. It is the continuation and the sublimation of warlike feuds by other, nonviolent means. This is exactly what occurred on the domestic level in all high cultures when the retaliatory justice of the feud was superseded by adjudicatory rule-of-law principles. We can be certain that the advent of world order will require extending the same process to international feuds.

At a minimum, international peace requires the continuation, or sublimation, of war by other means. But if one eliminates the violence, but retains all else of war, the result must be some form of politics. It may not be politics at its highest, but it will be politics rather than war. More important, the possibility of a higher form of political development in the future is not foreclosed. But the crucial problem is how to initiate the process that leads to the creation of a political order.

Let us return to the beginning of things according to Hobbes: war. The end of a war is signaled by the beginning of a peace conference. We sometimes think of a peace conference as the occasion for the victor to impose his demands on the vanquished. But the case is never really quite this simple. The victor never has the vanquished completely at his mercy. In actual practice there is no such thing as unconditional surrender. The vanquished party still exists. It will in due time recover from its defeat. It may even dedicate itself to resuming the war as soon as it is able.

The victor can neither expect, nor truly desire, the absolute and permanent subservience of the vanquished. What the victor does desire and can expect is a treaty—a contract—which will express as accurately as possible how the future relations between the two parties are to be conducted and what will be the degrees of superiority and inferiority between them in the foreseeable future. If these contractual arrangements are designed carefully and accurately, the result will be a good and fair treaty of peace upon which both parties can base their future actions.

However, the provisions of a peace treaty are unlikely to be lasting for two reasons. In the first place, war ends with a distortion of the true forces available to both sides. The victor, merely by having won, appears to be more powerful than he truly is. This is so even apart from the case of the Pyrrhic victory.

The condition of England after World War II is a good example. In order to wage the war England was forced in effect to sell her empire—to dispose of the foreign investments through which her imperial position had been maintained and to cash in her foreign sterling balances. England "won" the war, but she did so at the cost of becoming a smaller and less significant England in the scale of world power. However, the true effect of this imperial disinvestment was not to become apparent until several years after the end of World War II. Accordingly, at the end of World War II England appeared to be a more powerful nation than did the Germany that was defeated, dismembered, and in seeming industrial collapse. But matters changed quickly. Germany quickly demonstrated that she was not nearly so weakened by war as first had been thought.

Any treaty between the two nations based upon their apparent conditions as World War II ended would have been unenforceable because of the doubly unreal distortion in favour of England that her victory and Germany's defeat seemed to have brought.

But even if the distortions that follow wars could be avoided, peace would be precarious for another reason. This is because peacemaking tends to be approached as if it were a one-shot affair.

## After the Peace Treaty

A peace conference is conducted in the same way a tournament is staged. It is an event that is scheduled for a specific date. It takes place. It accomplishes its purpose. Then it ends, with all results final. There are delegates who attend.

They participate. They sign their names. Then they close down the affair and return home. The error is in assuming that a peace conference ends with the final ceremonial affixing of signatures. The mistake is in closing down and going home. A peace conference provides merely the initial, not the ultimate, terms of peace. The treaty it produces, like any contract or law, is but the beginning of a relationship, not the complete determination of its future course. The error nations and statesmen make concerning peace conferences is to regard them as finite, terminable bargaining sessions, like the dickering of barter and sale.

This is never truly the case in actual practice. Sooner or later misinterpretations or misunderstandings or unforeseen contingencies arise. But as the peace table machinery for discussion and bargaining has been closed down, it is hard to get such disputes aired. They fester unattended until they become so irritated and so close to breaking into violence that a new conference cannot be avoided. But by this time affairs too long unattended have deteriorated too far. The mistake was the initial one of thinking of peace negatively, as a kind of vacuum inaugurated by the signing of a peace treaty. This amounts to assuming that peace somehow keeps itself. But peace, like Bob Cratchit's Christmas, doesn't exist if nobody "keeps" it.

Peace doesn't mean simply not going to war. For appearances to the contrary, peace is not negative. It is not a vacuum. It is a positive occurrence: the specific moves required to substitute political for violent means of resolving conflicts. It means staying in the peace conference permanently.

This has been true of politics always. Politics taken at its simplest, and at the same time its most universal, amounts to what can be called a permanent peace conference. If the political process has its own essential "constitution," this is it. This is so, not because politics assumes peace is assured but because, on the contrary, it assumes peace is always in danger. In every peace conference, just as in every effort to negotiate a strike settlement, the conferees are always aware that their efforts may not succeed, and that a new resort to violence may be the outcome of their failure. However, there are occasions, occasions of high political achievement, in which the opposite may occur.

Each conference participant has a rudimentary vision of the better world his effort—and the joint efforts of his colleagues—may create. They strive for a good that is common, or public, as well as private. When the process succeeds it verifies a maxim of ancient political theory. For politics, to paraphrase Aristotle, comes into existence in order to safeguard life; it is maintained in order to safeguard the *good* life. Politics is like money. Once its benefits are experienced nobody wants to give them up.

Moreover, in politics (as distinguished perhaps from law and economics) no agreement or treaty is self-enforcing. At no time in politics can the participants really sign their treaty of peace and go home. This is why politics can be compared to a permanent peace conference. Each element in a political settlement must be watched over constantly by all parties as it is being followed out. The consensus that results from the political process is not static. It must be constantly reinterpreted. It must be applied and reapplied to new or possibly analogous situations. It is the *permanence* of the peace conference that really keeps the peace, not the content of the power settlement nor the spirit of the consensus.

There is a difference between two types of agreement that occur in a political situation. One is the familiar agreement on substantive issues. Examples would be the specific wage features of a strike settlement, or the prisoner exchange agreement in a peace treaty. The other type of agreement is like that represented by the American Constitution. It is the agreement on how to provide for the ongoing conduct of affairs so that the substantive agreements of the first type can be agreed to and carried out. This second type of agreement, or contract, is procedural rather than substantive. It need not be written out—witness the unwritten constitution of the English. But whether it is written or customary there is always a fundamental contract that lies at the base of every political order.

This is what gives 18th-century theories of the social contract their eternal validity. The most fundamental contract of any political order may be only implicit, but it is nonetheless necessary. It begins with the mutual recognition of the necessity of staying in permanent (even if intermittent) session. A political order starts from the recognition that the peace conference cannot be disbanded. From this beginning, specific political institutions such as parliaments and courts develop. But even in advanced nations one can still observe the rudimentary principle at work. Every legislature is a permanent peace conference.

Prior to the advent of the thermonuclear era it could have been maintained that there was a fundamental difference between the domestic politics played out inside nations and the international politics they carried out between themselves as nations. There would have been some justice to this claim. For the underlying assumption of the domestic politics of all nations is that war cannot be an instrument of policy, whereas the assumption of international politics had been that war was a proper instrument of foreign policy. Now this has changed. Among the great powers war has become just as ineffective in settling international disputes as it is in resolving domestic conflicts.

This means that in both arenas the same political imperatives apply. The world, for the first time, can and must consider all its political relationships on the same terms. It is true that wars can still be permitted among the smaller nations and between the smaller and the larger nations. But the penalty of power is that once a nation has joined the ranks of the great thermonuclear powers she deprives herself of resort to war in disputes with her peers. This is true of East-West relations despite the suspicion in the West that Russia intends to make her system victorious in the world and despite the suspicion in Russia that capitalism will never bow voluntarily to the spread of socialism.

Such suspicions are not incompatible with the maintenance of political order. Until quite recently there was a similar condition inside the Western nations. Their religions lived in a perpetual Cold War with each other. Of course much earlier there had been actual wars of religion. But for all their violence the religious wars settled nothing and they were finally abandoned in exhaustion.

The conflicting religions, like the conflicting nations of the Cold War, agreed to maintain a hostile, but a permanent peace conference.

Today there is an implied contract that places the world's nations in one political community, despite their persisting ideological struggles. This means that the general propositions that are valid for any political order are applicable today on the international as well as on the domestic level. The issues dividing the liberal and the collectivist democracies are not qualitatively different from those that once divided Catholics and Baptists, Roundheads and Cavaliers, Negroes and Caucasians. This is proved not only by the force of analogy but also by the terms of the "new balance-of-power" politics now obtaining in international relations.

The world and all its parts are now in the same universe of political conflict. The problem that remains is to discover how this world political community can first find its identity, then concentrate upon its areas of agreement, and finally produce its implicit social contract. This does not necessarily make the problem of world order easier, but it does force us to consider it on a different level.

## The Impediments to Innovation

It is the easiest thing in the world to "prove" that the world cannot, or will not, form itself into a true political community in the near future. But the same "proof" often applies to any proposed political innovation and to any novel legislative measure even in the most sophisticated political order. The reason is plain. A new law, a new constitution, or a new organic union requires that people change their traditional behaviour to conform with the proposed political innovation. They are asked to follow completely new and unaccustomed channels of behaviour. They are asked to accept on faith the fact that the new order will work and also that things will be better if they give it a try. But here is the rub. For whether or not things actually will work and be better under the new order depends upon how successfully people can be induced to accept their new roles as valid before any evidence of their validity exists.

This marks one of the great differences between the political order and the natural order. In science, workability is established quite differently. We do not frame scientific laws on the basis of the entirely new patterns of behaviour nature might choose to follow tomorrow. In politics, however, the workability of new laws does depend upon what people will decide to "make" workable by adopting them and giving them a try.

A political innovation presents people with the proposition that if the proposed new pattern of behaviour is installed, or substituted for an old pattern, a decided improvement will result. It founders on the impossibility of demonstrating that this is so in advance of being tried. Advance demonstrations of this sort are only possible in the physical sciences because we can count on the fact that there is sufficient determinism in nature to permit predictability. In nature we can know in advance what will probably happen if we introduce a change and with this confidence we can make changes and adapt our actions accordingly. But the material comprising the political order is patterns of human behaviour and these possess a characteristic indeterminism.

Politics turns the table on nature. For political "experience" tends to prove that any proposed innovation probably will be *un*workable and *un*necessary. This is so because the only evidence about its workability comes from what has been done in the past. But what has been done in the past cannot possibly contain any evidence at all supporting the workability of a novel proposal. Take the example of a bank. It is almost impossible to see how people could be induced to institute a bank if they had never before had any experience of one. The idea of a bank is that if people let it keep their money, and if they trust it, their money will be kept secure against theft. Next, however, the bank will lend their money out to others. It will make profits, pay interest, and increase the wealth of the community. Everything will be safe so long as people believe their money is safe. Any one person can get his money back so long as all don't demand their money at the same time. If they do, the whole thing collapses and many people lose money because there isn't really enough to pay them all what the bank owes them. The entire bank proposition is so inherently implausible that no primitive people can assimilate the idea abstractly. They learn it only by a gradual, unreflecting experience of banks introduced among them without their political consent.

In short, the only things that can be proved to be definitely workable and beneficial in politics are things that have already been made to work by the people concerned. Anything else tends to be regarded as being utopian regardless of how workable it might actually turn out if it were adopted. On the other hand, to maintain traditional practices usually appears to be the "scientific" and practical thing to do no matter how badly they actually work.

There is at the heart of politics a built-in bias against innovation because the only way novel patterns can become practical is by people making them practical by changing their behaviour to conform with them. But this requires making them traditional instead of novel. Dynamic societies partially overcome this difficulty through what was earlier called a dual-myth system, one possessing utopian as well as conservative goals. Charismatic leaders also may serve as a force for innovation by inducing blind faith in their followers. However, both devices have grave deficiencies. They can never fully overcome the a priori quality of impracticability that surrounds any proposal for a fundamental change in the established political system.

The a priori invalidity of every new plan means that the argument that a given new proposal—such as a proposal for world government—is impractical is not by itself a valid criticism of the plan. World order actually may be the most practical and scientifically valid thing that can be done and yet people might have no greater a priori conviction of its validity and practicability than do primitive peoples when told they ought to adopt a banking system: it seems like a fanciful dream to make men behave like angels.

For example, it is apparent to historians that the ancient Greeks might have preserved their culture had they been able to institute some form of federal or organic union. It is incontestably true that the Greeks would have been far better off had they done this. The benefits for everyone concerned would have far outweighed the attendant difficulties. And yet the Greeks, who were not ignorant of federative organizational forms, were like 20th-century men. They believed that all would be lost if they permitted the slightest abrogation of the sovereignty of their *polis*. But all this did was render them helpless before the armies of Alexander the Great, who forced upon them a much more drastic degree of centralization than would have sufficed earlier.

The practical conclusion usually drawn from this line of speculation is that politics is the art of the possible, and the possible is defined by the paths of the past. However, there is a deeper sense in which politics is in truth the art of the "impossible." For what is deemed to be politically possible is circumscribed by apparent power relationships. Any new proposal that threatens apparent power relationships in a fundamental way—requiring their reorientation—appears to be politically impossible from the power standpoint. This is almost a tautology of politics. Those who hold power will struggle to keep their interests from being harmed by innovations. To propose such innovations seems almost like proposing that the earth change its rotational orbit.

Yet we know that occasions do occur in which "impossible" and "utopian" political innovations are adopted. Indeed, it is part of the history of the West that proposals that were impossibly utopian and unworkable one day became the conservative foundation of established power relationships the next. After such changes—or revolutions—have occurred we then discover that they actually conform to the "true" state of power relationships better than did the old arrangements, even though we could not perceive this in advance. And this new "true" state, in its turn, seems to be just as imperishable as was its predecessor, though in fact it is just as perishable as was the old. For ultimately politics must register and legitimize fundamental changes in power relationships, even though the unwelcome midwife of change may be crisis and violence. The *tranquil* registration of change is difficult for the political process to accomplish because it is almost impossible to know with certainty when fundamental changes of power have taken place.

## Changes in Power

Several devices have been employed in attempting to measure changes in power and to translate their implications into new laws. Periodic elections help to do this in permitting different social groups to register their comparative changes in power through their support of issues, candidates, and parties. The expansion of the suffrage during the 19th century in Europe was an example of this and it was because of this that the labouring classes were able to assume an influential role in the political order.

Secondly, there are special occasions when adjudication procedures may register power changes in society. This happened during the 17th and 18th centuries in France and England when the courts of both countries gradually recognized the commercial and property needs of the bourgeois class. Arbitration procedures are specifically designed to make accommodations in accordance with power changes. Strike threats between workers and employers, between prison inmates and authorities, and between the officials of conflicting organizations and firms are examples of how arbitration adjusts customary arrangements as power positions change.

Third, in the Western tradition it has been customary to associate power with financial status. Large financial redistributions have often brought about corresponding redistributions of political power and social prestige. In socialist societies it is not money that measures power, but the other way around. Power changes among individuals are reflected by their changing tides of influence in the ruling party.

These are a few of the legitimized forms through which changes in power relationships may be registered politically. Moreover, as was seen earlier, dynamic societies have dual-belief systems. The progressive, utopian part of the myth system provides some degree of friendly receptivity for new proposals, providing they do not seem too revolutionary and providing they can be identified with the spirit of the utopian component of the myth system.

Even so, crisis is usually required to jolt politicians from their habitual conservatism to the support of utopian reforms. Examples of this occurred in the

Soviet Union following the death of Stalin, when pressures for reform had to be accommodated, and in the United States when the demands of Negroes and other minorities had to be granted. In both cases the ultimate effect of the legislation was to curtail the power of established economic and social elites and elevate the status of those they had formerly suppressed.

Similar events characterized the reforms that were initiated in Yugoslavia in 1966. Throughout the collectivist world cultural and economic development brought increased power to the intellectuals and experts who had helped make it possible. Gradually, they gained an improvement in status and a degree of freedom that would have seemed quite revolutionary only a few years previously.

Yet in all these examples the readjustments were just that. They were accommodations and alterations rather than fundamental innovations. Critics and reformers had been proposing the changes for many years. They had argued not only that the new freedoms and protections were just but also that everybody else would be better off if they were adopted. Their proposals were discredited as being visionary, utopian, impractical, impolitic, and so on.

This teaches us an important lesson about "practical" politics. The more practical and power-oriented politics is, the more shortsighted and static it tends to become. For when existing political forces are projected into the foreseeable future, effective reforms never appear to be within the realm of the politically possible. But as we study the teachings of history we can see that what, at the time, seemed to be the most practical, conservative, and hardheaded approach to politics was, in fact, the most erroneous approach, and the one most disadvantageous for all parties concerned.

Truly practical politics requires the adoption of more radical and visionary policies. This is a paradox of power. It must transcend its ostensible limits in its own best interests. This is why the opening definition of politics as the architectonic art is ultimately valid. It is especially valid for times in which the balance of political forces is changing rapidly. These are times when established institutions cannot adjust to change adequately enough. In such times the truly practical and conservative solutions to pressing problems always seem utopian and impractical. The world is at such a time today.

Proposals for world order have *always* been discredited as being utopian and visionary. It is possible, as we have just seen, that this never was true. It is possible that already many decades ago the institution of world order had become a practical and conservative necessity. We have seen how this could have been the case without the bulk of mankind ever having become aware of that fact. But even if objections to world order were valid prior to World War II, this alone does not mean that world order is still impractical and utopian today. There is mounting evidence that today all mankind is in the same position regarding world order that the United States occupied regarding labour legislation before the great depression of the 1930s; in the same position as was Russia prior to the death of Stalin.

Today the immediate institution of world order is the only practical, conservative, and hardheaded political solution to world problems. Putting it off is possible, just as it was possible for the Greeks to put off unification. But the price is a fearsome one. It must be paid in the violence and warfare of Korea and Vietnam, in border incidents in India, and turmoil in Africa and Latin America—just as domestic violence was produced in the United States by the seemingly practical politicians who always claimed that legislation guaranteeing labour and Negro rights was premature, visionary, and utopian.

There is one difference, however. Nations may be able to afford the luxury of "practical" politics; the world cannot. For so-called practical politics is the politics that accepts innovation only in response to crisis and violence. This kind of politics will destroy us all if it is applied to the problems of the world. And yet, this proposition can be as true as the law of falling bodies and at the same time appear to be only a visionary dream.

## The Price of Practicality

Let us assume that the world is confronted with the following alternatives. The first alternative is for every country that can do so to move underground, to prepare deep-level bomb and radiation shelters, and to devise ever ready protections against death rays and against chemical and bacteriological agents. The defense of such actions is, first, that they are necessary in order to insure that there will be a few survivors from a thermonuclear war. Second, they are necessary to convince other thermonuclear powers that an attack could not completely disable the population. There would be a surviving force capable of instigating counterdevastation.

To prepare such shelters and adopt such protections seems to be "practical" and "scientific." It appeals to the commonsense view of affairs. For it is obvious that if the most powerful nations remain organized as they now are and continue the heedless belligerence they now exhibit, cataclysmic war is statistically probable in any practical view. President Kennedy thought the odds were 50-50 that such a war would occur within ten years of his inauguration. A country would not be realistic if it did not prepare for this probability. Prudence would seem to dictate that every effort be made to visualize concretely the kind of conditions that would result from a third world war and to prepare for life under those conditions.

Realistic scientists who study such matters and proffer practical advice to their governments estimate that the most practical and scientific shelter programs might preserve as many as one-tenth of their nation's people. This is not only a hardheaded approach, it is the scientific way to insure victory in the event of thermonuclear war. If one country has ten percent survivors and her opponent only five percent, the one with a ten percent survival rate will be the winner. At least this is what the strategists have declared in advance.

But who will these "winners" be? It is true they will be "alive" in some sense. Their future offspring will be "men-children" by definition because they will be the offspring of the surviving men. However they will not be men-children in any sense that men-children have been defined before because they will show the genetic effects of radiated germ plasm, and genetics has discovered that most radiation-induced changes are detrimental. In some way that we cannot now calculate precisely, these future men will have grotesque bodies, reduced physical capabilities, and diminished mental capacities.

Even the immediate survivors themselves will be different men. For as the *Perspectives* article on HUMAN NATURE shows, man is defined not only by his personal physical characteristics but also by his material and cultural environment. Survivors of a thermonuclear war will have to blast out of their deep shelters through several feet of burnt-over cinder crust left in the wake of blast-induced fire storms. They will emerge into a world denuded of most of the biological and material surroundings that always in the past have been associated with human life. Possibly after a century or so has elapsed the least damaged peoples could even rebuild their industrial capabilities so as to be able to engage in another catastrophic war.

This is the practical view. However, to be fully realistic we must add that there is little reason to expect that anything would ever again be quite the same as in the past, not only because of the alteration of the material environment and the physical condition of man but more importantly because the alteration of man's cultural environment would be quite drastic. We can be sure that there would no longer be institutions like capitalism and socialism. These things that would have caused the war, the very things whose preservation men had thought they were fighting for, would be the war's first casualties.

A realistic consideration of the immediate postwar culture indicates that it would have to be something literally unimaginable now. This means that it is not possible to plan now in any way for the cultural conditions following a thermonuclear war. The most important problem might be that of finding and preserving those with the least damaged germ plasm. A simple factor such as that would be sufficient to change the family system, the class system, the incentive system, and so on. But there would be many other elements of novelty we cannot now foresee.

In short, we cannot say anything at all about what sort of cultural, legal, or political institutions the world would require after a thermonuclear war. The practical fact of the matter is that a post-World War III world would be in every sense something we have no possible way of imagining. Yet this is what "practical" politics will visit upon the world.

The second alternative is world order. Here the story is that nearly everyone believes that to undertake any action designed to avert catastrophe by instituting world order would be hopelessly impractical and utopian. Unfortunately, as we have seen, the *only* reason for this conviction is that every fundamental political innovation appears to be impractical and utopian before people have put it into operation through their actions. The fact is that what most men call practical politics contains a built-in tendency toward catastrophe.

Man may be, as Aristotle said, a political animal. Aristotle meant that man was, by nature, an animal who built political communities. But it also happens that man is by nature an animal who tends naturally to produce crisis. This results from man's predisposition to do only those things that appear to be practical and scientific—until forced to change by crisis.

It is evident to every thinking man that only slight modifications of our present modes of life through the inauguration of world order would insure a future little different from that we know at present. It would be peopled with human beings exactly like those we now have. Its physical environment would be the same one familiar to us now. It could even cope with the population explosion and insure affluence to all the world's peoples. The conclusion is inescapable that building a world order (though difficult and "utopian") is the cheapest, the most truly practical, and the easiest alternative for man to choose. To prepare for a catastrophic war is the costliest alternative, the most difficult to carry out, and at the same time the one designed to produce an unimaginably horrible future.

What is the conclusion? It is that the world is at the point of the reversal of practicalities and utopianisms. The future that practical politics leads to is unthinkable. The blind faith that a postthermonuclear world would work at all, much less be desirable, is not only blind, it is impractical. Creation of an effective world order would not only preserve our familiar way of life in its chief essentials, it would also be a vastly cheaper and more practical undertaking. Probably this has been true for more than a century, but it has certainly been true since 1950. World order is now the only truly practical and scientific alternative open to man. It is not possible to take exception to this proposition. It is demonstrably self-evident.

## Barriers to World Order

This places the discussion on a different level. Suppose we now assume it to be a fact that world order is intrinsically practicable and is not in fundamental contradiction with world power relationships. What then stands in its way? For one thing, there is the problem that people in general cannot be given sufficient faith in its practicability to lead them to engage in the collective entrepreneurial venture of putting it into practice.

The article on NATURE shows that the laws of nature are phenomenological rather than intrinsic to nature. They are the logical forms man projects onto nature. But the laws men make for their own government are not phenomenological. They are logical forms in one sense, but they are also concrete "things." They are made concrete when men put them into practice. One can "see" the concrete existence of a law each time a policeman issues a ticket for a traffic violation. The laws of physics can be descriptive because of the helpless, inanimate character of the natural order. The laws of government must be prescriptive because of the willful nature of man in politics.

The moment we can prove that nature operates differently from the description contained in a law of physics that law becomes invalid. However, man acting contrary to the laws of government is not in itself sufficient to discredit the law. Despite widespread violations of a law we may still believe that men ought to behave according to the law, and we seek for new ways of enforcement to make the disparity between law and behaviour disappear.

The authority of the state, backed up by police coercion, is the most familiar way of making human behaviour conform to the prescriptions of the laws of government. However, we also know that authority will never work well in this task if men do not fundamentally believe in the law—if they do not think it is just and if they do not truly wish to conform to it. Accordingly, something in addition to authority is necessary to influence the wills of men so that human behaviour will conform to the prescriptions of law. Men in general must believe in the law, or at least in the validity of the process through which the law was devised and promulgated.

We have seen earlier that a society's system of goals and beliefs furnishes its members with a general predisposition to believe in the justice of its system of laws. We have also seen how, first in the United States and then in the most advanced industrial nations, the goals and beliefs associated with the earlier stages of the industrial revolution have begun to lose their accustomed vitality. New goals and beliefs appropriate to the scientific revolution are beginning to inspire loyalty. Nonetheless, the older industrial goals still impart a degree of unity to the world. So much is this the case that we expect all societies, liberal and collectivist alike, to look pretty much the same in the near future.

Another thing shared by the liberal and the collectivist democracies is their approach to world order. They are exceedingly wary of it. The most they might admit is that some degree of international cooperation, though disagreeable, is necessary in order to avoid a greater evil. This leads both antagonists to adopt minimalist positions concerning world order. World order is not thought of as being good in itself but only good so as to preserve things that cannot be safeguarded any other way. It has value only to the degree it appears to be a necessary extension of their own preestablished goals. That is, both the United States and the Soviet Union have *conservative* goals and beliefs when it comes to the issue of world order. The *utopian* part of their belief systems continue to look inward and regard only domestic problems. World order is not a part of the utopian myth of either side in the Cold War.

This means that whatever validity the goal of world order possesses derives from its ability to reinforce the static and conservative elements in the goals held by the great nations. The problem obviously is to change this so that within each nation world order becomes a positive goal in its own right. This would make world order a part of the separate utopian myths of the world's autonomous nations. If this were to happen the world would then possess a sphere of separatism. It would be unified on the level of its utopian myths but remain divided on the level of its conservative myths.

The utopianism usually associated with the ideal of world order could turn out to have the virtues of its defects. For although a people's utopian myth always has the aura of impracticability its name implies, yet in the case of world order, the only hope it has of being realized lies in its becoming the dynamic, utopian component of the myth systems of the world's separate nations (and recall that affluence and democracy have furnished the dynamic and utopian components in the past).

This requires that we engage in a little practical utopianism. The beginning steps are easy enough to visualize. First would come the recognition of world order as a goal valuable in its own right rather than as an alternative to something worse. Second would come the "nationalization" of this supranational goal within the myth systems of the various countries. The achievement of world order would then make up the utopian component of each country's myth system. The nations of the world would recover the dynamism that is now being lost. The dynamic trend working its way within each nation would carry all of them along in the same direction. This in itself would amount to a preliminary form of world order. For one can imagine the new goal of world order as something hovering above the particular goals of each nation. The more distant, but also higher, loyalty to world order would constitute an area of spiritual union in the world. Moreover, individuals would owe allegiance to the larger goal without being guilty of disloyalty to their nation.

## Pacem in Terris

This is neither as novel nor as visionary as it might seem. Progressive cultures, as we have already seen, are those with dual-myth systems. The world was given its first concrete step in this direction when Pope John XXIII issued the encyclical *Pacem in Terris*. It was a direct appeal for world order in terms that transcended the antagonisms of the Cold War. But this was not its most important feature. There had been many such appeals and schemes for world order in the past. What was epoch-making about *Pacem in Terris* was that for the first time in history the highest authority of one of the world's largest and most powerful organizations (in international law the Roman Catholic Church's Vatican City is a sovereign state) officially established the dual-allegiance system referred to above. *Pacem in Terris* made it mandatory for Catholics the world over to realize their allegiance to world order by working to make it come about. Never before had a comparable organization or government done so. Were other nations to follow suit, world order would be well on its way toward establishment.

There were several likely candidates. Britain would be capable of declaring her allegiance to world order almost without internal opposition. So would several others of the Commonwealth nations: India and New Zealand, for example. Japan would be an excellent candidate. So would be Sweden, Switzerland, Israel, Yugoslavia, Uruguay, Tanzania, and a host of others. Once the trend had started it would spread with growing momentum throughout the world.

In 1965 the Center for the Study of Democratic Institutions called a worldwide conference in New York City. It was attended by the most famous philosophers and statesmen alive. They were convened for the purpose of discussing the extent to which *Pacem in Terris* provided a basis for world order. The response was favourable in the highest degree.

In May of 1967 the Center for the Study of Democratic Institutions conducted a second, somewhat smaller Pacem in Terris conference in Geneva. This was concerned more with the politics than with the philosophy of world order. Again, it appeared that the world was much more ready to take actual steps toward a genuine world order than its chanceries were willing to admit.

The mere fact that prominent personages from both the liberal and the collectivist democracies could be gathered together under the auspices of an encyclical by a deceased pope was significant in itself. A decade earlier no one then alive would have believed such a thing to be remotely possible.

One explanation was that *Pacem in Terris* was not a blueprint for world government. On the contrary, it expressed the ideology of world order. And it did so in a way that preserved the integrity of each person's allegiance to his own country. This meant that *Pacem in Terris* solved the problem referred to earlier. It provided a dual-myth system. It was a device for adding the realm of world order to each of the world's already existing nations. Beyond this, it avoided a problem that had plagued the previous efforts to frame a government for the world.

The problem is stated briefly: How is it possible to devise statelike institutions to facilitate world order when the collectivist democracies believe the "state" as such bears the congenital curse of despotism? How is it possible to visualize a form of government for the world to which the collectivist democracies could belong and to which their members could grant allegiance? The seriousness of the first problem is easy to illustrate from the typical world government constitution produced by Western intellectuals. Such schemes tend to be simple extensions of the forms of government familiar in the liberal democracies. Usually their unifying device is some form of federalism patterned more or less closely upon the American federal union. This kind of territorial federalism has been criticized above. But the more difficult question concerns the general problem of the state itself. How can we devise a form of union capable of exerting some degree of coercion against its members and yet absolve that coercive authority of the charge Marxism levies against all Western state forms?

It is plainly true that no plan for world order that possesses the birthmarks of imperialism, class bias, and political alienation, which Marxists attribute to liberal democracy, can possibly attract the allegiance of the collectivist democracies. This fact may help explain the relative acceptability of *Pacem in Terris* as a basis for inaugurating a dialogue on world order between East and West.

The underlying reasons are not hard to find. The Catholic Church has possessed its own distinctive body of political philosophy for many centuries. It is a philosophy which, whatever other objections may be raised against it, is innocent of one charge. It does not possess the characteristic economic and political conceptions lying at the base of Western liberalism. Thus it avoids entirely many of the problems about which the collectivist democracies feel quite strongly. Secondly, the Roman Catholic Church has never been wholeheartedly sympathetic to the European nation-state. For one thing, its own historical position was underminded by the rise of the nation-state. Its way of thinking about politics does not tie it automatically to the state so fulsomely disparaged in the doctrine of Marxism. Thirdly, Catholic political philosophy has retained many of the conceptions of civic order that were embedded in the political theory of the Roman city and in Roman jurisprudence. One example of this is in the theory of the corporate state. This is a theory that stands in some degree of bad repute because it was the official doctrine of Fascist Italy. But it is not intrinsically evil. The famous Guild socialists of the 1930s—Ernest Barker, Harold Laski, and G. D. H. Cole—all adopted the corporate state as the most promising form of humanitarian government.

The corporate state possesses an entirely different theory of political union from that found in liberal theory. Liberalism links together autonomous provinces, territories, and states into a larger entity. Corporate theory links together groups and associations. It conceives of a type of federalism based upon prin-

terpart of the medieval king's body politic would be created and it would furnish the world's peoples with an added object of allegiance. Ultimately, institutions follow allegiances. An island of world order ultimately would arise inside each nation just as in medieval times officers of the crown, representing the overall unity of the kingdom, gradually appeared in each locality. Of course, in the medieval world this form of federalism required centuries in order to produce unitary nation-states. Today world order is needed in a much bigger hurry.

## The Problem of Scale

The problem is that world politics presents itself to us in atavistic forms. The same problem that the ancients solved on the scale of the city and the problem modern Europeans solved on the scale of the nation now must be solved by all mankind on a world scale. This is the problem of supplanting the primitive retaliatory justice of the feud with civilized rule-of-law adjudication. And even though at each prior level, city and then nation, the introduction of the rule of law has involved the same process, each new setting into which it has been imported has involved a process no less arduous for being an old one.

Men seem completely unable to apply the lessons of politics they have learned on one level to the same problems when they occur on another. Seventeenth-century Europeans profited daily in their cities from the lessons of civic order made patent as a result of the urban revolution bequeathed them by the ancient world. Yet 17th-century Englishmen were unable to extend the same principles of civic order to the nation as a whole, short of revolution. Twentieth-century man now threatens to be equally obtuse about the inauguration of civic order on a world scale.

This is not to argue that the problems of achieving world order are simple or that they are the direct mirror image of the problems met in the inauguration of urban and national rule-of-law systems. For this would be like saying that whistling a tune and conducting a symphony orchestra involve the same underlying process. Each extension of rule-of-law principles ran into a series of special complicating factors. It was these novel complications rather than the familiar underlying processes which dominated men's attention.

The urban revolution required the invention of law. The nation-building revolutions required the invention of constitutions and mass political parties. The revolution for world order presents its own unique problems. For example, in the beginning, at least until industrialization and bureaucratization have stamped their homogenizing image on every corner of the world, the separate social and belief systems of the various nations must remain intact. Previously union has required some agreement on fundamental beliefs. Today's men will have to devise a union that leaves room for separate ideological autonomy— just as American and Russian federalism left room for territorial autonomy.

215

ety's more immediate bonds were held firm through this second network of allegiances that ended in the king's person.

The operation of this dual system of allegiances was revealed for all to see in 17th-century England when James VI of Scotland became James I of England. That event united two previously independent realms under one crown. Englishmen and Scotsmen remained disunited on one level for a hundred years after that event. Yet during that time they were spiritually united in the sense that they all owed a loyalty to the larger union. Among other things this meant that war between them was impossible.

This was a form of federalism: a realm of union together with a realm of separatism in the allegiances of subjects. It was a more spiritual form of federalism than became familiar afterward because the area of union was essentially a matter of allegiance to shared goals rather than to laws, institutions, or territories.

This is the sort of federalism—a federalism of world allegiances—that is again possible today. Just as in 17th-century England, it would not require supplanting the citizen's allegiance to his own nation. However, its dynamic would imply the ultimate overthrow of the nation-state system, just as the dynamic of medieval Double Majesty led to the ultimate overthrow of the network of particularistic allegiances to feudal lords.

This is a form of federalism that contains a prescription for a world political union and for a revolution as well. The creation of the nation-state was a revolutionary event and so will be the creation of its successor. But it is necessary to distinguish this revolution-bearing form of federalism from the territorial federalism that was later made familiar in places such as the United States and the U.S.S.R. For contemporary efforts at world order are often modeled on these later, territorial types of federalism. American federalism has even come to be referred to as a "dress rehearsal" for world union. However, the American example contains a grave defect as a model for world order.

American federalism was not an example of the inauguration of union, as had been the case with the union of England and Scotland. Rather, it was a device for recementing a union that had been shattered. The American colonies had been unified already under the British crown just as England and Scotland had been. Federalism was the device through which that ruptured union was re-established in a republican form. The two types of federalism were quite different. In the American case the states gave up some of their functions to a new government whose powers consisted of what it received from its members. In the other type of federalism none of the states give up anything. Rather, they all have something added to them from above.

If one thinks in terms of world order this would amount to installing something like medieval Double Majesty as the pattern of world order. A world coun-

ciples of association rather than upon principles of territorial autonomy. It is what might be called a political theory based upon human functions rather than upon property relationships. This means it is essentially civic—that is, city-oriented—rather than property—that is, state-oriented. This is related to the charge made earlier in discussing the nation-state.

It seems plainly true that world order, when it shows us its true political face, will turn out to have a civic complexion. This may be the most important explanation for the acceptability of *Pacem in Terris* as a basis for East-West discussions of world order.

Finally, the Roman Catholic Church has never made peace, so to speak, with capitalism. It always maintained a critical position toward capitalism's amoral stance on economic justice. It always identified itself—at least on a doctrinal level—with the cause of the poor. For all these reasons *Pacem in Terris* turns out to provide what few would have thought the Catholic Church could possibly produce: a neutral ground upon which East and West can meet and discuss the terms of the political order under which they can proceed in unison toward the future. At the very least it points out how the nations of the world can produce a dual-myth system, with world order as an object of allegiance inside each nation in the world.

## Dual Allegiances

The existence of dual allegiances has been quite common in history. This was the case all during medieval Christendom. All subjects owed allegiance simultaneously to a local political authority and also to a universal spiritual authority. During the late Middle Ages European states were themselves dualistic. The German scholar Gierke gave the name "Double Majesty" to this form of government.

Subjects owed allegiance to their crown, but the crown was organized on the basis of two distinct principles which were expressed in the doctrine of the king's "two bodies." What was called the king's "body politic" represented the area of overall union in the realm. Everyone owed allegiance to the whole through their direct allegiance to the king's body politic. But in addition to this, each man owed also a different kind of personal allegiance to his next higher superior. All these personal allegiances pyramided up through society till they ended finally in the king.

Medieval kingship was very much like the world order described above. The king was a personal ruler as well as the body politic. Through his "body politic" the king received the allegiance of the highest lords. Through the network of personal allegiances that spread downward through all the strata of feudal ties the king held feudal society together. However, overall union existed through the direct allegiance of each subject to the king's body personal. Soci-

World order will require a new kind of ideological federalism. It is easy to forget that a similar problem occurred at the inauguration of the nation-state. The early nations were often multilingual. Provincial and regional cultures persisted for several generations after the beginning of national regimes. Federative and commonwealth-of-nations devices permitted a considerable degree of autonomy among the various belief systems contained within one nationwide rule-of-law jurisdiction.

World order must devise a new way of applying this early lesson of federalism. It must be possible for the various cultures of the world to develop according to their own logics and yet maintain allegiance to a world rule of law. Again, there are a few hopeful examples. Great Britain never fully homogenized Ireland, Scotland, or Wales, yet all flourished under the same regime. America was never the same nation for New England, the South, the Midwest, and the Far West, but it always *aimed* at becoming one nation, indivisible, with the same liberty and justice for all. The same has been true of Germany, Italy, the Soviet Union, and of all nation-states.

Indeed, as the nation-state now begins to wither away, we discover how tenuous was the unity it once expressed. Scottish nationalism is of a piece with Ukrainian nationalism. Pakistanis and Indians are not much different from French and English Canadians. Each Western nation was once composed of as diverse ethnic and cultural ingredients as now characterize the world as a whole. What was true of the nation-state in amalgamating itself will also be true of world order.

World order does not require complete world uniformity. It merely requires that antagonisms not be allowed to activate the institutional detonators which are capable of igniting full-scale thermonuclear warfare. No conflict which may arise can be allowed to escalate into progressively more antagonistic retaliatory aggressions. Whenever a potential escalation presents itself, counterescalating procedures and forces must be available immediately. At the same time, it must be possible for regional blocs, spheres of influence, or "empires" to wax and wane nonviolently. This is a modest goal. It is simple in itself. It is easy for each great nation to advocate. Yet to the ordinary view it is heavy with the aura of utopian romanticism.